THE GRAMMAR OF THE UNCONSCIOUS

THE GRAMMAR OF THE
UNCONSCIOUS

The Conceptual Foundations
of Psychoanalysis

CHARLES R. ELDER

The Pennsylvania State University Press
University Park, Pennsylvania

Library of Congress Cataloging-in-Publication Data

Elder, Charles R., 1950–
    The grammar of the unconscious : the conceptual foundations of
psychoanalysis / Charles R. Elder.

        p.   cm.
    Includes bibliographical references and index.
    ISBN 0-271-01310-9 (cloth : alk. paper) — ISBN
0-271-01311-7 (paper : alk. paper)
    1. Psychoanalysis—Philosophy.   2. Subconsciousness.   3. Analysis
(Philosophy)   I. Title.
    [DNLM: 1. Freudian Theory.   2. Unconscious (Psychology)   WM
460.5.U6 E37g 1994]
    BF175.E444   1994
    150.19′5—dc20
    DNLM/DLC
    for Library of Congress   93-35531
                                                                            CIP

Published by The Pennsylvania State University Press,
University Park, PA 16802-1003

It is the policy of The Pennsylvania State University Press to use acid-free paper for
the first printing of all clothbound books. Publications on uncoated stock satisfy the
minimum requirements of American National Standard for Information Sciences—
Permanence of Paper for Printed Library Materials, ANSI Z39.48–1984.

FOR MY FATHER,
C. R. ELDER, JR.

Grammar tells us what kind of object anything is.
—*Wittgenstein*

CONTENTS

PREFACE

This work grew out of my dissatisfaction with poststructuralist readings of Freud and especially with the kinds of radical claims that are made on behalf of Freud in Lacanian psychoanalysis (e.g., the claim that the subject is ex-centric to itself, that Freud stands humanism on its head, and that the unconscious marks an irreducible cleavage between signifier and signified). There was a time when Lacan's strategy of self-subversion, together with his so-called mystical theology of language, held an enormous fascination for me—a time, too, when only the most radical form of thinking seemed adequate to the intellectual, cultural, and ecological crisis of our contemporary world. But Lacan has long since lost his appeal, and I no longer believe that the most radical form of thinking is necessarily the most adequate. (In the end, nonsense is nonsense, no matter how sophisticated its theoretical pretensions.) It seems to me now that what is important—and indeed all that really matters—is that we learn once more what it means to be human. Everything else is subterfuge or evasion.

I am no longer sure whether I learned these lessons from Wittgenstein or whether he merely confirmed what I had already begun to suspect. In any case, it was largely under his influence, and through his guidance, that I came to terms with many of the conceptual problems that had both plagued and fascinated me for a very long time. I do not claim to have solved these problems or to have surmounted them once and for all. All I can say is that I have personally found a certain freedom from the *compulsion* they once exercised over my life. If this work can do the same for someone else, it will have achieved the most I can hope for it.

Freud once characterized the task of analysis as one of relinquishing neurotic suffering for ordinary unhappiness. In much the same way, it seems to me, Wittgenstein demands that we give up our fascination with the illusions of philosophy for ordinary human reality, together with all the pain and suffering and uncertainty this reality exacts. This means,

among other things, that we renounce the solace of even the most radical
of philosophical posturing, that we learn to live modestly within the
reality of a world that we can finally neither master nor escape—a world
less enchanted, perhaps, but also more substantial. With respect to
Freudian theory, it means that we learn to resist the temptation to derive
metaphysical implications from the metapsychology, that we affirm both
the validity and the limits of the psychoanalytic truth, as it applies not
only to the innermost conception of the self but also to the understanding of our contemporary historical and cultural situation. As I try to
show in what follows, the real significance of Freud lies not in his
discovery of the unconscious, or in his critique of the Western notion of
the subject, or, finally, in his acute reflections on our culture of
renunciation; rather, the real significance of Freud consists in his articu-
lation of an entirely new form of psychological discourse (or, if you
prefer, a new form of "introspective consciousness"), a new set of
terms, images, and analogies for the description of human experience,
together with a new frame of questions for psychological and cultural
inquiry. Whether this new discourse is adequate to the full range of
human experience, values, and aspirations, whether it is ultimately
viable as a way of ordering our world, both conceptually and morally,
is a question we are only now beginning to ask, much less answer. It
remains, nonetheless, a question we must address more fully and more
adequately than we have to this point (though surely the works of critics
such as Philip Rieff, Alasdair MacIntyre, Christopher Lasch, Peter
Homans, and others have provided a basis for these efforts).

The present book was never conceived as anything more than a
prelude to this larger task of cultural analysis. It is intended as a primer
in a particular style of thinking about such questions, an introduction to
a method. This means that it does not represent a comprehensive
treatment of even the most basic themes in psychoanalytic theory and
practice (excluding any reference to symptom formation, the neuroses,
the structure of the personality, case studies, sublimation, and the
theory of culture, for example, to name only the most obvious, though
some of these topics—specifically, Freud's theory of culture and cultural
symbolism—I hope to treat in another volume); nor does it present
anything like a thorough and systematic response to the questions raised
in the current debate about the status of psychoanalysis as a science
(most prominently, in the recent works of Adolf Grünbaum and Marshall Edelson). There are many reasons for this, but the most important
is simply that I wanted to write a book that would be more generally
accessible to anyone with an interest in these kinds of questions—
questions, for example, about the nature of truth in psychoanalysis and

related disciplines, about the character of self-knowledge, about the nature and limitations of psychoanalytic and similar explanations, and about the character of Freud's discovery—rather than just one more scholarly treatise of interest only to a handful of other scholars. (Of course, whether I have succeeded is another issue altogether.) At the same time, I certainly hope that specialists in various fields—not only in psychoanalysis but in philosophy, in critical theory, and in the social sciences—will find something of interest in the approach that I offer here to some long-standing problems in these areas.

This book was originally part of a dissertation written in the Divinity School of the University of Chicago. I would like to thank those people—teachers and friends—who served on my dissertation committee: David Tracy and W. W. Tait, coadvisors; together with Peter Homans and Françoise Meltzer, both readers. Their patience, criticisms, and unwavering support were worth far more than they probably ever suspected. I am very grateful to all of them.

Judith van Herik, at Pennsylvania State University, not only read sympathetically and commented at length on an earlier version of the work but also offered invaluable suggestions for further reflection. I want to thank her for all that she has done.

Finally, I would like to acknowledge my gratitude to various members of my family: to my two children, Sam and Kate, for the joy that their presence brings to each new day; to their mother and my companion, Elizabeth, for her love, her wisdom—and her staying power; and to my father, Charles R. Elder, Jr., for his unquestioning support, even of that which he did not understand. I dedicate this work to my father, not to repay a debt, but as a sign of my enduring gratitude, respect, and admiration.

One never relinquishes one's work without misgivings, and this is particularly true of the present work. Rarely have I experienced more acutely the tension between what was necessary and what was possible, between what I sought to express and my ability to express it. I believe that the questions I raise here are important and that the method I use for dealing with them—the method of grammar, properly understood— is the right one. But I know that I am still a long way from mastering this method and that though these questions may be recognizably "Wittgensteinian" in tone and subject matter, I lack Wittgenstein's genius for dissipating the confusions that surround them. I have no doubt that this is a moral failing as much as an intellectual one. Of what is essential, we only understand what we are compelled to understand.

ABBREVIATIONS

I. Freud

ATI   "Analysis Terminable and Interminable" (1937)
CA   "Construction in Analysis" (1937)
EI   *The Ego and the Id* (1923)
ID   *The Interpretation of Dreams* (1900)
IL   *Introductory Lectures on Psycho-Analysis* (1916–17 [1915–17])
OD   "On Dreams" (1901)
OP   "An Outline of Psycho-Analysis" (1940 [1938])
PEL   *The Psychopathology of Everyday Life* (1901)
QLA   "The Question of Lay Analysis" (1926)
SAND   "Some Additional Notes on Dream-Interpretation as a Whole" (1925)
SELP   "Some Elementary Lessons in Psycho-Analysis" (1940 [1938])
TEA   "Two Encyclopedia Articles" (1923 [1922])
U   "The Unconscious" (1915)

II. Wittgenstein

BC   Bouwsma, *Wittgenstein: Conversations, 1940–51*
BlB   *The Blue Book* (1933–34) (in *The Blue and Brown Books*, 1–74)
CV   *Culture and Value* (1914–51)
L I   *Wittgenstein's Lectures, Cambridge, 1930–1932*
L II   *Wittgenstein's Lectures, Cambridge, 1932–1935*
LC   *Lectures and Conversations on Aesthetics, Psychology, and Religion* (1938–46)

MM   Malcolm, Norman, *Ludwig Wittgenstein: A Memoir*
ML   Moore, "Wittgenstein's Lectures in 1930–33"
OC   *On Certainty** (1949–51)
PG   *Philosophical Grammar* (1930–33)
PI   *Philosophical Investigations*, vol 1* (1936–45), vol. 2 (1947–49)
PR   *Philosophical Remarks* (1929–30)
RFGB   *Remarks on Frazier's "Golden Bough"* (1931, 1948?)
RFM   *Remarks on the Foundations of Mathematics* (1937–44)
T   *Tractatus Logico-Philosophicus** (completed 1918)
WVC   Waismann, *Ludwig Wittgenstein and the Vienna Circle* (1929–32)
YB   *The Yellow Book* (1933–34) (in *Wittgenstein's Lectures, Cambridge, 1932–1935*, 43–73)
Z   *Zettel** (1945–48)

*An asterisk indicates that reference is to remark, or section, numbers; all other references are to page numbers.

INTRODUCTION

What follows is intended both as an inquiry into certain long-standing conceptual problems and as the exemplification of a method. The problems are, for the most part, those which surround the question of the status of psychoanalysis as a comprehensive theory of symbolism, psychosexual development, and culture. The method is Ludwig Wittgenstein's method of grammar—or, as it is sometimes called, grammatical analysis. The point of the work is to clarify the distinctive features and applications of the language of psychoanalysis—particularly, the central concepts of the unconscious, repression, sexuality, and the like—and thus to reveal something significant about both its validity and its limits as a mode of explanation.

There is, I think, a very real need for this kind of inquiry. Put simply, it seems to me that much of the current controversy surrounding the questions about the status of psychoanalysis—especially in the protracted and largely sterile debate over its scientific validity—derives from a failure to comprehend the grammar of its characteristic expressions and terminology.[1] In other words, we consistently misunderstand Freud because we are consistently misled by the language he uses, his oddly

---

1. This is not to suggest that questions about the scientific status of psychoanalysis are unimportant, or that they have no bearing on issues of grammar as such. On the contrary, asking how and whether psychoanalytic propositions can be verified represents a contribution to the grammar of those propositions (see Chapter 6 below).

constructed idiom of unconscious drives, mechanisms, and ideation. When Freud says, for example, that "the unconscious is the true psychical reality," or "repression consists in keeping an idea from consciousness," or "the meaning of a dream is a wish," and so forth, we are inclined to take these as factual propositions, statements that should be open to certain kinds of evidential—which is to say, either experimental or clinical—confirmation. But this, I believe, is a mistake, one that is based on a confusion about the way in which these kinds of statements actually function in psychoanalytic discourse. This same mistake persists even into the most recent round of debates about the nature and status of psychoanalysis as a systematic discipline.[2]

"A substantive makes us look for a thing that corresponds to it," Wittgenstein notes in a different connection (BlB, 1). Asked, What is repression? What is the ego? What is an unconscious idea? and so forth, we find ourselves frustrated by our inability to designate the thing to which these words are supposed to refer; we feel as if we need to point to something and yet find it impossible to do so. Indeed, ever since Freud, we have been trying, in one way or another, to point to something called the unconscious—without any notable success.

By contrast, I proceed here on the assumption that questions such as Does the unconscious exist? and Is there such a thing as repression? are properly not factual questions but—at least initially—*grammatical* ones. They pertain to conventions of linguistic usage, to the various ways we speak about, describe, and organize our inner, psychological experience, rather than to immediately given empirical or psychological realities. What the unconscious is, how it is established and known, reveals itself

2. In other words, it seems to me that the interminable debate about the scientific status of psychoanalytic claims—including the most influential recent discussions in the works of Adolph Grünbaum and Marshall Edelson—largely misses the point. Briefly put, I would suggest that many of the central claims of psychoanalysis that have hitherto been taken as factual and hypothetical are actually grammatical and paradigmatic—including, for example, the entire theory of repression: such claims are properly neither true nor false, but rather set forth rules for the use of language ("We will call an event an instance of 'repression' when . . ."). Hence, the search for evidential foundations for Freud's repression etiology—such as we find in both Grünbaum and Edelson—is at best, I think, misguided. Whatever the final value of psychoanalytic theory, it cannot be judged "true" or "false" according to its correspondence to "the facts." (Though, of course, this fact alone does not rule it out as "unscientific," since it is the condition of any science that certain propositions have this paradigmatic status.)

By Grünbaum, see *The Foundations of Psychoanalysis: A Philosophical Critique* (Berkeley and Los Angeles: University of California Press, 1984) and "Précis of *The Foundations of Psychoanalysis: A Philosophical Critique*," in *Mind, Psychoanalysis, and Science*, ed. Peter Clark and Crispin Wright (Oxford: Basil Blackwell, 1988). By Edelson, see *Hypothesis and Evidence in Psychoanalysis* (Chicago: University of Chicago Press, 1984) and *Psychoanalysis: A Theory in Crisis* (Chicago: University of Chicago Press, 1988).

first *in grammar*, not evidence; what this and related expressions mean shows itself in the way they are used. (If we want to know the value of the rook in chess, we have to look at what can be done with it; if we want to know the meaning of the term "the unconscious," we must look at how it is actually used in the context of the theory and practice of psychoanalysis, its various roles and applications.)

The question posed here in relation to Freudian theory is not, therefore, Is it *true*? but rather, Does it *make sense*?—and if so, What *kind* of sense?[3] This is a question, we might say, about the logical or grammatical *possibility* of the Freudian unconscious, rather than the evidence for or against it.[4] It pertains to conditions of meaning, not to facts; to human conventions and practices—and, more specifically, to the rules embodied in those conventions—not to immediately observable realities. My aim, in part, is to show these conditions and to clarify these rules.

To avoid misunderstanding, let me insist at the outset that I am emphatically *not* saying that facts have nothing to do with the truth of psychoanalytic claims or that appeals to evidence are irrelevant, even in the case of the truth of some of the higher-level theoretical claims of the metapsychology (e.g., claims about the unconscious, about the nature and function of the psyche, and about the etiological role of sexual trauma). Given a proposition like "The unconscious exists" or "Infants have an active sexual life," it ought to be possible to attribute sense to the idea that these are indeed factual claims and that they refer to

3. The distinction between the truth and the sense of a proposition is reflected in the debate over logical positivism and problems of falsification. The question of verification has to do with the *truth* of propositions, and thus generally with appeals to evidence of some sort, whereas the question of falsification has to do with their *sense* and thus with logical and grammatical possibilities. In other words, part of what is involved in determining whether a proposition makes sense—that is, whether it conforms to accepted linguistic conventions—is asking whether it can be falsified by any possible or conceivable state of affairs. At the same time, however, falsification alone is not—as Karl Popper and others have maintained—an adequate criterion for the determination of sense.

4. In the opening pages of his influential work, *The Unconscious: A Conceptual Analysis* (New York: Humanities Press, 1958), Alasdair MacIntyre states his intentions in pretty much the same terms, but the analysis he subsequently offers is actually more philosophical and critical than grammatical. In general, as I understand him, MacIntyre's point is to show how Freud's use of language is confused and, in particular, to criticize Freud's understanding of the unconscious as something "substantial" (see esp. 71–79). My own purpose, by contrast, is simply to illuminate the various ways Freud uses the terms and to show the kind of sense—or senses—which it has. In my view, it is not a criticism of Freud to say that he treats the unconscious as something substantial; it remains to be shown what *kind* of substance the unconscious is. (Though of course, this is not to deny that Freud sometimes draws mistaken inferences from his way of conceptualizing the reality of the unconscious.)

something besides rules for the use of language. (For there is a sense in which we are *in fact* motivated by unconscious wishes and fantasies far more than we realized before Freud, just as there is a sense in which children are *in fact* sexual and not just called so by Freud.) Nonetheless, I would argue—and it is the burden of what follows to show—that much of what Freud sets forth as hypothetical or factual is actually rooted in the grammar of theory, in its distinctive terminology, syntax, and conceptual framework, and that much of what Freud claims to have discovered factually is more in the nature of a grammatical movement: what it offers above all is a new way of looking at things, a new way of making sense of our experience. It is not enough, however, simply to state this; rather, we must work through the language of Freudian theory piecemeal and in such a way that we begin to *see* that this is so. As Wittgenstein writes in his remarks on Frazer, "To convince someone of what is true, it is not enough to state it; we must find the *road* from error to truth" (RFGB, 1). This is precisely the purpose of the method of grammar as I use it here.

How does this kind of grammatical inquiry proceed? To begin with, it is not a matter of forming one more theory about the status of psychoanalysis (surely we have more than enough already); in fact, it isn't a matter of *theory* at all. Grammar is not theoretical but descriptive. "There must not be anything hypothetical in our considerations," Wittgenstein tells us. "We must do away with all *explanation*, and description alone must take its place" (PI, 1:109). Grammar describes how we use particular words and forms of expression, as well as, in the process, displays the contexts and conditions of these uses.[5] Put simply, our question is about the meaning of Freudian language—and we need no theory to talk about meaning. Meaning is something revealed *in* language, through the way in which words and expressions are actually used. In most instances, however—and particularly in dealing with philosophical and theoretical problems of the sort represented here—this meaning and its conditions can only be *shown*, not stated (for reasons I try to make clear later). Hence, this work presents, not a theory, but a description of how language is actually used in psychoanalysis, a description aimed at displaying those logical and grammatical relations that are relevant to the sense of psychoanalytic concepts and propositions. The point is to show how certain forms of expression do or do not have a

5. Like the words "history" and "logic," the word "grammar" has two senses: first, as the method of study, and second, as its object. Hence, for Wittgenstein, "grammar" is not simply the description of the rules and conditions of linguistic usage but also those rules themselves (in roughly the way that the word "logic" means both the science of logical structures and the structures themselves).

coherent application and to show what role they play, rather than to argue for the truth of this or that theoretical claim or to set forth opinions about the status of the theory as a whole. Indeed, this "antitheoretical" stance represents an important part of what I take to be the originality of Wittgenstein's method (which is not to say that certain of Wittgenstein's claims—and my own—cannot be construed theoretically).

This work is not only an inquiry into the conceptual foundations of a particular style of thinking, then, but also, to the extent that it is successful, an exemplary exercise in the application of the method of grammar—a method that, it seems to me, has been largely misunderstood. This is my pretension in relation to Wittgenstein, as distinct from my pretension in relation to Freud.[6] Without trying to give an exhaustive account, let me offer just a few words about my understanding of this method. (For further discussion, see Appendix A, "The Method of Grammar.")

As a philosophical strategy, grammar can be broadly defined as a description of the various ways and contexts in which particular linguis-

6. It is worth emphasizing that this is not a work about Wittgenstein and that it is no more than incidently related to his views on Freud and psychoanalysis (although, as will be obvious, I am indebted to Wittgenstein for many brilliant and provocative suggestions). Indeed, it is one of the ironies of Wittgenstein's legacy that although he is, in the words of one interpreter, "the major ideological influence upon the contemporary critique of psychoanalytic theory," his published remarks on psychoanalysis bear little relation to his own grammatical method. This is true not only of the well-known and frequently anthologized comments on Freud in the *Lectures and Conversations* but also of the less familiar Cambridge lectures. In fact, almost all of Wittgenstein's major points about Freud and psychoanalysis in these two sources (with the possible exception of his distinction between "cause" and "reason")—that is, the criticism of Freud's determinism and, more generally, of any attempt to found a psychology on the principles and methods of the natural sciences, the characterization of the notion of the unconscious as purely "a way of speaking," the rejection of the attempt to explain dreams, the judgment of psychoanalysis as a "myth" and of interpretation as a form of persuasion, and so forth—whatever their validity, are more philosophical and critical than grammatical: that is, they are based on an appeal to some external standard of truth (or even, one sometimes suspects, on certain deep-rooted prejudices), rather than on an analysis of the language of the theory and a representation of the way in which this language actually *works*. It is only in *The Blue Book*—and in a few scattered references in his notebooks—that Wittgenstein sketches what could really be called a *grammatical* approach to psychoanalysis, one that takes seriously his own injunction to *describe* linguistic usage rather than criticize or reform it, and to *display* the grammatical relations rather than pronounce judgments on the truth of its theoretical propositions (see BlB, esp. 22–24, 57–59).

Hence, although many of his explicit criticisms of Freud are consistent with the grammatical approach to be employed here, I want to insist that what follows is *not* intended to be an account of Wittgenstein's opinions about psychoanalysis, whatever their interest or validity. It is instead an attempt to apply his method to the language of psychoanalytic theory.

tic expressions are used, a description aimed at revealing the underlying logical—or deep grammatical—structure of those expressions, in contrast to their surface grammatical form.[7] For Wittgenstein, the purpose of this kind of description is predominantly negative and critical; his overriding aim is to show that most philosophical—which is to say, metaphysical—statements involve either a misuse of language or, more often, a misperception about what actually occurs when we use language, and that philosophical problems are largely the product of a failure to comprehend the deep grammatical conditions for making meaningful statements. Philosophical problems are, for Wittgenstein, problems of language; thus, they can only be resolved by attending to the ways in which we actually use language, by obtaining a "clear view" (*Übersichtlichkeit*) of the grammatical and logical relations between words, expressions, and segments of language, of words as they are used in the context of ordinary linguistic practices.[8] "Your questions refer to words," he writes, "so I have to talk about words" (PI, 1:120). By describing and comparing the different uses of superficially similar expressions (e.g., "I have a headache" and "I have five dollars," or "There is no one in the room" and "There are no physical objects"), Wittgenstein wants to dispel the illusions created by certain false analogies in language, illusions that lead the philosopher to make statements that are either nonsensical (e.g., "Only *my* sensations are truly real" or "Only consciousness exists") or else merely disguised expressions of grammatical rules (e.g., "I cannot feel your pain" or "Only *I* perceive *this*").

Wittgenstein himself was concerned almost exclusively with the conceptual problems of professional philosophy (philosophy of mathematics, philosophy of language, philosophy of mind, etc.), and he had very little to say about the technical languages of the natural and human sciences. Hence, his purpose was critical and largely limited to showing how certain kinds of utterances fail to meet the conditions of meaning in language (i.e., that they are senseless) or how they fail to accomplish

7. "In the use of words one might distinguish 'surface grammar' from 'depth grammar,' " Wittgenstein writes in the *Investigations*. "What immediately impresses itself upon us about the use of a word is the way it is used in the construction of a sentence, the part of its use—one might say—that can be taken in by the ear.—And now compare the depth grammar, say of the word 'to mean' [*meinen*], with what its surface grammar would lead us to suspect. No wonder we find it difficult to know our way about" (PI, 1:664).

8. Despite the appeal to our ordinary linguistic practices, it seems to me that Wittgenstein's method of grammar should be sharply distinguished from so-called ordinary language philosophy, such as that represented, for instance, in the work of J. L. Austin, John Searle, and Stanley Cavell. In my understanding, Wittgenstein's sole concern is *to dissolve philosophical problems*, not to provide a philosophy of language or a theory about the conditions of sense. His aim, in other words, is critical and therapeutic, not constructive.

what they are intended to accomplish (i.e., that they do not represent reality). In applying this method to the technical language of psychoanalysis, my own intention is somewhat different, since, by and large, my purpose is less to condemn it as nonsense than to clarify its unusual, perhaps even unique, grammatical and semantic features, what might be termed its grammatical specificity. This kind of activity is more of the order of housekeeping than of razing buildings—or even of destroying houses of cards: for what is essentially at issue here is the character and function of this language, rather than its legitimacy. In the course of scientific investigations—and particularly in the case of elaborating new scientific perspectives, whether in the natural or the human sciences—we are almost invariably led to say more than we really mean, or understand ourselves to mean, whether out of habit, negligence, or (less often) sheer stupidity. Then it becomes necessary to go back over our language and try to determine which of its aspects are "useful" (in the sense of having coherent and significant applications) and which are not. In one of his recently published notes, Wittgenstein describes the situation as follows:

> In the course of a scientific investigation we say all kinds of things; we make many utterances whose role in the investigation we do not understand. For it isn't as though everything we say has a conscious purpose; our tongues just keep going. Our thoughts run in established routines, we pass automatically from one thought to another according to the techniques we have learned. And now comes the time for us to survey what we have said. We have made a whole lot of movements that do not further our purpose, or that even impede it, and now we have to clarify our thought processes philosophically. (CV, 64)

It is precisely to this task of trying "to clarify our thought processes philosophically" that this work is devoted. In psychoanalysis, we might say, our words have effectively outrun our understanding; now we must go back over the language to see how its different terms and conceptual aspects (including syntax and methodology) actually work in practice, that is, how they are used to produce the effects of meaning that they do in fact produce, both in the sense of representing significant psychical realities (e.g., unconscious mental processes and motivations) and in the sense of establishing certain analogical relations between what were previously viewed as widely disparate symbolic and cultural phenomena (e.g., money and shit, or obsessive acts and religious practices).[9]

9. I believe that it is one of Wittgenstein's real limitations that he fails to allow for what might be called creative nonsense, not only in philosophy, science, and mathematics but also—and perhaps especially—in the human sciences.

(A brief aside: Many of Wittgenstein's followers talk rather freely about philosophical problems as the product of, in the famous phrase from the *Investigations*, "language on holiday" [PI, 1:38], as if it were the most obvious thing in the world to recognize such language. Although this may be more or less true of the language of metaphysics—in the rather weird claims of some philosophers that, for example, "only my pain is real" or "naming is a remarkable act of mind"—it is far less obvious when one looks at the technical languages of the human sciences. Sociologists and cultural anthropologists, for example, are fond of making statements such as "Culture is a purely human product" or "Myths and symbols are culture's way of organizing thought." Well, what kind of statement are these? Are they useful scientific theorems—or merely instances, once more, of language "on holiday"? I want to suggest that there are in fact no easy answers to these questions and hence, too, no readily available rule for deciding when language belongs to the one category and when it belongs to the other.)

There are a number of logically different kinds of questions that can be asked about a theory like psychoanalysis. The questions with which grammar is concerned are, one might say, logically peculiar.

Consider, for instance, the following questions as illustrations of the different logical types of questions one can ask about the game of chess:

1. How many pawns does white have?
2. Why can't the bishop move along the edge of the board?
3. Did Fischer make the best possible move at 15?
4. Why do you speak so highly of Capablanca's game of 1925?[10]

Now, notice how differently we go about trying to answer each of these questions, and the different kinds of criteria to which we appeal in each case. In the case of the first question, for example, all that is necessary is to look at the board and count the number of white pawns. In the case of the second, we must refer, not to the board, but to the rules of the game that tell us how pieces are supposed to move. In the case of the third, what is involved is a complex matter of strategy, the history of the game, and even, perhaps, an assessment of the relative skills and propensities of Fischer and his opponent. In the case of the fourth, we might well appeal not only to strategy and judgments of skill but to criteria that border on the aesthetic—for example, the dramatic

10. Based on Norwood Hanson, *Perception and Discovery: An Introduction to Scientific Inquiry*, ed. Willard C. Humphreys (San Francisco: Freeman, Cooper, 1969), 17–18.

rhythm of the game, its cadence, the unique situations that were met and overcome.

In much the same way, grammatical questions *about* or *within* psychoanalysis are logically distinct from other kinds of questions and even, as I have suggested, logically *peculiar*, though perhaps one cannot say precisely what it is that makes them so. To clarify the point, consider now the following kinds of questions:

1. Are protozoa one-celled organisms?
2. What are the meanings of "principle" in the expressions "principle of least action," "principle of the rectilinear propagation of light," or "principle of natural selection"?
3. What are the meanings of "law" in "laws of nature" (e.g., Snell's law, Boyle's law, Kepler's law, and Pauli's law), and does this compare to Freud's understanding of certain "laws of the mind"?
4. How, and to what extent, is the character of our research and observation influenced by the form of notation in which we choose to express our questions?
5. How much of what we call observation is simply a working out of the grammatical resources implicit in our notation?
6. What do we mean by the word "exist" in the following sentences: "A striped coelacanth exists," "Carbon 14 exists," "Submicroscopic particles exist," "A contradiction in his proof exists," "A solution to this problem exists," "Red exists," "The unconscious exists," "God exists"?[11]

All of these questions are, I submit, "grammatical," though this is not to suggest that the distinction between grammatical questions, on the one side, and factual questions, on the other, is always easy to draw. On the contrary, the boundary between fact and grammar, symptom and criterion, is a fluid one and constantly shifting, for, as Wittgenstein puts it, "what today counts as an observed concomitant of a phenomenon will tomorrow be used to define it" (PL, 1:79). Nonetheless, to call our own inquiry grammatical orients us toward certain kinds of questions and away from certain others; it suggests that what we are about, once again, is clarifying the logical and grammatical *conditions* of facts as opposed to determining or explaining the facts themselves; or, as we might also say, we are looking here at the *rules* that underlie the use of

11. Again, based largely on Hanson's discussion of this issue in *Perception and Discovery*, 16.

language in psychoanalysis rather than at the relation between psychoanalytic propositions and the realities to which they are supposed to refer.

One of the presuppositions of posing the problem in this way is the idea that psychoanalytic language does not provide a description of "psychic realities" in anything like the manner in which Freud supposed—that is, as a matter of observation validated through consensus, the formation and testing of hypotheses, or the verification of hypotheticals through the accumulation of confirmatory instances (inductivism). Indeed, it is one of the basic assumptions of this work that the foundational terms and propositions of psychoanalytic theory are—by the standards of common, or ordinary, usage—grammatically *deviant* and that therefore they cannot be evaluated in any straightforward manner (e.g., by appeals to facts or by deductions based on observations). The language of psychoanalysis—especially the so-called metapsychological propositions relating, for example, to unconscious ideation and affect, to the nature, structure, and functions of the mind—represent, in my view, *utterly novel forms of expression for the description and representation of psychical reality*; consequently, the rules for their application must be determined, for the most part, *within* the practice of psychoanalysis itself (since none is given in advance, according to the established linguistic practices) and evaluated relative to other conceivable conceptual constructs (since they cannot, as it were, be set against "reality" as such). In other words, to overstate the case a bit, the core propositions of psychoanalytic theory are not—and, I think, cannot be—directly grounded in empirical or clinical evidence, precisely because *they are not "empirical" in the usual sense of this term* (any more than the poetic statement "The mind is brushed by sparrow wings" or the mathematical proposition "$4 + 2 = 6$" can be verified by reference to empirical, factual realities, though for different reasons in each case).

On the other hand, precisely because they are grammatically deviant, the actual applications of the concepts and propositions of psychoanalytic language can only be determined by a process of analysis; that is, short of analysis, we have no idea what these concepts and propositions really *mean*. (Freud is constantly misled about the proper application of his own theoretical constructs, in large measure because he bases his thinking on false analogies with the natural sciences.) For example, when Freud sets out certain propositions about "*the* unconscious," as a substantive, he effectively invents a new concept.[12] This concept has a

12. At least, as it concerns his own scientific investigation of psychological realities. For my purposes here, it does not matter that the term "the unconscious" was current in the popular philosophy of the time.

meaning, then, only to the extent that it has a consistent and significant use—a coherent application—and this use can only be determined contextually: that is, relative to other logically related and cognate terms (e.g., "consciousness," "repression," and "defense"), on the one hand, and in the context of the practice in which it occurs (viz., in the act of interpretation and construction of certain life narratives, in the process of treatment, in the construction of a theory of culture, etc.), on the other. This means, among other things, that the use of the concept is ultimately justified solely by the validity—that is, the logical coherence and instrumental value—of the theory as a whole.[13] Note, too, that much will depend here on the question of what criteria are judged relevant to the determination of the validity of the theory and, further, that this is once again largely a grammatical, rather than an empirical, question; it pertains to our linguistic practices, rather than to any immediately observed realities. (The idea to be avoided here, of course, is the notion that there are "facts" that transcend the language in which we express them—psychical facts, in this case—and that adjudicate the correctness of our forms of expression.) Similarly, with respect to technical concepts such as "cathexis," "energy," "repression," "instinct," and even the apparently common notions of "sex," "pleasure," and "anxiety"—however familiar these words may *appear*, Freud uses them in ways previously unheard of, and hence it becomes necessary to justify that use by prescribing a consistent and proper application. ("Don't ask for the *meaning*," Wittgenstein declares, "ask for the *use!*" The best way to teach children the meaning of money is to show them what it will and will not buy. The best way to teach someone the meaning of a concept is to show him or her what it can and cannot do. Knowing what a concept can and cannot do means knowing its proper applications.)

Consider the following propositions: (1) Motor-impaired behavior is consistently manifested among the aged, and (2) Sexual behavior is consistently manifested in infants. Despite their outward, formal similarity, there are profound differences between these two statements. The

13. By suggesting a correspondence between the "validity" of the theory and its "coherence and instrumental value," I do not mean to prejudice the question of the nature of scientific truth (as conceived according to the different options of inductionism, falsificationism, objectivism, realism, and so forth). Nonetheless, in adopting the language game as the basic unit of analysis, it would seem that Wittgenstein commits himself, at least implicitly, to an instrumentalist conception of scientific theory, since, in his own account, the relative autonomy of language games disallows appeals to independent, objective "facts" as grounds either for verification or for falsification of the theory as whole. Hence, in this account, not only must a theory be justified only by its instrumental value, but in the end this value itself can be judged solely by the fact that *it is thus used.*

first proposition uses the expression "impaired behavior" as a shorthand for behavior that falls short of accepted norms; an instance of motor behavior is called impaired when it is judged to represent something less than optimal or normal functioning. To the extent that it describes a familiar state of affairs in a relatively common idiom ("*This* is the behavior in question" and "*This* is what we mean by 'motor impaired' behavior"), verification of this proposition is largely a matter of direct observation (allowing, perhaps, for some minor deviations in what will be called "optimal" or "normal" functioning). Is *x* an instance of motor-impaired behavior? Well, look and see. Describe the behavior, then compare it to other instances of observed behavior and ask whether it conforms to the established standards of normal functioning.

But now consider the second statement, "Sexual behavior is consistently manifested in infants." How do we go about deciding whether this is true? The problem here, of course, is that we are not sure about the meaning of the term "sexual behavior." For Freud, as we know, "sexual" can refer to all kinds of behaviors that were not previously regarded as sexual, that is, behaviors that are not related to the genitals or to the activity of reproduction (a child sucking its mother's breast, playing with its feces, etc.). In this case, then, we are dealing with a new, extended meaning of the word "sexual," and thus it is not immediately obvious how we go about determining the truth of the statement in question. Do infants manifest sexual behavior? It is no longer clear how we are supposed to proceed with this question. Minimally, we can say that is not simply a matter of looking. (Nor, I think, is it merely a matter of deciding what we will call sexual, for it seems to me that decision plays very little part in this process. In fact, it makes sense to say that the redefinition of sexuality that we find in Freud theory can actually bring about a new, changed perception of behavior, in the case of both infants and adults, a new way of seeing and describing this behavior that goes significantly beyond the now common platitudes about perception being "theory-laden.")

To repeat, grammatically deviant concepts must be given an application. Most often this means that the rules for the use of these concepts must be capable, at least in principle, of being clearly formulated and having their mutual interrelations defined. "Just because a sentence is constructed after a model does not make it part of a game," Wittgenstein remarks in one of his lectures. "We must provide a system of applications" (L II, 19). To the extent that psychoanalysis, as a general theory of human development and motivation, claims to be *true*, showing what sense the theory has requires that we show how—and to what extent— the propositions that constitute that theory can be verified or falsified;

that is, it requires that we show what can be *done* with these propositions. Such a demonstration, then, will be a contribution to the grammar of the concepts involved. For just as the introduction of a third king into the game of chess means nothing until we have given the rules for it, so the concept of "repression," for example, has no meaning until it is shown how we know that such a thing as repression actually occurs; the concept has meaning, in other words, only to the extent that statements about repression can be shown to have, first, an application within the system of propositions that constitute the theory as a whole and, second, some "grounding" in our common forms of life (though the nature of this grounding may be extremely complex and resistant to explicit formulation).

So much for the positive and more theoretical aspect of the grammatical enterprise; there is also, and more to the point, a negative and critical implication. For the aim of grammar, as Wittgenstein never tired of insisting, is not to find an answer to conceptual problems but to see the impossibility of coherently posing certain kinds of conceptual questions. "Philosophy, by clarifying, stops us asking illegitimate questions," Wittgenstein says in one of his lectures (L I, 111). In relation to psychoanalysis, an important part of the effect of determining the context and conditions of the application of such terms as "sexual," "repression," "the unconscious," and "ego" is to show—not abstractly but concretely, through perspicuous examples and comparisons—that certain questions (and certain general kinds of questions) *cannot meaningfully be asked* and therefore, by any standard of common sense, *ought not to be asked.* These questions include many of those which have dominated a good deal of the literature on Freud and psychoanalysis—questions such as, Is there an unconscious? Do unconscious thoughts have causal efficacy in relation to conscious ideation? Does psychoanalysis actually *explain* the motivations behind human behavior and cultural creativity? Must we now, as a result of Freud's discovery, redefine the nature of the human subjectivity? These kinds of questions, though not entirely senseless, are potentially vicious and stultifying, especially when posed—as they normally are—as demands for factual information or evidence of some sort. I try to show in this work that the import of these questions is actually far more *rhetorical* than empirical, in a sense that should become clearer as the discussion proceeds. (Though let me add here, by way of avoiding potential misunderstandings, that I emphatically do not mean "merely rhetorical," as if all that were at stake in this issue were some kind of wordplay.)

Once again, I am not interested here in whether psychoanalytic theory is "true," but rather in clarifying what it would mean to call it so.[14] My aim is not to pronounce on the truth of psychoanalysis but to show the grammatical specificity of its language and, in the process, to determine what kinds of statements within psychoanalysis might legitimately be called true or false and what kinds of criteria are relevant in making such judgments. Freudian language about unconscious psychical processes is not a mistake but, at least as Freud himself uses it (and many after him), an expression of linguistic confusion. To oversimplify a bit, we might say that Freud was mistaken not in *what* he said but in the implications he drew from his theory (as, for example, when he claimed to show that the ego is not master of its own house). Some of this confusion derives from the distinctive grammatical characteristics of terms like "the unconscious" and its cognates, some from more general misconceptions about the grammar of such concepts as "mind," "thinking," and "feeling"—that is, confusions having to do with notions of interiority, the privacy of sensations, ideas, and so forth. The more important point about trying to clarify these confusions, however—the moral implication, as it were—is this: *what is necessary with respect to psychoanalytic theory is not the correction of this or that theoretical error but the resolution of a certain urge, a certain need for and fascination with the kinds of explanations that psychoanalysis offers.* In the end, we need to learn what can and cannot be legitimately expected from psychoanalytic theory (and, I would add, from the human sciences generally); we need to be freed from the compulsion to see things too narrowly, according to false and misleading analogies, whatever the security or consolation such a limited perspective may offer.

As an exercise in the method of grammar, the purpose of this work is to shed some light on the way language is actually used in psychoanalysis, as well as on the semantic, logical, and grammatical conditions of that use. It is also intended, in the process, to break the hold of certain deep-seated and misleading linguistic pictures (e.g., the picture of the unconscious as something mysterious and inaccessible). While this is, on the whole, a negative operation, there is no denying that it is

14. Much of the contemporary debate about the status of psychoanalysis revolves—openly or implicitly—around the issue of determining the criteria relevant for judgments about its truth, both as a theory and a method of interpretation. There are those who argue that the relevant criteria are—or ought to be—those of the physical, or naturalistic, sciences (e.g., Grünbaum); others who maintain that such criteria must be derived from the humanistic disciplines, and especially from philosophical hermeneutics (e.g., Habermas and Ricoeur); still others who argue that there are and can be no fixed criteria, that such criteria can only be determined relative to certain broadly social, cultural, and historical conditions (e.g., Wittgenstein).

informed by certain positive assumptions—especially assumptions about both the nature of psychoanalysis and about the function of language in psychoanalytic theory (just as Wittgenstein's philosophical inquiries are informed by certain positive, if largely unacknowledged, assumptions about the nature of language, meaning, the true aims of philosophy, etc.). Briefly stated, these assumptions are

1. that what is involved in psychoanalysis, as a comprehensive theory of human psychology and development, is *something like* a paradigm shift as it is described by Thomas Kuhn in relation to the natural sciences—that is, it represents a fundamental change in the frame of questions for psychological inquiry, along with a corresponding redefinition of the range of possible answers;[15]
2. that the decisive aspect of this shift occurs through specific innovations *in language*, that is, through certain semantic and grammatical movements that produce "a new way of seeing" psychological, social, and cultural phenomena;

15. Although a definitive statement of the differences between psychoanalysis and the natural sciences is beyond my competence, I would suggest that the Freudian innovation is *like* a paradigm shift in the natural sciences in this one primary respect: that what it fundamentally provides is not a body of hypotheses or a general theory of human behavior but a paradigmatic set of concepts, syntactical relations, and interpretive practices, and that its real significance lies, therefore, not in any factual discovery (e.g., the discovery of an unconscious mind or of the etiological importance of infantile sexuality) but in the elaboration of a new set of terms, images, and models for the description of human experience, along with a corresponding framework for psychological inquiry. On the other hand, it *differs* from the natural sciences in the following respects: (1) in contrast to the so-called hard sciences, psychoanalytic theory rests on certain analogical correlations that are not subject to verification through prediction and experiment (e.g., the analogy between infantile and adult behavior, or that between pathological and religious behavior) (in the actual practice of interpretation, these correlations might be characterized as *figural and rhetorical* rather than *causal*, pertaining to the *sense* of human experience—construals of meaning—rather than to the organization of a physical field); (2) in psychoanalysis there is no clear separation between *method* and *object*—the very nature of psychoanalysis as an essentially interpretive and heuristic enterprise disallows independent confirmation of "facts" and their theoretical explanation (this has to do, most generally, with the contrasting grammars of such terms as "physical object" and "personal motivation," "external phenomenon" and "internal need"); and finally, (3) in contrast to the paradigms of empirical science, those of psychoanalysis are, in an important sense, unsurpassable: they are not subject to more than minor modifications and can never be disconfirmed by the accumulation of further evidence—and this, of course, because they are not grounded in observable facts to begin with, but rather in intentions, needs, avowals, and the like. This much said, I will be the first to admit it is less than fully adequate. It seems to me that we are still some distance from reaching a consensus about the character of the differences between the natural and the human sciences, though I am not in a position to argue this view here.

3. that the Freudian metapsychology—minimally defined by the distinction between conscious and unconscious psychical processes—represents an attempt to set forth the basic terminology and conceptual framework for this new perspective and that, as such, it remains indispensable to any purportedly psychoanalytic account of these different psychological and cultural phenomena, their character, function, and mutual relations.

4. that the propositions that constitute the metapsychology are largely—though not exclusively—*grammatical and paradigmatic* rather than hypothetical and factual; that what is fundamentally at issue in the metapsychology—and particularly in language about unconscious thoughts, affects, acts of volition, and so forth—is *not* the discovery of objective, independently verifiable "facts," or the deduction of an explanatory hypothesis from empirical evidence ("observation statements"), but rather *new forms of description and representation* of what are actually familiar, though perhaps unrecognized, psychological intentions, motivations, and reactions, a new system of notation that introduces covertly revised criteria for the use of certain accepted words and phrases (e.g., "unconscious," "ego," "thought," "pleasure," "energy," and "sexuality"); and

5. that the validity of any given psychoanalytic interpretation resides essentially in its *persuasive power* that is, in its capacity to elicit agreement through the rhetorical force of its redescription and especially in its display of previously unnoticed analogies between different symbols, images, and patterns of behavior.

Let me stress once more that these various theses are more strategic and heuristic than substantive. They are neither propositions whose truth I intend to prove nor components of a theory about psychoanalysis, its scientific status or epistemological foundations. They are instead more of the order of methodological recommendations, suggestions for fruitful ways of looking at and approaching certain kinds of philosophical problems that seem consistently to arise in connection with psychoanalysis.

The most that can be accomplished by grammatical analysis is *a change in our way of seeing*, and hence of conceptualizing, certain problems. In describing language—grammatical relations and actual linguistic practices—grammar proceeds by way of elucidation, by showing, or "making manifest," rather than by explanation or theoretical exposition. By bringing out certain analogies and connections, by arranging our familiar knowledge in unfamiliar ways, a grammatical analysis leads us to view certain features of our language differently; it dissolves theoretical problems by showing the confusions that underlie them. In and of itself, however, grammar contributes nothing to our fund of factual knowledge, nor does it provide a foundation for theoretical judgments.[16]

Somewhat ironically, then—in view of Wittgenstein's pointed criticism of Freud on this issue[17]—it turns out that the force of a grammatical analysis is itself fundamentally rhetorical rather than demonstrative. Like psychoanalysis, grammar is a matter of persuasion rather than logical or empirical demonstration; its aim is to change our way of looking at particular conceptual problems rather than our way of looking at solutions to the problems as such. In his 1938 lectures on aesthetics, Wittgenstein acknowledges this explicitly. Having argued at length that psychoanalysis, like aesthetic criticism, is essentially a form of persuasion, he goes on to add, "What I'm doing is also persuasion. If someone says: 'There is not a difference', and I say: 'There is a difference' I am persuading, I am saying 'I don't want you to look at it like that.' " And a bit later, in the conclusion to the same lecture:

> I am in a sense making propaganda for one style of thinking as opposed to another. I am honestly disgusted with the other. Also I'm trying to state what I think. . . .
>
> How much we are doing is changing the style of thinking and

16. It cannot be *proved*, for example, that the basic theoretical objects of psychoanalysis are the product of linguistic innovations, since, within a given conceptual framework, fact and paradigm are mutually constitutive. Indeed, not only are the relevant facts largely determined by the theory, but much of what can be described from one perspective as the product of observation and inference can also, from a different perspective, be attributed to grammatical resources implicit in the terminology itself (e.g., the notion of the symptom as compromise formation, as something causally conditioned by repression and its effects). (To the best of my knowledge, Kenneth Burke was the first to argue that it is possible to "deduce" a great deal of Freudian theory without any appeal whatsoever to observation, merely by tracing out the grammatical implications of its key terms. See especially "Terministic Screens" and "Mind, Body, and the Unconscious," both included in *Language as Symbolic Action: Essays on Life, Literature, and Method* (Berkeley and Los Angeles: University of California Press, 1966).

17. In his 1938 lectures on aesthetics, Wittgenstein repeatedly insists on the essentially rhetorical character of psychoanalysis, charging Freud with having "cheated" his patients through his reductive interpretations and characterizing psychoanalysis as a "dangerous" and "powerful" mythology that exercises an enormous appeal on those who fall under its influence (see LC, esp. 18, 23–27, 43, 50–52). "If you are led by psychoanalysis to say that really you thought so and so or that really your motive was so and so, this is not a matter of discovery, but of persuasion," Wittgenstein says at one point. "In a different way you could have been persuaded of something different" (LC, 27).

how much I'm doing is changing the style of thinking and how
much I'm doing is persuading people to change their style
of thinking.
(Much of what we are doing is a question of changing the
style of thinking.) (LC, 27–28)

Like both psychoanalysis and aesthetics, the method of grammar consists in "placing things side by side" so as to exhibit certain features;
and in each case, the intended effect is to change our way of looking at
things (see also L II, 39–40).[18]
Properly speaking, a grammatical analysis is not "wrong," or "false,"
but only, perhaps, "irrelevant," or "unconvincing." Indeed, it seems to
me that this is at once the most distinctive and most neglected feature of
the later Wittgenstein's new style of thinking, the hallmark of his
innovation in philosophical and pedagogical method. What matters in
grammar is not the right theory or opinion but the right way of seeing
things, the appropriate perspective. "What I want to teach you isn't
opinions but a method," Wittgenstein writes in one of his notebooks.
"In fact the method to treat as irrelevant every question of opinion."[19]
(Once again, I refer the reader to Appendix A, "The Method of
Grammar," for further discussion of these points.)
In keeping with this understanding of the grammatical method, the
character of this work is—or at least should be—primarily rhetorical
rather than theoretical or explanatory. This means that whatever else
may be said about what follows, it should not be possible to say that I
have set forth a wrong opinion about the nature of psychoanalysis—not,
of course, because I found all the answers to the philosophical problems
surrounding Freudian theory but because all I am trying to do here is to
describe how language is used in psychoanalysis, to lay out its most
obvious terminological and grammatical features, to describe the contexts in which it is applied, and to make significant comparisons where
it seems helpful to do so. Nothing I say here should be controversial,
though it may certainly happen that the way I present it may be
unpersuasive or confused—or, in a different way, wrong in its representation of what Freud actually said or intended.
This brings me, then, to the last point of these introductory remarks:
namely, the *style* of this work. Against the prevailing trend in Wittgen-

18. This is not to say that there are not important differences between aesthetics, psychoanalysis, and grammar, just as there are important differences between, say, theoretical physics and
biology, even though both are rightly considered natural sciences.
19. Quoted in S. Stephen Hilmy, *The Later Wittgenstein: The Emergence of a New
Philosophical Method* (Oxford: Basil Blackwell, 1987), 5.

steinian scholarship,[20] I am convinced that Wittgenstein's style of writing—that is, the form in which his ideas are expressed, the actual structure of the text—is inseparable from his method of analysis. The reason for this is basically twofold. First, it has to do with the nature of a grammatical investigation as a kind of "metalogical" inquiry: what we attempt to say in metalogic—the attempt to set forth, linguistically, the logical and grammatical conditions of sense in language—cannot really be said, but only *shown* (e.g., in the attempt to characterize the relation between theory and fact, or grammar and object, in psychoanalysis or, more generally, in the analysis of the applicability of certain terms and forms of explanation). The conditions of sense in language cannot be made the object of linguistic description. Grammar, then, is not merely a description of language but also a form of representation: it *represents* grammatical relations and conditions rather than (because impossible) simply stating them.[21]

The second reason has less to do with the method as such than it does with the peculiar nature of the problems toward which that method is directed. For it is in the nature of such problems as, for example, the reality of sensations or the existence of external objects or even the reality of the unconscious that different positions on these issues *cannot be coherently formulated*, much less denied. Hence, in the popular Wittgensteinian parlance, these kinds of problems cannot be solved, but only *dissolved*, and the dissolution of a problem proceeds by a much different strategy and logic than does its solution. In particular, it requires a kind of multivectored approach, one that employs not only argumentation but also pointed presentation in the form of questions, examples, hypothetical and parallel constructions, poetic allusions, even jokes and anecdotes. The proper response to a nonsensical question is *to show* its nonsense, and showing nonsense requires a style of presentation that departs from the usual expository form. With respect to the problem at hand, it does no good to insist that it makes no sense to ask

20. With the exception of, most prominently, O. K. Bouwsma, Stanley Cavell, and, more recently, Henry Staten (see Bouwsma, *Toward a New Sensibility* [Lincoln: University of Nebraska Press, 1982]; Cavell, "The Availability of Wittgenstein's Later Philosophy," in *Must We Mean What We Say?* [Cambridge: Cambridge University Press, 1976], 44–72; and Staten, *Wittgenstein and Derrida* [Lincoln: University of Nebraska Press, 1984]).

21. Doubtless the case of technical languages, such as found in psychoanalytic and other scientific theories, is different from a consideration of language as a whole. One wants to say that these technical languages are, in one way or another, *grounded in* ordinary language and experience and hence should be subject to an analysis that is not merely "presentational." However, the problem with this line of reasoning, it seems to me, is that it begs the question how we are to differentiate between technical language, on the one side, and ordinary language, on the other.

whether the unconscious exists: we must *show* that it is senseless; we must lay bare the grammatical confusions that lie at the root of the urge to pose such questions. This requires that we look at the problem from a number of different perspectives, that we examine it in different lights and in various contrasting contexts.

I believe that these two facts account for many—though certainly not all—of the distinctive qualities of Wittgenstein's style, and it is for this reason that I have adopted certain of the basic features of that style in this work. Of course, there is the further fact that Wittgenstein had genius, whereas I do not, so there is no question of my duplicating his accomplishment here. Like Freud's self-analysis, Wittgenstein's achievement in philosophical method will always remain, in a sense, unsurpassable: no one can repeat the original movement with the same degree of grace, intelligence, and disclosive power. Still, if his method is teachable, as I believe it is, then it ought to be possible for any reasonably competent person to apply it. Whether this is in fact the case remains to be seen.

1

THE UNCONSCIOUS IN PSYCHOANALYSIS

Die Rückkehr von der Überschätzung der Bewusstseinseigenschaft wird zur unerlässlichen Vorbedingung für jede rightige Einsicht in den Hergang des Psychischen. Das Unbewusste muss nach dem Ausdrucke von Lipps als allgemeine Basis des psychischen Lebens angenommen werden. Das Unbewusste is der grössere Kreis, der den kleineren des Bewussten in sich einschliesst; alles Bewusste hat eine unbewussten Vorstufe, während das Unbewusste auf dieser Stufe stehen bleiben und doch den vollen Wert einer psychischen Leistung beanspruchen kann. Das Unbewusste ist das eigentliche reale Psychische, *uns nach seiner inneren Natur so unbekannt wie das Reale der Aussenwelt, und uns durch die Daten des Bewusstseins ebenso unvollständig gegeben wie die Aussenwelt durch die Angaben unserer Sinnesorgane.*[1]

(It is essential to abandon the overvaluation of the property of being conscious before it becomes possible to form any correct view of the [course of the psychical] [*Hergang des Psychischen*]. In Lipps's words, the unconscious must be assumed to be the

---

1. Sigmund Freud, *Die Traumdeutung* (Frankfurt am Main: Fischer Taschenbuch Verlag, 1982), 497.

general basis of psychical life. The unconscious is the larger
sphere, which includes within it the smaller sphere of consciousness. Everything conscious has an unconscious preliminary
stage; whereas what is unconscious may remain at that stage and
nevertheless claim to be regarded as having the full value of a
psychical process. The unconscious is the true psychical reality;
*in its innermost nature it is as much unknown to us as the reality
of the external world, and it is as incompletely presented by the
data of consciousness as is the external world by the communications of our sense organs.*) (ID, 612–13 [Freud's emphasis])

1.1   This passage gives us a certain picture of the human mind, or
psyche.[2] The picture is something like this: The mind is composed of
two parts, consciousness and the unconscious, of which the latter is by
far the more extensive and important. Consciousness is the surface; the
unconscious, the depth of psychical life. Consciousness is merely the tip
of the iceberg. The unconscious is the true matrix of psychical life, the
"first cause" in the chain of mental events, as well as the ultimate source

---

2. It has often been observed that there are no German equivalents for the English "mind"
and "mental." What becomes "mind" in English is most often *Psyche* or *Seele*, sometimes
Geist, and occasionally *Intellekt*; what becomes "mental" is generally either *seelisch* or *geistig*.
The Strachey (*Standard Edition*) translation has been criticized for failing to take these
differences into account, and especially for conflating "psyche" and "mind," "psychical life"
and "mental life," while omitting entirely any reference to "soul." Bruno Bettelheim, in
particular, has argued that this represents a fundamental distortion of Freud's meaning. "Freud
never faltered in his conviction that it was important to think in terms of the soul when trying
to comprehend his system," Bettelheim writes, "because no other concept could make equally
clear what he meant; nor can there be any doubt that he meant the soul, and not the mind,
when he wrote '*seelisch*' " (*Freud and Man's Soul* [New York: Alfred A. Knopf, 1983], 73).
Soul, of course, is the more comprehensive term, embracing both mental and emotional life
while transcending immediate awareness: "By 'soul' or 'psyche' Freud means that which is
most valuable in man. . . . For him, the soul is the seat both of the mind and of the passions,
and we remain largely unconscious of the soul. In important respects, it is deeply hidden,
hardly accessible even to careful investigation. It is intangible, but it nevertheless exercises a
powerful influence on our lives. It is what makes us human; in fact, it is what is so essentially
human about us that no other term could equally convey what Freud had in mind" (Bettelheim,
Freud and Man's Soul, 77–78).
    Generally speaking, since I am at least as interested here in *how Freud has been appro-
priated*—for example, in the construction of "models of the mind"—as I am in what he
originally meant, this poses less of a problem than one might at first suppose. What really
matters is not what Freud intended but how he has been used. Still, there is no question that
the *Standard Edition* translation is, at times, profoundly misleading. In the discussion that
follows, therefore, I have occasionally taken the liberty of altering the translation. (I am
indebted to Judith van Herik for having rightly insisted on the importance of this issue, as well
as for clarifying some of its implications.)

of all psychological realities, both normal and abnormal. Thus, the unconscious is "more real" than consciousness, even though it can be known only incompletely, through the data of consciousness, just as the external world can be known only incompletely through the data of the senses. The unconscious is the source of our most intimate but hidden motives; it moves us out of unknown depths, stirring us to actions whose meaning we can ultimately neither deny nor comprehend.

Now, this picture of the unconscious as something inaccessible, as something deep and mysterious, *seems* comprehensible; it seems to provide its own meaning; it seems to tell us, in our use of the concept, "what we have to do, what we have to look for, and how" (PI, 2:112). For example, we imagine consciousness as an island surrounded by a great sea or as a thin surface stretched across an inconceivable depth; or we think of it as something that is located "behind" or "beneath" consciousness, in back of the head, perhaps, just above the neck, or something of the sort; or we imagine our relation to the internal object of the unconscious on the analogy of our relation to the external reality of the world, except that the one, of course, is "inward" and the other "outward," and so forth. All of these pictures suggest themselves at one time or another; they seem almost to *impose* themselves on us, especially when we try to think philosophically about the reality of the unconscious and its implications. Nonetheless, I want to propose that all of these pictures are, without exception, profoundly misleading, that there is in fact a real discrepancy between what these different pictures suggest and how the concept is—and how it legitimately can be—used in psychoanalysis, a discrepancy between what these pictures indicate about its use and how the concept is actually *applied* in psychoanalytic practice and theory. (It is as if, in learning to play chess, we became fascinated with the figure of the bishop, its physical appearance, and came to believe that it, and not the queen, was the most powerful piece on the board. But all that really matters, of course, is what it can *do*, according to the rules of the game, how it can and cannot be used. The concept of the unconscious, like the bishop, may conjure up certain images that *seem* compelling; but like the bishop, it has only the value that we give it in use.)

It is this discrepancy between picture and use that we must try to clarify. We must learn to see *through* the image to the actual application; we must see how the image is and is not true to the reality.

1.2   Certain pictures are embedded in our language, in our grammatical forms; the image of the unconscious as something deep and hidden, as a kind of mysterious, occult entity "in the mind," is one such picture.[3] In order to free ourselves from the picture, we need to get clear about the actual use of the concept. (To begin with, do not immediately think of the unconscious as something *internal*. At the same time, of course, there is nothing *wrong* with describing the unconscious as "internal," provided that we are not misled by false analogies; what matters is how we understand this description, how we make use of it.)

1.3   The picture of the unconscious as something unknown and unknowable, as something dark and hidden, something uncanny, ominous, and perhaps even threatening—this picture emerges again and again in the course of our thinking about the phenomena that psychoanalysis describes; it literally forces itself on us. This picture belongs to our language. It is, as it were, a *shadow* of our language. (Through the method of grammar, we try to bring light to the shadows of our language.)

1.4   Our aim is, in part, to *deliteralize* the picture of the unconscious. We want to see the picture *as a picture* and not as the object itself. (Ask yourself: Where is the unconscious located? Is it powerful or weak? Large or small? Light or dark? Does it have effects on consciousness? Does it behave according to certain of laws, or is it, on the contrary, something wild and chaotic, "a cauldron full of seething excitations" [NIL, 73]? Now ask, *How do you know*? Do you know in the same way that you know, say, that this table is hard, or that this light is bright? Or in the way that you know that molecules are composed of atoms? Or that *this* is red? Or that clouds indicate the chance of rain? Or that *this* is the right sequence of notes to conclude a musical phrase? All of this concerns the grammar of the expression "to know.")

1.5   We can distinguish between two kinds of investigations: first, the investigation into the properties of an object, and second, the investigation into the grammar of the word referring to an object (YB, 51). The

---

3. There are, of course, many others. We speak, for example, of thinking as something that goes on "inside the head," or of the soul as something that inhabits and animates the body, or of earth as a ball suspended in space, or of a floor as composed of loosely connected atoms. These grammatical pictures are, as it were, "illustrated turns of speech" (PI, 1:295). They are the simplified, idealized images that are imbedded in our language, that inform and direct the way we speak about things. Such pictures are everywhere; they are natural, inevitable, and, in and of themselves, harmless. Difficulties arise only when we literalize these grammatical pictures, that is, when we take them as *representational* rather than figural. A grammatical *illusion* is neither more nor less than a grammatical picture that is taken literally. (For further discussion, see Appendix A, "On the Method of Grammar.")

former is factual and empirical, the latter grammatical (though the line between them is sometimes thinly drawn). If the unconscious is the distinctive domain of psychoanalysis, its privileged "object," we might say that the inquiry here concerns the grammar of the word that refers to that object—in other words, the grammar of "the unconscious."

Grammar does not give us facts about the object, but rather it "tells us what kind of object anything is" (PI, 1:373). This is a matter of *sense*, not truth.

1.6 "Does the unconscious exist?" We cannot answer this question until we know what kind of sense to attribute to the term "the unconscious," for the distinction between what exists and what does not exist is a distinction *in our language*; what is real and what is unreal shows itself in *grammar*, in the sense of the propositions about what is real and unreal. (One of the best ways to determine this sense—though not the only one—is to ask, How do we know, or find out, about an object like the unconscious? That is, by what procedures and methods?)

It is not reality that gives sense to language, but our use of language that determines what is "real" and what is "not real"—that is, it is our use of language that determines the *possibilities* of the real. Our problem, then, concerns the *concept*, not the thing, it concerns the use of the term "the unconscious" rather than its referent. (If we want to understand the sense of the concept, we must look at its actual use *in the language*, for it is the use of the term—in the context of certain activities, of certain social and technological practices—that, as it were, ties the word to its referent.)

What the unconscious is reveals itself in *grammar*, not evidence; what this and related expressions *mean* shows itself in the way they are *used*.

1.7 "But surely there are things that exist and 'are real' that have not been expressed in our language! (Science discovers more and more of such things every day.) And surely there is reality—a world—that exists independent of our speech about it. What you say seems to imply, on the contrary, that it is only our language that *constitutes* reality, that nothing exists except as it is expressed in language. This would seem to lead, then, to the most radical form of constructivism, or an extreme version of linguistic relativism."[4]

When I say that it is not reality that gives sense to language, but our use of language that determines what is "real" and what is "not real," I

4. I am indebted to Fred Berthold, of Dartmouth College, for having raised these general questions, though not necessarily in the form that I present them here.

don't mean that language determines reality, as, say, an optical lens determines visual perception, or as the relation of the various parts to one another determines the movement of a mechanism, but rather as the rules of a game determine which moves are allowed and which are not. (Can the pawn move diagonally in chess?) When I say that language determines the *possibilities* of the real, what I mean is (1) that we cannot appeal to some extralinguistic reality to adjudicate questions of language usage (sense is sense *within* our language: that is, the rules of grammar are independent of the facts, or states of affairs, that we describe in language—or, as we might also say, grammatical rules neither conform to nor contradict existing facts) and (2) that language, or linguistic conventions, alone determine what can and cannot be said to exist (questions of sense precede questions of existence: that is, what is "possible" or "impossible" is determined grammatically, prior to questions of fact).[5]

We say that though no one is sitting in this chair, somebody *could*. This means roughly that the sentence "The man sits in this chair" *makes sense*, or as we might also say, that there is a *logical possibility* of someone sitting in it. But if we ask whether there are square circles on the moon or whether the son of a barren woman might one day be elected president, we are talking nonsense; such things are ruled out grammatically, prior to any question of existence or actual possibility.

"Does language *determine* what is real?" Yes and no. Yes, if by this we mean that only certain grammatical combinations *have sense* and, therefore, the *possibility* of reference to reality; no, if this is taken to mean that nothing exists apart from its expression in language. (I don't know what this latter would *mean*.)

1.8   "So it would be true that mermaids don't exist even if no one ever said that mermaids don't exist?" Yes, of course; but I have no trouble imagining a world in which mermaids *do* exist; their existence, in other words, is *grammatically* possible, since the words have meaning and since I can formulate statements about their existence without logical contradiction. But now suppose I ask, "Do 'anaphylaxes' exist?" How

---

5. These two points correspond roughly to what are sometimes called in the literature—a bit confusingly, I think—"the doctrine of the autonomy of grammar" and "the doctrine of the arbitrariness of grammar." Wittgenstein says at one point that "the connection between 'language and reality' is made by definitions of words, and these belong to grammar, so that language remains self-contained and autonomous" (PG, 97). But I would add that definitions often involve more than mere words: for example, gestures, pointing, and other, more complicated social activities. In other words, the link between language and world is made in our *activity*, in our social practices, both linguistic and nonlinguistic.

would you answer? (What you would not do, presumably, is try to find one.)

1.9 "Returning to the question of the unconscious, if we say that it is the concept and not the referent that concerns us, then is it a matter of indifference that there are established procedures for knowing the contents of the unconscious mind (dream analysis, free association, interpretation of the transference, etc.) and that these procedures reveal the real, objective influence of what can be described as unconscious affects, ideas, and so forth?" Not at all. On the contrary, the procedures by which the unconscious is known, how unconscious ideas are made conscious, tell us something essential about the grammar of the concept (just as the procedures for knowing an atom and for verifying or falsifying propositions about atoms tell us something essential about how the concept of "atom" is to be understood and applied). Nonetheless, in dealing with questions of this sort, it is important that we not begin by looking for an object simply because we are confronted by a noun (the so-called reference fallacy), but rather describe particular instances of language use as they are embedded in various activities, practices, language games, institutions, and the like.

1.10 The idea of the unconscious is sometimes nothing more than a mythological way of marking *logical* boundaries. One says, for example, "The unconscious cannot be observed directly," "The unconscious is timeless," "The unconscious knows nothing of logic." Everything I want to say might be summed up in the remark that these are *grammatical* statements, not factual ones.[6] (But admittedly this distinction is itself far from clear, and therefore of little help at this point.)

1.11 In one of his last writings on the subject, Freud proposes that psychoanalysis is based on two fundamental hypotheses: first, with respect to what he calls the localization of psychical phenomena, that "mental life is a function of an apparatus to which we ascribe the

6. It is widely accepted that the unconscious system, or primary-process thinking, can be defined according to four distinctive characteristics: (1) it admits of no degrees of certainty or doubt and no forms of contradiction (i.e., it knows nothing of logic); (2) it is not temporally regulated (i.e., it knows nothing of time); (3) it is regulated exclusively by the pleasure principle (i.e., it knows nothing of external reality); and (4) the libidinal energies that constitute it have relatively free mobility by comparison to conscious and preconscious wishes (i.e., they are unbounded). In what follows, I try to show that this kind of characterization, while appropriate to the construction of a certain explanatory model of the mind, is profoundly misleading when taken as descriptive of an object ("the unconscious").

characteristics of being extended in space and of being made up of several portions—which we imagine, that is, as resembling a telescope or microscope or something of the kind" (OP, 145); and second, with respect to the general character, or "nature," of psychical phenomena, that the "true essence" of the psychical is unconscious—or, put differently, that "[psychoanalysis] explains the supposedly somatic concomitant phenomena as being what is truly psychical, and thus in the first instance disregards the quality of consciousness" (OP, 158). The first hypothesis pertains to the possibility of devising a spatial representation of the functional relations between different psychical processes; the second pertains to the methodological assumption of an explanatory category that exceeds conscious experience or is constituted by something *other than* what appears to consciousness. The question here is, Are these in fact hypotheses?—that is, propositions capable of verification or falsification—or are they something else, something of the order of definitions and standards that cannot, in principle, be judged either true or false, but only, perhaps, "useful" or "not useful" for specific purposes (just as the metric system may be useful for some kinds of measurement, less so for others)? How do we decide?

1.12   Asking about the *use* of the concept of the unconscious is a way of asking about its logical status: What *kind* of concept is it? To what logical category or class does it belong? Is the concept of the unconscious of the same logical type as, say, the scientific concept of "physical cause"? (That is, do we appropriately use the two concepts in the same way?) Or is it more like the concept of "gravity"? Or the concept of "the atom"? Or is it perhaps more akin to certain concepts in the human sciences, to sociological and cultural concepts like "class conflict," "agency," "interest," and "alienation"?—or to the psychological concepts of "identity," "personhood," "creative aptitude," and so forth? Again, the only way to answer these questions is to look at how the concept is used, to see how that use is like, how it is different from, the use of other, apparently similar kinds of concepts.

Or we might also ask, Is the unconscious a hypothetical construct, something about which it makes sense to say that it is or is not a demonstratable fact? Or is it rather a kind of notation, an element in a form of representation—that is, something that belongs to the *framework* rather than the data of psychoanalysis (i.e., a *condition* rather than the *object* of description)? This, too, would be a question about the logical status of the concept, but one of an order different from those just mentioned. (In considering the pieces of a chess game, we may ask how the rook is similar to the pawn or, in a different way, how both the rook and the pawn compare to the squares on the board, each as integral elements of the game.)

Here we are asking, in effect, Can propositions about the unconscious be significantly falsified?[7] And the answer to this question will be a contribution to the grammar of such propositions. (Notice that the problem of falsification is more basic than the problem of verification, since the one concerns the *sense* of the proposition, the other its *truth*.)

This is like asking of a chess piece, What are the rules for its movement? What can we do with it? (And we must always keep in mind that it may have more than one use.)

1.13   Wittgenstein tells us that the meaning of a word is its use in the language. This means that often—though not always—one can substitute "the use of a word" for "the meaning of a word," since the use constitutes a large part of what we mean by "meaning." Thus, understanding a term like "the unconscious" amounts to knowing its various uses, its different applications (and those uses may be *very* different from what the term itself seems to suggest).

Just as the best way to teach children the meaning of money is to show them what it will and will not buy, so the best way to learn the meaning of a concept is to see what it can and cannot do. And just as it may be difficult to explain what "money" is but not "how money is used," so it is less difficult to describe the uses of the term "the unconscious" than it is to explain what the unconscious *is*.

Consider, for example, the apparent paradox of unconscious ideas and affects. How do we comprehend the idea of, say, "unconscious pleasure," a pleasure, in other words, that is not experienced as such, that may in fact be experienced as pain? How do we make sense of this idea? To the extent that we *can* make sense of this notion, it is a matter, first, of situating this paradox in the context of a theory in which it has a definite use ("We call *x* an instance of unconscious pleasure when . . ."), then, of resolving this theory itself into a set of rule-governed activities (or language games). In this way, the concept of unconscious pleasure is seen to refer, not to some mysterious, occult event or subliminal experience, but to particular kinds of interpretation that themselves relate disparate kinds of events and experience, both pleasurable and painful.

1.14   What kind of discovery is represented in Freud's discovery of the unconscious? Did Freud discover the unconscious as Columbus

---

7. Following Popper's modification of the verification principle.

discovered America—or as Newton discovered gravity—or, in keeping with Freud's own favorite analogy, as Copernicus discovered the helio-centric principle of planetary movement? Here we would need to ask, too, about the nature of these other kinds of discoveries. Did Newton or Copernicus discover any new "facts," or did they merely propose new ways by which the known facts might be *organized*? And how do we go about trying to answer this? How do we make a distinction here between "theory," on the one hand, and "fact," on the other? *Can* we make such a distinction? (This concerns the grammar of "fact.")

What has changed as the result of Freud's discovery of the uncon-scious—or, if you prefer, of his discovery of the Oedipus complex as the basic structuring principle of both character and culture? Do we now understand something essential about human nature that we did not understand before?—For example, that we are less in control of our lives than we had previously thought, that we are more fragmented, less whole, than we may have liked to believe, or that our character, which we formerly believed was shaped for the most part by our will, is actually determined by a relatively limited set of experiences in infancy? We now discover, says Freud, that "the ego is not even master in its own house, but must content itself with scanty information of what is going on unconsciously in its mind" (IL, 285). But how did we *make* this discovery? Through introspection, perhaps? Then how do we verify its truth (or prove it to be false)? By what means do we demonstrate the truth of this idea? Are there such means?

1.15   Do I know myself *better* since Freud? What would "better" mean in this context? Do I know myself better than Plato knew himself—or only differently? How would we go about deciding a question like this? To what standards would we appeal?

Am I, perhaps, better adjusted to my environment, more capable of surviving, for having read Freud? Am I closer to some deep truth about myself? (How do I know?) Am I *happier* for having read Freud? (This seems doubtful.)

"But surely this much, at least, is certain: I know myself better, having read Freud, than so-called primitives know themselves, for a primitive is superstitious and ignorant in ways that I clearly am not."[8] In the first place, of course, it can be questioned whether I am "less

8. We *call* these people primitive. Social organizations and practices may become more complex over time, allowing us to speak of "primitive" phases and peoples, but this does not mean that earlier and less complex phases of the development were somehow deficient or that all cultures necessarily follow the same developmental path. In fact, part of what is being placed in question here is precisely the meaning of "primitive."

superstitious and ignorant" merely for having been exposed to Freudian theory (though reading Freud allows me to rationalize certain beliefs, that is, it gives me *reasons*). But isn't there still something odd about the idea? For what do we mean by "knowledge" here—and what is the object of that knowledge? Do I understand myself better in the same way that we understand better the causes of solar eclipses, or of rain? Do I *live better* than this "primitive"? Suppose we say that understanding myself in this sense is something like "knowing how to get on in the world." Do I get on better than the primitive does?

The primitive, we like to say, lives for the most part unconsciously, whereas we are conscious. But what are we really expressing here? What is the character of this difference?

Imagine that we tried to teach this primitive—a member of a remote tribe in Africa—the use of the concept of the unconscious. How and where would we begin? Why would it be not merely difficult but impossible for the primitive to understand (in a way that teaching the primitive physics, for example, would not be impossible)?

1.16   We are following Freud's usual procedure of beginning a discussion of psychoanalysis with a general account of the reasons for adopting the concept of the unconscious. How do we know that there is something like an unconscious or that there are such things as unconscious ideas, affects, and motivations? What justifies our use of the concept? What is it that we know when we know the unconscious?

Freud himself gives various arguments in justification of the concept, though he always comes back to the idea that the assumption of an unconscious is the necessary condition for explaining certain kinds of psychical phenomena, phenomena that would otherwise remain inexplicable. The concept of the unconscious is both useful and necessary, he argues, because there are many psychical acts or events—for example, dreams, neurotic symptoms, and hypnotic suggestion—that are utterly incomprehensible to any psychology that is based exclusively on the data of consciousness. These phenomena are rendered comprehensible, however, as soon as we assume the existence of something like an unconscious mind. Dreams and symptoms can then be explained as the distorted expression of repressed psychological conflicts, posthypnotic effects as the product of unconscious ideas, and so forth. In each case, it is only by presupposing certain acts other than those of consciousness—only by *interpolating* these acts between the disconnected and unintelligible phenomena of consciousness—that we are capable of constructing a comprehensive psychological explanation for virtually *all* observed psychological occurrences, both normal and pathological.[9] (To this we might add that it is the convergence of these interpolative acts on one unified object, one causal nexus, that allows the concept to relate widely disparate phenomena and to subsume both normal and pathological phenomena under a single explanatory category, "the unconscious.")

Let us disregard, for the moment, the question whether—and in what sense—the assumption of the unconscious actually allows us to *explain* psychical events like dreams and symptoms. Let us look instead at how the term functions in such explanations, how it is used.

1.17   Consider, first, the evidence of hypnosis, Freud's personal favorite.[10] The doctor places an umbrella in the corner, hypnotizes one of his patients, and says to him, "I am leaving now. When I come back you will meet me with my umbrella open and hold it over my head." The doctor awakens the patient, then leaves. When he returns, the patient does exactly as ordered. The doctor questions him, "What are you doing? What's the meaning of this?" The patient, embarrassed, remarks lamely, "I only thought, doctor, as it's raining outside you'd want your umbrella in the room before you went out" (SELP, 285). "It is a state of affairs of this sort that we have before our eyes when we speak of the existence of *unconscious mental processes*," Freud writes.

> We can challenge anyone in the world to give a more correct scientific account of this state of affairs, and if he does we will gladly renounce our hypothesis of unconscious mental processes. Till that happens, however, we will hold fast to the hypothesis; and if someone objects that here the unconscious is nothing real in a scientific sense, is a makeshift, *un façon de parler* we can only shrug our shoulders resignedly and dismiss what he says as unintelligible. Something not real, which produces effects of such a tangible reality . . . ! (IL, 277–78)

Okay, let us ask, then, Is there any evidence in this example of an unconscious mind, or unconscious will, that directs the patient's ac-

9. This argument, summarized here from a number of different sources, is set forth most fully in the opening section of Freud's famous essay, "The Unconscious" (U, 166–67).

10. Freud generally cites three facts as evidence for the existence of an unconscious mind: (1) the fact that thoughts suddenly come to consciousness without any conscious preparation or forethought; (2) the fact that slips—or parapraxes—occur that can be shown to be motivated by unconscious intentions; and (3) the fact of hypnotic suggestion (SELP, 283–86; see also, QLA, 197).

tions? All we actually *observe* is the fact that he is given a suggestion under hypnosis and later acts on this suggestion. Of course, we are inclined to say—and Freud would have us believe—that a suggestion is given to the unconscious mind, or placed in the unconscious, which asserts itself in the form of an irresistible directive: Open the umbrella. (Here we *picture* something hidden that suddenly emerges into light, or something of that kind.) But do we really gain anything by ascribing this motivation to the unconscious? Does the concept of the unconscious actually allow us to *explain* the fact of hypnotic suggestion? Or doesn't it rather give us a way of *describing* that fact, or representing it to ourselves, just as we might describe the soporific effect of a drug as following from an agent with "dormitive virtues"? (We say, "There *must* be a cause," and one presents itself.) Is the unconscious merely "*une façon de parler*," after all?

"He opened the umbrella because an idea that was preserved in the unconscious directed him to do so." But we know nothing of this unconscious apart from the fact that it connects event *A*, the hypnotic suggestion, and event *B*, the posthypnotic effect. All we observe are the two events, *A* and *B*, which we connect with the idea of the unconscious. But what does the explanation provide that we did not already know before? In this case, at least, the meaning of the concept of the unconscious is entirely exhausted by a description of the relations on which it is supposed to be based. (And this is part of what it means to say that the unconscious is a form of representation, or a notation.)

Where we want to mark a change or to account for some event but cannot see a cause, we postulate the existence of something unseen, an unseen psychical agent of some sort. After Freud, we call these unseen agents "unconscious." (False analogy: "unconscious thought" and "unseen cause.")

1.18 "But the correlation is nonetheless a *real* one, for it is not two randomly observed events that are at issue here, but the relation between a specific order and the patient's *acting* on that order, acting, moreover, without any awareness of the reasons for his action. Why then shouldn't we attribute his action to the effects of an unconscious idea?" Of course, we *can* say this, and we may even claim to have *explained* the patient's action in doing so, but we should be very careful about the kinds of implications we derive from this way of expressing the matter. We know that hypnotic suggestions have effects, and we can explain those effects by appeal to the notion of an unconscious, but when we describe the action as the effect of an unconscious idea, we are in danger of being captivated by a picture whose application is in fact quite limited. For, to repeat, what do I know of this unconscious apart from the observed connection? And what can I properly infer on *this* basis? (We have a tendency to extrapolate from the single instance much more than it can actually support.)

1.19 "In many cases, however—in the case of dreams, parapraxes, and symptoms, for example—the concept of the unconscious does more than merely connect two observed events; it provides the possibility of constructing a comprehensive theory of motivation. For it is only the concept of the unconscious—together with the model of wish fulfillment—that allows for a *dynamic* explanation of such psychical phenomena, one that provides a way of comprehending these phenomena and that clearly goes beyond mere representation or redescription."
    Doubtless the idea of the unconscious functions otherwise in the context of the psychoanalytic theory of dreams and neurosis than it does in the case of hypnosis (i.e., it has a different *use*), and noting this difference is itself an important step toward the clarification of the concept. *How* it functions, whether it is necessary to such explanations and the *kind* of necessity it possesses, is examined later. (Among other things, we need to ask what "explanation" means in this context.)

1.20 Another argument runs like this: "At any given moment I am conscious of only a very small portion of what can, at least potentially, be made conscious. The entire content of my memory, my knowledge of a large number of facts, my acquired dispositions, and so forth, are all outside of my immediate consciousness but nonetheless capable of becoming conscious; they exist, so to speak, 'in a state of latency.' These various ideational contents and dispositions are clearly mental, but unconscious. Their very existence is thus proof of the reality of an unconscious mind."
    This is precisely the kind of explanation that turns logical and grammatical differences into mythological ones. In the first place, to claim that memories, dispositions, and the like, are stored in "an unconscious" contributes nothing to our knowledge of them. We are all familiar with memories—which is to say, we all know how to use the term "memory"—and we all know that memories refer to such mental contents as may or may not be present at any given moment. In other words, it belongs to the grammar of "memory" that we use the term with reference to ideas and images, for example, that were are not always in our minds; "to remember" is precisely to bring something to mind that was formerly absent. This does not mean, however, that what was brought to mind must have existed somewhere—where?—prior to hav-

ing been remembered. Hence, nothing whatsoever is added by attribut-
ing these capacities and activities to an unconscious mind. (We think of
a memory on the analogy of an object and then we believe that it must
exist in a "place." We cannot designate this place directly but presume
that it is "in the mind." But now ask yourself, What is a place that
cannot be located, that is neither here nor there, but somewhere in
between? Indeed, what do we *mean* by the word "place" here?)

Moreover, the argument here pertains only to what might be called
descriptively unconscious, to what is merely latent, and not to the
dynamic unconscious—that is, to the explanatory concept Freud in fact
wants to establish. To say that memories are (most of the time) unconscious is to use the term "unconscious" very differently from the way
Freud uses it when he says, for example, that dreams are the expression
of unconscious ideas. (Again, ask yourself, in each instance where we
use the term, How do we know?) What is unconscious in the first,
descriptive sense has no necessary relation to what is unconscious in the
second, explanatory sense; and the fact that we commonly use the term
in the first sense does nothing to legitimate its use in the second.

1.21   It is important to recognize that the word "unconscious" has a
large variety of uses and many different senses, according to the context
in which it appears. We say, for example, "a man is unconscious," and
"a stone is unconscious," and "a memory is unconscious." All of these
represent legitimate uses of the word. But now, suppose we ask, Can an
idea be unconscious—or, still yet, a *feeling*? One person says yes,
another no. How do we decide who is right? (One thing we should *not*
do is conduct experiments, for what could experimental data—indeed,
what could any fact—tell us here that was not already built into the
meaning of the term? The issue here is not whether such and such is the
case in the world—that is, whether unconscious ideas "exist"—but
whether it *makes sense* to speak about such things. Similarly, it is a
matter of asking, not whether such a thing as *the* unconscious exists,
but whether the concept"the unconscious" has coherent use, or application. The first question orients us toward observed phenomena; the
second, toward linguistic *practices*, or what Wittgenstein would call
language games.)

1.22   Note that Freud adopts the concept of the unconscious not
because what appears to consciousness is *false* but because consciousness
is "incomplete," "discontinuous," or, taken by itself, "unintelligible,"
because the data of consciousness are *insufficient* to account for the
known phenomena of psychical life (e.g., dreams, hypnosis, and neu-

rotic symptoms).[11] The assumption of the unconscious allows us *to make sense* of things that would otherwise appear senseless; if, however, we then go on to claim that the unconscious is more true, or more real, than consciousness, then we must be prepared to give an account of what we mean by "true" and "real" here. (We cannot mean that consciousness is thereby deposed as a source of truth, since, of course, it is only through the data of consciousness that we arrived at the notion of the unconscious in the first place.)

"There is something profound and mysterious, something insidious behind or beneath the surface of consciousness." We have to see that what is mysterious here belongs to our form of representation and not to the object.

1.23 "When Freud writes that 'the unconscious is the true psychical reality,' his point, we might say, is methodological rather than metaphysical: what we means is not that consciousness is unreal, or false, but that consciousness as such—that is, what I immediately experience, what I think, feel, sense, and imagine—cannot provide the basis for a comprehensive psychological account of human behavior and pathology, that the postulate of the unconscious is necessary in order to *explain* certain psychical phenomena and occurrences, that it is part of the theoretical context within which these phenomena and events *make sense.*" But surely Freud wants to say much more than this. For it is not only that the postulate of an unconscious allows us to explain certain things, according to Freud, but that with the discovery and scientific description of the unconscious *as something objective and real*, as a locus of real psychical forces and cause, it now becomes possible for the first time to explain certain things that were previously inexplicable. In other words, for Freud, the unconscious is more than a hypothetical construct or a methodological postulate; it is a demonstrable fact with observable effects.

A practicing physicist does not adopt the law of gravity because it allows him to explain certain kinds of motion; rather, he sees certain kinds of motion *as instances of* the effects of gravity. The law of gravity is, as it were, built into his way of construing things. Likewise, Freud does not assume the existence of the unconscious in order to explain dreams; rather, he sees—and interprets—dreams as the manifestation of

11. This is very different from what many of the more radical reinterpretations of psychoanalysis—for example, Jacques Lacan and his followers—want to claim. It is one thing to say that mental life cannot be explained without appeal to the notion of an unconscious, quite another to say that consciousness is something essentially dissimulating.

unconscious conflicts, that is, *as instances of the effects of repression*. It is a matter not of adopting a hypothesis but of seeing things *this way* rather than some other. (What fact would count *against* my seeing dreams as the expression of unconscious conflicts?)

1.24   Can we imagine a situation in which it might actually make sense to say that the unconscious is "more real" than the conscious? Perhaps. But if such a situation were not the exception rather than the rule, if it were not ordinarily the case that we trust in our conscious perceptions, motives, and ideation, conscious and unconscious would no longer retain their customary meanings.[12]

(Remember: the point here is not to show Freud's theory to be "wrong" but rather to indicate how certain aspects of that theory—for example, the idea that the unconscious is *more real* than consciousness— cannot be coherently applied, or, put differently, to show that a certain *picture* of the unconscious cannot be coherently applied.)

1.25   "Our real desires are unconscious."[13] Why is this idea at once so disturbing and, on some level, so believable? Our real desires, according to Freud, are the desires of infancy. This *seems* plausible; it seems to make sense. More than that, it allows us to comprehend ourselves in an entirely new way, allows us to understand certain aspects of our behavior that would otherwise seem arbitrary or senseless.

I have no trouble believing, for example, that my desire to acquire material things beyond immediate needs represents a form of displace-ment, an attempt to compensate for some primal loss; moreover, believ-ing this allows me to explain certain things about myself and my behavior that would otherwise be inexplicable—for instance, why I sometimes feel compelled to buy something, then find the possession of it so unsatisfying. But suppose I ask, How do I *know* my desire for

12. For example, when Lacan proclaims that Freud "de-centers" the human subject, that as a result of Freud's discovery "the very center of the human being is no longer to be found at the place assigned to it by a whole humanist tradition" (Lacan, *Écrits*, trans. Alan Sheridan [New York: W. W. Norton, 1977], 114), we should take this as a paradox whose main value lies in its capacity to shock and stimulate. As a paradox, this statement is both true and not true, but it is neither true nor false in any conventional sense. For an illuminating account of the value of paradox, see John Wisdom, *Paradox and Discovery* (New York: Philosophical Library, 1965), esp. 114–38.

13. "It begins to be apparent that mankind, in all its restless striving and progress, has no idea of what it really wants," writes Norman O. Brown in his landmark study of psychoanalysis and cultural history, *Life Against Death*. "Freud was right: our real desires are unconscious" (Brown, *Life Against Death: The Psychoanalytic Meaning of History* [Middletown, Conn.: Wesleyan University Press, 1959], xviii).

material things derives from something else, from some more fundamental wish of childhood? How do I establish the truth of this idea? And here I am utterly at a loss. How *could* I know such a thing? How could such an idea be subjected to proof of any sort? What would count as evidence here? Moreover, if I go further and say that my *real* desire is not for this or that possession at all but for something else, then I seem to be verging on nonsense. (Imagine that I desire to buy something—say, a new tie or the latest recording of a favorite classical piece. Now suppose we ask, What is the actual character of this desire? Is it *wrong* to say that I desire the tie, if I also claim that, in fact, my *real* desire is for something else, that is, for some lost object of childhood? Yet if I say that what I *really* desire is the childhood object and not the material thing before me, aren't I simply introducing new criteria for the use of the word "desire," along with, perhaps, the terms "conscious" and "unconscious"? Aren't I actually inventing an entirely new game for the use of these words?)

The notion that our real desires are unconscious contravenes both common sense and ordinary language usage, and yet there is something so fascinating about the idea, so profoundly compelling, that we find it very hard to give it up—as if it were intrinsically convincing and stood without need of any proof or evidence.

1.26   "How are we to arrive at a knowledge of the unconscious?" Freud asks in his famous essay "The Unconscious." "It is of course only as something conscious that we know it, after it has undergone transformation [*Umsetzung*] or translation [*Übersetzung*] into something conscious." And he adds, "Psychoanalytic work shows us every day that translation of this kind is possible" (U, 166). Here Freud uses the term "unconscious" in what might be called a phenomenological sense: that is, as something having an *experiential* basis (I "know" the unconscious once it is translated into "something conscious," once it becomes something I can experience). Now, this is very different from his more usual "hypothetico-deductive," or "heuristic," use of the term (i.e., the unconscious as a condition of explanation or necessary assumption for establishing the continuity of psychical processes and events) and still more different from his frequent "objectivistic" use (i.e., the unconscious as an internal but quasi-empirical "object" or as an unobserved but inferred cause of certain observable effects). How are these different uses related?

Freudian theory, we might say, does not converge on a single, unitary phenomenon, or hypothetical construct, "the unconscious," but rather it provides a new terminology and syntax—and indeed an entirely new language—for both describing and forging connections between a multitude of different events, activities, symbolic relations, and so forth, that were perhaps already in a significant sense "known" but whose interrelations were largely unrecognized. Freud shows connections in a whole that had not previously been apprehended *as a whole* (e.g., the connection between dreams and neurotic symptoms), connections that he then represents theoretically with the use of the term "the unconscious."[14] (Freud's mistake was to claim to have *discovered* the whole as something objective, factual, and empirically demonstrable.)

1.27 "Does the unconscious exist?" Put in this form, one doesn't know where to begin with the question.

Compare "Does gravity exist?" and "Do atoms exist?" But surely we can say that we observe the *effects* of gravity and atoms! But now ask, How do we recognize these effects *as* effects? How do we explain the movement of planets, for example, as effects of gravity? (It is as if we needed to find something that *precedes* everything else, some kind of ground or protophenomenon, so as to build on it. But the more we press for such a ground, the more it seems to slip away.)

1.28 Someone once said it was his life's goal to know the unconscious *in its entirety*. Now, if you say that this is impossible, then ask yourself whether this impossibility is a practical or a logical one. (Is the unconscious really so *large*?)

1.29 The passage quoted at the beginning of this section suggests an analogy between knowing the unconscious and knowing the external world: the external world, Freud says, is known (incompletely) through the sense organs; the unconscious is known (incompletely) through the data of consciousness. The "innermost nature" of both the external world and the unconscious remain unknown and unknowable.

There are at least two ways in which this might be understood: first, in a strictly Kantian sense, as a metaphysical assertion about the unknowability of the object "in itself" (the unconscious as a kind of psychical noumenon), and second, as a methodological statement about the limitations, in principle, of inferential reasoning (the unconscious as the unobserved but inferred object of scientific description).

With respect to the first alternative, we should distinguish, in our use of the term "unconscious," between that which is unconscious *in*

14. See John Wisdom, "Philosophy, Metaphysics, and Psychoanalysis," in *Philosophy and Psychoanalysis* (Oxford: Basil Blackwell, 1964), 248–82.

principle and that which is unconscious *in fact*. It may be useful to say of certain psychological phenomena that they are unconscious "in principle," or "by definition." In cognitive psychology, for example, the mechanisms of memory—to the extent that we are not merely (in fact) unaware of them but *cannot* (in principle) become aware of them— are "unconscious in principle." So, too, we might say, the conditions of knowledge are "unconscious": whatever constitutes a *condition* of knowledge cannot—in principle—become its object, since whatever I can know is, by definition, no longer a condition but an object of my knowledge.[15]

The unconscious in this sense is a purely heuristic fiction (as in the case of the mechanisms of memory) or else a kind of negative metaphysical category (as in the case of a psychical noumenon): that is, merely a name we attach to the limits of our conceptualizations.

1.30   Freud wanted psychoanalysis to be "scientific," and this meant, among other things, that psychoanalytic knowledge should be "objectivistic" in a manner parallel to the natural sciences. Hence, he conceived the unknowability of the internal object as the logical counterpart of the unknowability of the external world:

> Just as Kant warned us not to overlook the fact that our perceptions are subjectively conditioned and must not be regarded as identical with what is perceived though unknowable, so psychoanalysis warns us not to equate perceptions by means of consciousness with the unconscious [psychical] processes which are their object. Like the physical, the psychical is not necessarily in reality what it appears to us to be. We shall be glad to learn, however, that the correction of internal perception will turn out not to offer such great difficulties as the correction of external perception—that internal objects are less unknowable than the external world. (U, 166)

But notice, once again, that the unconscious in this sense—that is, the unconscious as something that is *in principle* unknowable—has nothing to do with the dynamic, *psychoanalytic* unconscious, or what Freud usually describes by that name. The unconscious that concerns psychoanalysis, the unconscious that is the object of Freud's discovery, is not

---

15. The Lacanian conception of the unconscious as defined by the interval between signifier and signified, as well as Derrida's notion of "spacing," or "*différance*," both belong here—that is, to what is unconscious *in principle* rather than unconscious *in fact* (to an unconscious, in other words, that is not properly psychoanalytic).

some kind of unknowable "essence" but something that can in principle be known—and indeed *is* known by precisely those methods Freud himself describes (i.e., the procedures of free association, interpretation, construction, etc.). It is the unconscious *in fact*, the unconscious as it can be *made conscious* and interpreted—which is to say, the *dynamically repressed* unconscious—that is the object of psychoanalysis, not the Kantian thing-in-itself. Freud's concept is defined in positive terms by the logic and method that lead him to adopt it in the first place.

The problem here derives from Freud's failure to distinguish his *methodological* point (concerning the subjective conditions of knowledge and the logic of "nonobservables") from his *metaphysical* one (concerning the inaccessibility of reality as such). It is a problem that one meets frequently in social and psychological theory.

1.31   "The unconscious can only be described in terms of what is conscious." "The unknowable is forever condemned to being described in terms of the known." "Thoughts must be conscious." "Logic must be pure." And so forth. What looks as if it *had to be*, what cannot be imagined otherwise, belongs to *grammar*, not facts. It belongs to our form of representation, not to the thing represented.

"The unconscious can only be known incompletely and as mediated by certain representations." This tells us something important about the way the term "unconscious" is *used*. (But don't go looking for an object hidden, as it were, *behind* its representations.)

1.32   Freud sometimes speaks as if the unconscious were a kind of ever-receding conceptual horizon. The unconscious, he says, is not something observed but something *inferred*, and psychoanalysis, like the other natural sciences, proceeds by methods of observation and inference toward the progressive approximation of a reality, x, that exists independent of our perceptions. What resists any final description, then, is not so much the object of the unconscious as the ultimate nature of "the psychical" as such—that is, the psyche considered as the internal, psychological counterpart to the external, natural world.

"The hypothesis we have adopted of a psychical apparatus extended in space . . . has put us in a position to establish psychology on foundations similar to those of any other science, such, for instance, as physics," Freud writes in "An Outline of Psycho-Analysis." "In our science as in the others the problem is the same: behind the attributes (qualities) of the object under examination which are presented directly to our perception, we have to discover something else which is more independent of the particular receptive capacity of our sense organs and which approximates more closely to what may be supposed to be the real state of affairs" (OP, 196). Notice, first, Freud's insistence that the object of the psyche, or "psychical apparatus," is perfectly analogous to the objects described by physics. Now, ask, How far does this analogy actually extend? Do I observe the qualities of the psyche as I observe the qualities of an object? Do I *know* the psyche by the same procedures that I know the objects of the external world? Freud then carries this analogy still further—now in the direction of a kind of Kantian transcendental metaphysics—to claim that the true object of both physics and psychoanalysis is not that which is presented to perception but something "independent of the particular receptive capacity of our sense organs," something, as he goes on to say, that can only be "inferred," something that remains, in itself, resolutely "unknowable":

> We have no hope of being able to reach the latter itself, since it is evident that everything new that we have inferred must nevertheless be translated back into the language of our perceptions, from which it is simply impossible to free ourselves. But herein lies the very nature and limitation of our science. It is as though we were to say in physics: "If we could see clearly enough we should find that what appears to be a solid body is made up of particles of such and such a shape and size and occupying such and such relative positions." In the meantime we try to increase the efficiency of our sense organs to the furthest possible extent by artificial aids; but it may be expected that all such efforts will fail to affect the ultimate outcome. *Reality will always remain "unknowable."* The yield brought to light by scientific work from our sense perceptions will consist in an insight into connections and dependent relations which are present in the external world, which can somehow be reliably reproduced or reflected in the internal world of our thought and a knowledge of which enables us to "understand" something in the external world, to foresee it and possibly to alter it. Our procedure in psychoanalysis is quite similar. We have discovered technical methods of filling up the gaps in the phenomena of our consciousness, and we make use of those methods just as a physicist makes use of experiment. In this manner we infer a number of processes which are in themselves "unknowable" and interpolate them in those that are conscious to us. And if, for instance, we say: "At this point an unconscious memory intervened," what that means is: "At this point something occurred of which we are totally unable to form a conception,

but which, if it had entered our consciousness, could only have been described in such and such a way." (OP, 196–97; emphasis added)

There is much that merits comment in this passage,[16] but for the moment I am interested only in the kind of inference Freud is talking about. There are, it seems to me, two possible readings (both of which may be at work in Freud's thinking). Freud suggests at the outset that an inference of some kind is involved in the movement from the perception of the qualities of an object to the reality that stands behind it. This, of course, is the Kantian point, though Kant recognized that this movement is more properly described as a "deduction" than an inference. (Inference moves either from fact to fact or from fact to organizing principle, whereas deduction, in the sense that it is being used here, moves from fact to conditions.) Further along in the passage, however, Freud seems to shift from this more metaphysical point to talking about an inference from observed psychological facts, or "phenomena of our consciousness," to the underlying processes that allow us to explain, or make sense of, these observed facts. What kind of inference, then, is involved here? What kind of inference is involved in the movement from the observation of certain kinds of behavior or psychical events (e.g., the observation that a boy reacts to horses with excessive fear) to the idea that they are impelled by unconscious motives (e.g., unresolved Oedipal wishes and conflicts)? *Is* this a matter of inference?

Compare these two statements:

1. I see clouds and infer that it's going to rain.
2. I see a woman compulsively washing her hands and infer that she is motivated by an unconscious guilt of some kind.

Now, in the first instance, if it doesn't rain, then my inference is proved to be false, and I am forced to conclude that clouds do not always indicate rain. But what about the second instance? What subsequent occurrence—that is, what observation or fact—could possibly prove that my inference had been wrong? That she denies having any feelings

16. For example, the odd conflation of molecular physics and Kantian metaphysics in support of the claim that reality is unknowable, as if the limitations of perception might confirm the Kantian point or more refined instruments of observation deny it. Almost invariably when Freud draws analogies between psychoanalysis and the natural sciences, he weaves a conceptual confusion of such complexity that only extended analysis can untangle the mess. One could easily write an entire essay on this passage alone.

of guilt? That she behaves as if she were not in fact guilty? In any case, no single occurrence will either confirm or refute the inference as it stands; more important, *any* occurrence whatsoever can be made to accord with it. (This is related to the fact that the theory of the unconscious has an enormous explanatory capacity, that it is capable of explaining virtually everything that happens within its field and that whatever happens seems always to confirm it. On the other hand, of course, one would also argue that *nothing* is explained by it, since if any imaginable observation is consistent with the theory, then no possible occurrence is excluded and, therefore, none is explained. But suppose the point of some explanations is not to relate a given phenomenon to other phenomena through a theory but rather to redescribe the phenomenon in such a way that it *makes sense*. This "making sense" might involve an appeal to theory, but it need not. It may just be a recommendation to look at things in *this* way or in light of *this* analogy [e.g., the analogy between the stain of blood and the stain of guilt].)

1.33   Here we want to say something like this: the idea of the unconscious cannot be inferred from the facts of observation; rather, it is the assumption of the unconscious that determines, in part, the character of the facts, and also even what will count as a fact. (A sum of facts does not yield the organizing principle of those facts, nor is a fact a "fact" without some such organization.)

1.34   "Misleading parallel: psychology treats of processes in the psychical sphere, as does physics in the physical" (PI, 1:571). Freud, in his theorizing about psychical life and the unconscious, is constantly being misled by analogies, especially by analogies to the natural sciences. Sometimes this results in the creation of new meaning; sometimes in nonsense. Is there any way to decide, prior to analysis, which constructions will lead to which result? (How do we decide that a proposition has meaning, particularly if it uses terminology we have never encountered before? How do we know, in advance, how such propositions are to be employed? It is as if we were presented with a new game the rules for which had yet to be invented—or, better, a game for which the rules were vague, inconsistent, or incomplete. How are we supposed to play this game?)

1.35   Freud wants to say—and claims to demonstrate—that the unconscious "exists." But what exactly does this mean? We say, for instance, "A striped coelacanth exists," or "Carbon 14 exists," or "Red exists," or "Gravity exists," or "Mermaids exist," or even "God exists"—what do we mean by "exists" in each these cases? Does the unconscious exist as a striped coelacanth exists—or more as gravity exists? How do we go about deciding, in each case, whether the thing in question actually does exist? by what methods and procedures?

Compare the grammar of the statement "The unconscious exists" with that of "Red exists." To what extent are these two expressions analogous? That is, to what extent is our use of the word "unconscious" like our use of the word "red"? In the *Investigations*, Wittgenstein discusses the logic of the statement "Red exists" at some length:

> It looks as if we were saying something about the nature of red in saying that the words "Red exists" do not yield a sense. Namely that red does exist "in its own right." The same idea—that this is a metaphysical statement about red—finds expression again when we say such a thing as that red is timeless, and perhaps even more strongly in the word "indestructible."
>
> But what we really *want* is simply to take "Red exists" as the statement: the word "red" has a meaning. Or perhaps better: "Red does not exist" as " 'Red' has no meaning." Only we do not want to say that expression *says* this, but that *this* is what it would have to be saying *if* it meant anything. But that it contradicts itself in the attempt to say it—just because red exists "in its own right." Whereas the only contradiction lies in something like this: the proposition looks as if it were about the color, while it is supposed to be saying something about the use of the word "red."—In reality, however, we quite readily say that a particular color exists; and that is as much as to say that something exists that has that color. And the first expression is no less accurate than the second; particularly where "what has the color" is not a physical object. (PL, 1:58)

The proposition "Red exists" looks as if it were about the color red when in fact it expresses something about our use of the word "red": namely, that it can be meaningfully applied to certain objects, that it belongs to the description of the object, and so forth. Now, it seems to me that the statement "The unconscious exists" is similar to the statement "Red exists" in this respect: that while it looks as it were a statement about the "object," it actually tells us something about our form of representation, that is, what kinds of descriptions are possible, how these descriptions proceed, what semantic combinations do and do not make sense, and so forth. "The unconscious exists": this means merely that the term "the unconscious" *has meaning*—and it has meaning, as I have said, only to the extent that it has a legitimate and consistent use. (Those who deny the reality of the unconscious *want* only to deny that the term "the unconscious" has meaning, whereas those who affirm the reality of the unconscious too often fail to realize that they must yet show how the word is to be *applied*.)

1.36 We might want to say that the proposition "There is an unconscious" is *internal to the logic* of psychoanalysis. It is not in principle verifiable or falsifiable; rather, it belongs to the grammar of psychoanalysis that this kind of proposition is accepted, that such acceptance is the condition for engaging in the practice that *is* psychoanalysis (just as the rules of a game are neither true nor false, but make up part of the conditions for playing the game).

The form of psychoanalytic statements about the unconscious makes them look like factual propositions when they are really grammatical ones.

1.37 "Then statements about the unconscious are not literal but metaphorical. They describe, not what the reality is, but what it is *like*."[17] No, it would be a mistake to characterize language about the unconscious as metaphorical or even figural, for in order to call a particular instance of language use "metaphorical" we need to be able to indicate what a "literal" or "conventional" use would be like—that is, we need to be able, if not perhaps to translate the metaphorical expression into a literal description, at least to specify the criteria that would be relevant to such a translation (just as, in the interpretation of poetry, no matter how irreducible we may consider the poem *as a poem*, as a work of literary art, still we are able to speak of "good" and "bad" interpreta-

17. This is a position that is becoming increasingly popular and is perhaps most prominently represented in the works of Donald Spence (see, e.g., Spence, *The Freudian Metaphor: Toward Paradigm Change in Psychoanalysis* [New York: W. W. Norton, 1987], esp. 17–42). In the course of reviewing the various criticisms of the reality of the unconscious, for example, Spence writes, "Most damning of all, we have no independent evidence that the dynamic unconscious has an independent existence, and therefore that it is anything more than a metaphor" (25). Now, what could be meant by "independent evidence" here? What kind of evidence would be relevant here? Indeed, how do we make sense of the idea, in relation to the unconscious, of an "independent existence"? Independent *of what*? Moreover, what are the implications of saying that the unconscious is not "anything more than a metaphor"? What could it mean, in this context, to be "more than a metaphor"? Is gravity, for example, "more than a metaphor"? (What rides on the answer to this question? Our attitude toward falling bodies, perhaps?)

tions, "good" and "bad" translations in this sense). In the case of psychoanalytic language about the unconscious, however, *we have no such criteria.* (Ask yourself, What would a literal description of the mind—much less of the "unconscious mind"—look like? And if we can't describe something literally, then it doesn't make sense to say that we can describe it metaphorically either.)

1.38 Freud uses old words in new ways, words like "sexual," "ego," "energy," and even "the unconscious." We think, perhaps, "He is using chess pieces and a chess board to play, not chess, but a game of his own." (Of course, even in that case, the game must have *rules*, if indeed it *is* a game.)

1.39 Certain discoveries, we might say—both in the natural and in the human sciences—are more grammatical than factual: that is, they have less to do with the "facts" of the world than they do with innovations in our way of speaking about things, in our forms of expression. Freud's discovery of the unconscious might be characterized as a discovery of this sort.

"Doesn't this amount to saying, then, that talk about unconscious psychical processes really is purely a way of speaking, a *façon de parler*, and that the concept of the unconscious is no more than a notation? If so, then the whole thing seems to become merely a verbal dispute, a matter of words and of our preference for certain kinds of descriptions over others."

Is it merely a matter of words if I describe my behavior toward my wife as motivated by unconscious hostility toward women rather than, say, by her meddling nature? Is it merely a matter of words if, at the end of a long analysis, I come to understand my repeated professional failures as the expression of a fear of success? Is it merely a matter of words when we decide in a court of law that *this* is an instance of negligence? And how do we decide this? (It may happen in all of these cases that the *facts* are clear and accessible to everyone; what matters then is how those facts are interpreted or how they are *organized*.)

Or further: Is it merely a matter of words if I choose to measure the distance between two points in meters rather than miles? Maybe not; but then again, maybe so. (Suppose a typical American is lost on a European highway and running out of gas; suppose that he doesn't know the metric system or the rules for conversion.) Is it merely a matter of words if I describe the movement of an object in terms of

Newtonian rather than Einsteinian physics? (And here it seems that the distinction between grammar and fact begins to break down.)

1.40   Two men are walking beside a river when one of them makes a wild gesture with his arm, knocking the other into the water. The second man bears a marked similarity to the first man's father. There are two possible explanations: (1) the first man unconsciously hates the second, or (2) he was simply carried away by the conversation they were having.

Is our choice between these two explanations a purely arbitrary matter, a matter of choosing between two different but equally valid forms of expression? One might be inclined to say that *both* explanations may be correct: I can describe the first man's behavior according to either his "conscious" or his "unconscious" motives.[18] But, as Wittgenstein notes, "the games played with the two motives are utterly different" (LC, 23). The question is, What do we *do* with these different explanations? how do we *use* them?

Think about what is at stake in the matter of choosing one explanation rather than the other (e.g., the one man may well decide not to go walking with the other again, or he may decide to press criminal charges). With respect to its *consequences*, it is clearly not a matter of indifference which explanation one chooses.

1.41   "You say that Freud's discovery is grammatical rather than factual, but doesn't this distinction rest on a kind of naïve realism about the relation between language and world, theory and fact, one that Wittgenstein himself was at pains to deny? For how do we draw a line between grammar, on the one side, and facts, on the other? Isn't such a line, simply by virtue of being drawn *in language*, always on the side of grammar? The distinction between the real and the unreal, as well as the concept of agreement between theory and fact, belongs only to our language, not to the world."

This distinction is indeed a distinction made *in* our language; it refers, however, not to the relation between language and world but to the function, logic, and use—the grammar—of certain kinds of statements. Some statements are capable of, and are generally used in conjunction

18. Elsewhere, Wittgenstein suggests that our choice between these different explanations may come down to a "tendency of mind": "Should we say that there are cases when a man despises another man and doesn't know it," he asks, "or should we describe such cases by saying that he doesn't despise him but unintentionally behaves towards him in a way—speaks to him in a tone of voice, etc.—which in general would go together with despising him? Either form of expression is correct; but they may betray different tendencies of mind" (BlB, 30).

with, certain methods of verification and falsification; others not. What is important is that we learn to recognize which kind of statement we are dealing with, and typically we do this by seeing how the statement is used. (For further discussion, see Appendix B, "On Sense, Nonsense, Hypothesis, and Grammatical Rule.")

Like other of Wittgenstein's technical innovations—"language game," "form of life," the distinction between "symptom" and "criteria," and so forth—the distinction between grammatical and factual statements should be viewed as descriptive and heuristic rather than substantive: its purpose is to orient our inquiry in a particular direction (and away from others).

1.42 We are asking in what ways it makes sense to view Freud's discovery of the unconscious, on the one hand, as the discovery of something empirical and objective and, on the other hand, as purely an innovation in language, a change in our way of speaking about certain kinds of experiences and symbolic relations. I am trying to show that many of the puzzles that surround the concept of the unconscious can be dispelled by looking at it from the perspective of grammar—that is, by examining its uses and its distinctive grammatical features. If I say that statements about the unconscious are grammatical, I am making a statement about how the concept is *used* or about at least one of its uses. I am also suggesting that certain kinds of questions (e.g., What is the evidence for claiming that there is an unconscious?) are perhaps confused and misleading. Nonetheless, it would be too simple to say of Freud's discovery that it is purely grammatical (whatever that might mean) or that talk about the unconscious is mere rhetorical play.

1.43 Here we might take our cue from John Wisdom, who refers to what he calls "eccentric statements," that is, statements that are, as it were, only indirectly related to observations.[19] Such statements, he tells us, are logically peculiar, and their nature and role—both in the sciences and in everyday life—are exceptionally difficult to understand. (In science, for example, we often come across hypotheses that cannot be refuted and thus, in a sense, tell us nothing—hypotheses that nonetheless prove to be immensely fertile.)

People making statements of this type most often *believe* that they are reporting facts, as do the people who attempt to refute them; but this is because both *see* things in a particular way—or, as we might also say, they organize the facts differently.

19. Wisdom, *Paradox and Discovery*, esp. 123–38.

1.44   Let us look at another illustration from Wittgenstein. Suppose it were found helpful to call a certain state of tooth decay not accompanied by pain "unconscious toothache" and to use here the expression "I have a toothache but don't know it." Is there anything wrong with this? No, says Wittgenstein, for it is simply a new terminology that can be translated back into ordinary language at any time ("unconscious toothache" = "tooth decay without pain"). At the same time, however, we need to recognize that this form of expression makes use of the words "to know" and "toothache" in a new way that is not directly connected to our ordinary ways of knowing whether we have a toothache (i.e., our experience of pain in the tooth).[20] Hence, if we want to understand the meaning of a term like "unconscious toothache"—if, in other words, we are to use the term properly—we need to ask how we "know" or "find out" about such things: that is, how are the words "unconscious" and "to know" *used* here, and how is this use similar to and different from other, more familiar uses (BlB, 22–23)?

There is nothing wrong with introducing a new convention like "unconscious toothache," since all it really does is allow us to mark the distinction between a bad tooth that aches and one that doesn't.[21] Certainly, we can imagine situations in which this distinction might be useful. The problem, however, comes from the fact that this new form of expression evokes certain pictures and analogies that lead us to see it as something *more* than a convention, something that seems to challenge our accepted notions of what is real and what is possible. In particular, to the extent that we construe it along the lines of conventional grammar, the phrase "unconscious toothache" may begin to sound either nonsensical or fantastic (in a manner exactly analogous to Freud's talk of unconscious psychical processes—"unconscious pleasure," "unconscious idea," "unconscious wish," etc.). Thus, says Wittgenstein, on hearing this expression "you may either be misled into thinking that a stupendous discovery has been made, a discovery which in a sense altogether bewilders our understanding; or else you may be extremely puzzled by the expression (the puzzlement of philosophy) and perhaps ask such a question as 'How is unconscious toothache possible?' " (BlB,

20. We may even ask whether it makes sense here to speak about "knowing" whether I have a toothache. Do I *know* I have a toothache, or do I simply "have a toothache"? How do I find out if I have a toothache? Suppose I am wrong. *Can* I be wrong? What procedures do I have for checking? And so on.

21. According to Moore's account of Wittgenstein's discussion of this issue in one of his lectures, Wittgenstein at the time also proposed that the term "unconscious toothache," if "unconscious" were used as Freud used it, might necessarily be bound up with the physical body, whereas this is not the case with the expression "conscious toothache" (ML, 311).

23). In either case, you fail to grasp the convention *as a convention*, as a specific innovation in language, suited to specific and limited purposes, and thus you find far more behind it than is actually there.

So, too, in psychoanalysis, Freud's talk about unconscious psychical processes—thoughts, feelings, volitions, and the like—conjures up all sorts of misleading images (e.g., images of things hidden deep in the mind, things dark and sinister, and realities incapable of being known directly) and false analogies (e.g., the analogy between "unconscious motives" and "unseen causes," or between "knowing the unconscious" and "knowing the reality of physical objects"), pictures and analogies that lead us to ask such questions as "Can there *be* unconscious thoughts, feelings, etc.?" "Does the unconscious actually *exist*?" "Are dreams truly wish fulfillments?" "Can we ever *really* know the unconscious?"[22]

22. In contrast to what I am suggesting here, Wittgenstein himself seems to think that psychoanalytic language about "unconscious thoughts," like the notion of "unconscious toothache," can be translated without remainder into ordinary language. Thus, in the same discussion, he continues as follows: "The idea of there being unconscious thoughts has revolted many people. Others again have said that these were wrong in supposing that there could only be conscious thoughts, and that psychoanalysis had discovered unconscious ones. The objectors to unconscious thought did not see that they were not objecting to the newly discovered psychological reactions, but to the way in which they were described. The psychoanalysts on the other hand were misled by their own way of expression into thinking that they had done more than discover new psychological reactions; that they had, in a sense, discovered conscious thoughts which were unconscious. The first could have stated their objection by saying 'We don't wish to use the phrase "unconscious thoughts"; we wish to reserve the word "thought" for what you call "conscious thoughts" ' " (BlB, 57; cf. L II, 40). The implication here is that psychoanalysis simply describes common "psychological reactions" in a new idiom—namely, one that involves reference to unconscious thoughts, feelings, and the like—and that such descriptions can at any point be translated back into ordinary language. I want to say, on the contrary, that psychoanalytic language is in an important sense *irreducible*, that it does more than simply redescribe what we already know, that in fact, through its grammatical innovations, it *creates* a whole new area of meaning and experience.

For Wittgenstein, it is perfectly acceptable to use the expression "unconscious toothache," since (1) it has a legitimate use (i.e., it allows us to distinguish between two kinds of bad teeth, those which ache and those which don't) and (2) it is merely a linguistic convention that can always be translated back into ordinary language. Notice, further, that these two points are logically related: it is *because* there are accepted independent criteria for making judgments about the soundness of one's teeth (bad looking tooth = state of decay) that we can translate our convention into ordinary language ("unconscious toothache" = "state of decay without pain"). If it were impossible to know when a tooth is actually decayed, if there were no independent ways of "finding out" by inspection, that is, by looking at and perhaps by touching the tooth in question, then our convention would lose all sense. It is only because we can recognize a bad tooth when we see one that we can also speak of a bad tooth that doesn't cause pain—in other words, "unconscious toothache."

But it is here, I think, that the analogy between the two forms of expression, "unconscious toothache" and "unconscious thought," breaks down. For in the case of the latter, there are

As in the case of "unconscious toothache," the best way to avoid this kind of confusion is to ask, with respect to these unconscious psychical processes, *how do we know—or find out about—them*? Indeed, what do we mean by "knowing" in this context? How is this concept of knowing like—and how unlike—other conceptions of knowing? This is, once more, an extension of the verification principle: it states that "the unconscious," as a theoretical concept, gets its meaning from the kind of verification that is relevant to propositions *about* the unconscious or about unconscious psychical processes. In short, the meaning of the concept is the method of its verification—except that now we understand this, not as a principle of meaning, but as a methodological prescription, a way of clarifying the grammar of the terms and propositions involved. "What counts as an adequate test of a statement belongs to logic," Wittgenstein writes in *On Certainty*. "It belongs to the description of the language-game" (OC, 82).

1.45 One way of clarifying the meaning of propositions about the unconscious is to ask, How are they verified? Another—and perhaps just as useful way—would be to ask, How is the term "the unconscious" actually *learned*? How did *we* learn the use of the concept? How would we go about teaching this word to a child? Think about the actual process of trying to teach this concept to a child or even to someone for whom it had no previous meaning (e.g., the "primitive" of my earlier discussion).[23] Now we begin to see how much is presupposed by the concept, how very complicated and context-bound its use actually is.

If I try to imagine teaching the concept to a child, one way I might begin is to say the following: "When certain things happen to you, or when you find yourself doing things you don't really want to do, this is because there is something inside of you, a kind of second self, that causes these things to happen. This self is something you cannot see, something, perhaps, you cannot even feel, but it is there nonetheless. So, too, in your dreams; what happens in dreams, confusing as it may sometimes seem, is actually this second self trying to speak to you in a strange language of images and figures." And now we see, too, part of the reason that the notion of the unconscious is so easily misconstrued.

There is perhaps a certain irony in this: that the unconscious, which

---

no independent criteria for determining the nature or content of these thoughts comparable to those by which we determine the state of a tooth. By the same token, in contrast to the example of "unconscious toothache," the psychoanalytic form of expression *cannot* be translated into ordinary language, and this precisely because there are no available criteria for such a translation.

23. See section 1.15.

is supposed to function as a *critique* of fantasy, as a corrective to wishful thinking, is itself all too often the *expression* of such thinking (like the childhood fantasy of an invisible companion or of some evil person who makes us do things that we don't want to do). Talk to a true convert to psychoanalysis: the most fantastic things are, for that person, as real as tables and chairs—and very nearly in the same sense.[24]

1.46   In calling a feeling, idea, or whatever "unconscious," we are not saying that it is like a conscious feeling in all other respects except that it is not conscious (the use of the expressions "feeling" and "unconscious feeling" are, in fact, *very* different); rather, we are saying something about its relevance—and especially its causal relevance—to the interpretation and explanation of certain kinds of behavior or symbolism. (This is part of the reason why psychoanalysis is not, strictly speaking, a form of psychology.)

1.47   We tend to construe the relation between a conscious and an unconscious idea on the analogy of that between a "seen" and an "unseen" chair or, in a different way, that between an observed and an unobserved "cause." A "conscious idea" is one of which I am aware (just as I see this chair); an "unconscious idea," we are inclined to think, is just like a conscious one, except that I'm unaware of it (like the chair in the next room). Or: a "conscious motive" is one of which I'm aware at the time that I act (as when I see one ball cause another to move); an "unconscious motive" is just like a conscious one, except that I'm not aware of it at the time (as when a ball is moved by a hidden magnet).

Or consider now the relation between "preconscious" and "unconscious." According to Freud, this difference is based on the distinction between that which can be easily remembered (the preconscious) and that which can be remembered only with difficulty (the unconscious); in other words, the distinction seems to be based on different aspects of memory. In fact, however, this way of conceptualizing the distinction conceals some profound differences between our relation to what is called "*un*conscious" and our relation to what is "*pre*conscious." First, for example, whereas the former is the product of interpretation and of procedures specific to psychoanalysis, the latter is simply a function of memory. Second, the content of the former is always, or almost always, a *wish*, whereas the content of the latter can be virtually anything. Third, the former pertains to my *intentions*; the latter, to my memory

24. Frank Cioffi makes these and related points in his brilliant—though somewhat skewed—discussion of psychoanalysis in "Wittgenstein's Freud," included in *Studies in the Philosophy of Wittgenstein*, ed. Peter Winch (New York: Humanities Press, 1969), 184–210.

as a whole. Fourth, the former refers, in most instances, to something I have actively *denied*; the latter, to the sum total of my memories, regardless of my relation to them—and so on. Indeed, the very terms, "preconscious" and " unconscious," suggest a certain symmetry that is misleading: "preconscious" denotes a mental *capacity* (i.e., my capacity to remember things); "unconscious" denotes a function or aspect of my character (i.e., what I have repudiated or disavowed).

Generally speaking, to say that something is the product of the unconscious or the product of a compromise between conscious and unconscious is to say that it has (1) a certain *meaning*, or significance (that it can be *interpreted* psychologically: e.g., as the expression of a wish or a conflict between wishes), (2) a certain *origin*, source, or etiology (that it can be *explained* genetically or causally: e.g., as having arisen from a particular event, or a past repression), and (3) a certain *function* (that it can be *explained* economically: e.g., as serving to "release" certain internal pressures). Each of these different aspects, then, is essential to the grammar of the term, and each marks an important difference from our ordinary, commonsense understanding of psychological language.

1.48   If you want to know what the unconscious means, you must look above all at the ways in which we can legitimately speak about *knowing* the unconscious: What does Freud *call* knowing the unconscious, or knowing an unconscious thought? Is his use of this expression consistent? Does it have a coherent application? Once again, this is a question of grammar and not epistemology; it concerns the way in which these words are used in the context of a specific theoretical framework and relative to specific kinds of activities, interests, and purposes. As Wittgenstein notes in one place, there is a temptation to believe that this question, How is the unconscious known? is only indirectly relevant to the question, What is it like in this case "to get to know"? But in fact the question concerning the unconscious is really a question concerning the grammar of the term "to know," and this becomes clearer if we put it in the form, What do we *call* "getting to know"? For just as it belongs to the grammar of the word "chair," for example, that *this* is what we call "to sit in a chair," and it belongs to the grammar of the word "meaning" that *this* is what is called "explaining meaning,"[25] so it belongs to the expression "unconscious thought" that *this* is what Freud calls "knowing an unconscious thought."

---

25. " 'The meaning of a word is what is explained by the explanation of meaning,' " Wittgenstein writes in the *Investigations*. "I.e.: if you want to understand the use of the word 'meaning,' look for what are called 'explanations of meaning' " (PI, 1:560).

To explain the criteria for someone's having unconscious thoughts, feelings, and so forth, is to give a grammatical explanation of the meaning of the term "unconscious thought."

Let us look, then, at how Freud describes this process of knowing unconscious psychical processes. For this purpose, I propose that we examine Freud's theory of dreams, as well as the procedure of dream interpretation, as the most characteristic, and in a sense paradigmatic, example in psychoanalysis of "knowing an unconscious thought."[26]

26. In the preface to the first edition of *The Interpretation of Dreams*, Freud calls the dream "the first member of a class of abnormal psychical phenomena of which further members, such as hysterical phobias, obsessions and delusions, are bound for practical reasons to be a matter of concern to physicians." He continues, "As will be seen in the sequel, dreams can make no such claim to practical importance; but their theoretical value as a paradigm is on the other hand proportionately greater. Anyone who has failed to explain the origin of dream-images can scarcely hope to understand phobias, obsessions or delusions or to bring a therapeutic influence to bear on them" (ID, xxiii). Much later, in the *New Introductory Lectures*, Freud had this to say about the importance of his theory of dreams: "[The theory of dreams] occupies a special place in the history of psychoanalysis and marks a turning point; it was with it that analysis took the step from being a psychotherapeutic procedure to being a depth psychology. . . . Whenever I have begun to have doubts of the correctness of my wavering conclusions, the successful transformation of a senseless and muddled dream into a logical and intelligible mental process in the dreamer would renew my confidence of being on the right track" (NIL, 7).

As Paul Ricoeur has pointed out, dreams are paradigmatic for psychoanalysis both with respect to the *method* (free association) and to the *conceptual model* (the model of repression and "wish fulfillment") (see Ricoeur, *Freud and Philosophy: An Essay in Interpretation*, trans. Denis Savage [New Haven: Yale University Press, 1970], 154–55, 159–62, 174–75.)

2

KNOWING THE UNCONSCIOUS
The Interpretation of Dreams

2.1   "During the long years in which I have been working at
the problems of neurosis I have often been in doubt and sometimes
shaken in my convictions," Freud writes in 1908. "At such times it has
always been the *Interpretation of Dreams* that has given me back my
certainty" (ID, xxvi). If the concept of repression is the cornerstone of
psychoanalytic theory, dream interpretation is surely the foundation of
its method. "The interpretation of dreams," according to Freud, "is the
royal road to a knowledge of the unconscious activities of the mind"
(ID, 608). What we know of the unconscious, what we can understand
of the meaning of the concept, its uses and applications, comes first and
foremost through the process of dream interpretation.

What does it mean to interpret a dream? What does it mean to
say that dreams are "meaningful"? (Leading analogies: "Words are
meaningful." "Music is meaningful." "Dreams are meaningful.") How
do I *know* that this is the meaning of my dream? That is, what are the
criteria for judging the correctness of an interpretation? How is it that I
recognize the dream as the expression of *my* unconscious thought, *my*
wish, *my* desire?

2.2   It is often said that Freud's great discovery was his recognition that
dreams have a meaning. Here one wants to ask, *When* did dreams
become meaningful? Were dreams *not* meaningful before Freud?

It is as if our dreams were saying something over a long period of time, but we did not hear, or could not understand, what they were trying to express. Then along came Freud with a new procedure of interpretation, and we were suddenly able to decipher their language: dreams now had a meaning, as if for the first time. But then it seems odd that they were willing to go on speaking for so long without being properly understood.

2.3   For centuries, we did not understand the function and movements of the blood; then William Harvey discovered the basic principles of the circulation of the blood, and what had formerly seemed senseless, even contradictory, suddenly made sense. In this case, however, what is involved in the discovery is a change in the way in which we organize and explain certain observed anatomical phenomena (the sizes of cardiac chambers, the relative sizes of the conduits, the spasmatic character of bleeding from the heart, etc.), not the *kind* of sense that we attribute to these phenomena (i.e., whether they are to be regarded as organic, neurological, psychological, as causally determined, as motivated, etc.).

The kind of sense that we ascribe to dreams is very different from the kind of sense that we ascribe to the movement of blood; indeed, what we mean by "sense" is very different in each case. (We could even say that much of the current debate about psychoanalysis is focused on the question of the kind of sense, if any, that ought to be attributed to Freud's discoveries.)

2.4   The basic theory of dreams can be described in terms of four propositions: (1) every dream has a meaning (*Sinn, Bedeutung*) that can be interpreted; (2) the meaning of a dream is the fulfillment of a wish; (3) this wish—a repressed wish, ultimately from childhood—is the motive for the dream; and (4) this wish arises from the unconscious (hence, the concept of the unconscious is a necessary assumption both for the interpretation of dreams and for the explanation of their construction). Let us look at each of these propositions in turn.

2.5   "Every dream has a meaning." At first glance, this looks like a hypothesis, comparable to the proposition "All crows are black." In the case of the latter, if we find a white crow, the proposition "All crows are black" is falsified. Similarly, if a substance is found that does not expand when heated, the proposition "All substances expand when heated" is falsified. Presumably, then, if we find a dream that cannot be interpreted, the proposition "Every dream has a meaning" is likewise falsified. (In order to be "scientific," Popper said, a statement must be falsifiable; in order to be falsifiable, it must be capable of conflicting with possible or conceivable observations.)[1]

But now ask yourself, What would an *un*interpretable dream look like? Can we *imagine* such a dream? Would it simply be more absurd than the dreams with which we are familiar, and therefore less interpretable? Would it, perhaps, be a dream to which one has no associations? (According to Freud, of course, the answer to this last question is no, that, on the contrary, it is often precisely those dreams that do not immediately provoke associations that are in fact the most significant.)

There is no such thing as an uninterpretable dream for psychoanalysis, not because of the nature of dreams but because of the nature and presuppositions of the method: every dream, without exception, is interpretable simply by virtue of being reported as a dream. Hence, we know that we are dealing here not with a hypothesis but with a statement of method. To say, "Every dream has a meaning," is not to set forth a generalization based on evidence, or facts of some sort, but to state an axiom; it tells us that dreams are to be regarded as *symbols* as things to be interpreted, rather than as chance, random occurrences. Moreover, the fact that *every* dream can be interpreted is significant in another way as well: it tells us something about the grammar of "interpretation" in this context (viz., that its application is not limited by anything in the nature of the dream as such, that it can be applied to all dreams without exception).

2.6   To say that dreams have meaning is, for Freud, to say that they are "mental," or "psychical," acts.[2] Indeed, it is now widely accepted that dreams are, as it were, "the most personal, private, and individual of

1. Karl Popper, *Conjectures and Refutations: The Growth of Scientific Knowledge* (New York: Basic Books, 1962), 39. Of course, taken as normative, it is now generally accepted that Popper's criterion of falsification involves too limited a notion of scientific rationality. For a good discussion—and critique—of the principle of falsificationism, see A. F. Chalmers, *What Is This Thing Called Science? An Assessment of the Nature and Status of Science and Its Methods* (St. Lucia: University of Queensland Press, 1976), 38–76. Chalmers formulates the second part of the principle more fully and adequately as follows: "An hypothesis is falsifiable if there exists a logically possible observation statement or set of observation statements that are inconsistent with it, that is, which, if established as true, would falsify the hypothesis" (40).

2. For the purposes of this discussion—and in view of the way that Freudian theory has been translated into the English idiom of mind—I am using the terms "mental" and "psychical" interchangeably here, though I recognize that they are, at best, only roughly synonymous and that there is no German equivalent for the former. It may well be that I am speaking here more about the way that Freud has been appropriated than I am about Freud himself. (See Chapter 1, note 2.)

mental actions."[3] Well, *are* dreams "mental actions"? How would we go about deciding this?

We say that thinking, willing, and wishing, for example, are mental acts, but how do we know this? How dow we decide that, say, thinking is a mental action? But now notice: as soon as we pose the question, it seems utterly nonsensical, for it belongs to what we mean by "thinking" that it is a mental act, that it occurs "in the mind," that it is, to some extent at least, volitional, or motivated, and so forth. Indeed, thinking is perhaps the foremost example of what we *mean* by "mental act."[4]

But what about dreaming? Is dreaming, perhaps, thinking *in images* (as opposed to words)? If this means that dreaming is an inner process, like thinking, that tells us nothing that we did not already know, for it is not the fact that dreams are mental that is in question here, but the fact that they are "acts." Well, suppose we ask, *who* acts in dreams? *Are* dreams motivated as thinking, for example, is motivated? Freud puts the answer in the form of a rhetorical question: "If we are not responsible for our dreams," he asks, "then who is?"[5] But here one wants to say, why must *anyone* be responsible? I am responsible for what I do, for the way that I act; but dreams seem much less things that I *do* than things that *happen to me*. If I say that I am responsible for my dreams, then surely I have extended the range of my responsibility, perhaps even redefined what it means to be responsible. (Freud redefines the meaning of responsibility; after Freud, we are both more and less responsible for our acts.)

2.7 When we say that dreams are "mental acts," we should distinguish between the dream as dreamed (the nocturnal event) and the dream as remembered and interpreted (the dream report). For the sense in which the actual dream can be called a mental act is, it seems to me, very different from the sense in which the interpreted dream—this most personal and private affair—can be so called. Among other things, I might conduct certain kinds of neurological tests to show that dreams are mental acts in the first sense (demonstrating that dreams are *"mental* acts," with correlations to other kinds of mental activity), whereas in the second sense I will probably be much more concerned to show that

3. Peter Homans, *The Ability to Mourn: Disillusionment and the Social Origins of Psycho-analysis* (Chicago: University of Chicago Press, 1989), 125.

4. As Judith van Herik has pointed out to me in conversation, it may be questioned whether thinking is equally the foremost example of what goes on *in the psyche*.

5. "Obviously one must hold oneself responsible for the evil impulses of one's dreams," Freud writes. "What else is one to do with them? Unless the content of the dream (rightly understood) is inspired by alien spirits, it is a part of my own being" (SAND, 133).

dreams express something about my motivations, wishes, feelings, and the like (to show, in other words, that dreams are "mental *acts*," products of my personal psychological makeup).

2.8   Of course, it might be the case that dreams represent facts—states of affairs—without their being, in consequence, "mental actions." That is, dreams could be a "thinking in images" that is more or less random, arbitrary, and, in the ordinary sense, unmotivated. But even then we would need to ask what we mean by "representation" here, for—at least according to psychoanalytic theory—there is no immediate likeness, no structural or thematic similarity, between the manifest dream and that which it is supposed to represent (i.e., the dream thoughts). The translation from manifest dream to latent dream thoughts requires both certain rules of procedure (i.e., the method of free association and interpretation) and a theory, one that links the different elements of the dream report not only to various common themes (e.g., themes of being exposed, of being guilty, and of having sexual intercourse) but also to certain general truths about human beings (e.g., that they have a fear of being exposed, that they experience guilt that they cannot express, and that the desire for sexual intercourse exceeds the constrictions that are placed upon it). And now it begins to seem that in order for the dream to be representational *in this sense*, it must also be called a mental action, for it clearly has a psychological significance. But then we can also raise questions about this particular use of the term "representation," for if meaning in this case must be mediated by a theory, then one can ask whether it makes sense to say that the dream *represents* a meaning. (A work of art may be meaningful, but it seems odd to say that it *represents* a meaning.)

2.9   Consider how we learn and teach the use of the expression "I dreamt." A child on awakening tells us about seeing dragons and dinosaurs, about ships and castles and queens, and we respond by saying, "You dreamt about . . . ," and "Wasn't it wonderful?" and "Weren't you scared?" and so forth. In this way, we teach children to preface their narratives with the expression "I dreamt." In time we can ask them if they dreamt the previous night, and they can answer yes or no and perhaps give an account of the dream. This, then, is the language game; it involves a complicated process of repeated interaction, communication, and exchange (PI, 2:184). (Telling dreams is one language game; interpreting them is another; forming a theory about dream construction is a third. Each of these games has different rules, though they are related to one another—just as we might say that chess is related to checkers.)

Does it matter, Wittgenstein asks, whether children are deceived by their memories, whether they actually had these images while they slept or merely believed so on waking? Usually not, since the distinction between really having certain images and merely seeming to have them rarely plays a role in the game itself. On the other hand, it wouldn't be absurd to raise such questions. In the end, as Wittgenstein says, "it will turn on the use of the question"[6] (PI, 2:184).

And now we might ask, What would be the criteria for determining whether someone remembered a dream accurately or not? Could there *be* such criteria? That is, can I *imagine* what these criteria would be like?

2.10   Suppose that there were some kind of sophisticated video machine that allowed us actually to see and record the dreams of other persons while they slept. Suppose, further, that what we recorded was later contradicted by the accounts of the persons who had the dreams. What would be at stake for the dreamers if it were shown that they had misremembered their own dreams, not merely in some minor details but as a whole? If I were such a dreamer, this *might* be very much like being told that I was no longer the person that I believed myself to be, for if I can be wrong about *that*, I might think, then of what can I be sure? If this was in fact *not* my dream, then mustn't I begin to doubt my own sanity? (Just as if I were to remember clearly having been to the store on the previous day and then be shown that this was wrong.)

On the other hand, I can also imagine that the contradiction might be of little or no consequence to me, for how much is really at stake in my being able to remember my dreams truthfully? Indeed, how much is at stake in my being able to remember my dreams at all? (If I don't remember my dreams, or if I remember them wrongly, does this mean that I am less able to learn about my own unconscious? Consider what is at stake in this question.)

6. For example, we might want to insist that the dream report correspond in all significant respects to the actual dream and that this be the measure of the dream's truthfulness. In this case, however, it is important to recognize that we have introduced new criteria for determining what "truth" means, criteria other than those which Freud himself proposed. Wittgenstein writes, "Assuming that dreams can yield important information about the dreamer, what yielded the information would be truthful accounts of dreams. The question whether the dreamer's memory deceives him when he reports the dream after waking cannot arise, unless indeed we introduce a completely new criterion for the report's 'agreeing' with the dream, a criterion which gives us a concept of 'truth' as distinct from 'truthfulness' here" (PI, 2:222–23).

2.11 We hear about people for whom dreaming is *not* something "mental" at all but something real that occurs, as it were, in another place, in a second world parallel to this one (a belief that is also common among children). How would we go about convincing these people that dreaming only occurs "in their heads"? What are *our* criteria for determining that dreaming is purely mental? Other people watch us as we sleep and report that we do not actually move, even when in dreams we experience ourselves walking, jumping, climbing, and so forth—but then couldn't we also say that it belongs to the nature of this other world, the dream world, that we move freely within it, without having to move physically? Is there anything *in the nature of the experience itself* that would indicate that it all occurs "in our minds"? And what do we actually convey when we say this? (Where is this "in the mind"?)

It is true to say that the idea of a separate world doesn't "fit" with our conception of the way things are, of what is real and not real; but then how did we learn this conception? How do we know that there is only *one* world to be inhabited? To take a similar example from Wittgenstein's *On Certainty*, how do I *know* that this world—the world in which we all live—did not begin with my birth?

I know these things because they form an integral part of my conception of the world, the system of ideas, propositions, and ways of doing things that has been taught to me, directly or indirectly, from the moment I was born. "Our knowledge forms an enormous system," Wittgenstein writes. "And only within this system has a particular bit the value we give it" (OC, 410). I do not normally question whether dreams occur "in the mind" or in some other, separate reality, but it makes sense to ask such questions. How, then, do we go about answering them? And how would we convince those who did not believe as we do, those of another culture, that our view was correct and theirs false? "At the end of reasons comes *persuasion*," Wittgenstein writes (OC, 612); and, we might add, at the end of persuasion comes coercion. (If I am convinced in this way of the location of dreams, mightn't I be similarly convinced of their meaning?)

2.12 "Every dream has a meaning." This means, for Freud, dreams are "symbolic structures," that is, things that *can be interpreted*. But then doesn't this amount to saying that dreams have meaning because they can be interpreted and that they can be interpreted because they have a meaning?

2.13 "The meaning of a dream is the fulfillment of a wish." Here again the analogy suggests itself: the meaning of a word is what the word signifies, the object to which the word refers; the meaning of a dream is what the dream signifies, namely, a wish.

First, we may ask why Freud finds it necessary to insist that *all* dreams are wish-fulfillment dreams. Why not allow that there are other kinds of dreams, anxiety dreams, for example, or even dreams that are purely incidental or unmotivated? (Though for Freud, of course, an unmotivated dream would be uninterpretable, and this has already been ruled out on principle.)

One explanation for this insistence—the one that Wittgenstein puts forward—has to do Freud's general obsession with finding the *essence* of a thing. What Freud wanted was not merely a method for interpreting dreams but a comprehensive, scientific theory about the nature of dreams in themselves, a theory that explained the essence of the process. To claim that only *some* dreams are wish fulfillments would be to fail to find that essence. Wittgenstein comments, "Freud was influenced by the 19th century idea of dynamics—an idea which has influenced the whole treatment of psychology. He wanted to find some one explanation which would show what dreaming is. He wanted to find the *essence* of dreaming. And he would have rejected any suggestion that he might be partly right but not altogether so. If he was partly wrong, that would have meant for him that he was wrong altogether—that he had not really found the essence of dreaming" (LC, 48). Freud insisted on a single form of explanation for all dreams, one that would explain dreams according to their essence: the "wish," or "wishful impulse," was his name for this essence.

2.14   Let us look more closely at what this means. To begin with, the statement "All dreams are wish fulfillments"—like the statement "All dreams are meaningful"—is clearly not a factual proposition; rather, as Wittgenstein notes, it is more like the statement of the hedonist who says, "All men desire nothing but pleasure." "The hedonist does not find this out by going around asking people what they want," Wittgenstein remarks. "He has no statistics about this. And yet he knows very well that people want all sorts of things. So it isn't at all like: Everybody wants a motorcar. If someone wants a motorcar, then he wants pleasure, and if he wants to smoke or to write a letter, then he wants pleasure. *Pleasure is another word for whatever anyone wants.* In other words it's a *tautology.* Everyone prefers the preferable. So pleasure is the desirable, the preferable" (BC, 58). The statement "All men seek pleasure" is grammatical rather than factual: it is not a generalization based on evidence but a recommendation for how certain words are to be used; it tells us nothing about the character of human beings, but rather it indicates something about the meaning of "pleasure" in this context (i.e., pleasure is that which all men seek, however they may go about it). Still, the *form* of the statement is deceptive, and thus when someone announces that he has found out that "all men seek pleasure," there is the illusion of having discovered something, of having ascertained some deep truth about human nature and motivation.

So, too, when Freud says that all dreams are wish fulfillments, this sounds like an inductive generalization, as if he had patiently proceeded from the examination of one dream after another—the hungry man dreams of food, the thirsty man of water, the child of ice cream, and so forth—then suddenly come upon the truth: *This* is what *all* dreams really are! *This* is the *essence* of dreaming! "This is a generalization," says Wittgenstein, "and the clarity and the fascination of the one case deludes one" (BC, 59). In fact, however, Freud has not demonstrated the truth of a proposition; rather, he has recommended a particular use for the terms "dream," "wish," and so forth. He has given us a new way to talk about the meaning of dreams.

Of course, once the generalization has been set out, all sorts of qualifications are introduced, to the effect that dreams are not "simply" wish fulfillments but *fundamentally*, or *in essence*, wish fulfillments, and so on. Then it becomes a matter of the proper interpretation—the interpretation, in other words, that invariably *shows* the dream to be the distorted expression of a wish. (This is the cunning logic behind the manifest/latent distinction on which the whole of the psychoanalytic method rests, a logic that guarantees the truth of its theory, for whatever appears on the surface as a disconfirmatory instance can be interpreted, on the latent level, as a confirmatory one.)[7]

2.15   Freud says that all dreams are wish fulfillments; when someone produces a dream that runs counter to the wish, he answers, "But the dreamer *wishes to be frustrated*." Heads I win, tails you lose![8]

2.16   A painful dream may be wishful insofar as it provides a desired punishment of the dreamer for some repressed wish-impulse. In other

7. This distinction between "manifest" and "latent," "surface" and "depth," is undoubtedly the most fundamental category in psychoanalysis and governs the whole of Freudian discourse. ("Repression" is merely another name for this distinction.) It prescribes both the logic (syntax) and grammar (application) of the basic terms in Freudian theory. For a fascinating development of this idea from a rhetorical, or "tropological," perspective, see Nicolas Abraham, "The Shell and the Kernel," trans. Nicolas Rand, *Diacritics* (March 1979): 16–29.

8. For an insightful discussion of this strategy in Freud, see Edmund Burke, *The Philosophy of Literary Form: Studies in Symbolic Action* (Baton Rouge: Louisiana State University Press, 1941), 233. In Freud, see esp. CA, 257.

words, the painfulness of the dream is intended by one sector of the personality (e.g., the superego) to serve as punishment for the reprehensible desires of the other (e.g., the ego). But here we want to ask, *Whose* wish are we to look for in the dream, that of the ego or that of the superego? And why should it happen that one sector of the personality prevails this time, the other the next? To say that the dream is a representation of *my* wish is at best misleading if one then goes on to add that my personality comprises mutually conflicting agencies and wishes, any one of which may be represented in the dream in any given instance. (Whatever wish is supposed to be represented may always be assigned some aspect of the psyche.)

2.17 Once the dream is defined as the product of conflicting wishes—as a compromise between conscious and unconscious intentions—one can in principle *always* find an unambiguous wish behind its construction, a wish that the dreamer is inclined to repudiate, precisely because the wish that is represented in the dream need no longer, according to the logic of interpretation, be one that I recognize or acknowledge as my own.[9] For Freud, this wish is the *meaning* of the dream. ("How, then, do I recognize this wish as *my* wish?")

"Then is it wrong to say that dreams are wish fulfillments, if in fact this can neither be confirmed nor denied by appeals to evidence?" No, there is nothing wrong with the use of this expression, provided we are clear about *how* it is used; what is wrong is to think that such statements refer to facts in the world rather than to matters of expression. The mistake, in other words, is to think that the proposition "All dreams are wish fulfillments" is an empirical generalization rather a grammatical and methodological proposal. The designation of dreams as wish fulfillments provides a new way of speaking about dreams (and wishes) and thus also of understanding and interpreting dreams, a new way of making sense of them. This is not a hypothetical generalization but a recommendation of method: it tells us what dreams are and, therefore, how the interpretation is supposed to proceed. As Wittgenstein puts it, "To say that dreams are wish fulfillments is very important chiefly because it points to the sort of interpretation that is wanted—the sort of thing that would be an interpretation of a dream" (LC, 47). It is, in other words, part of what Freud *calls* interpreting a dream.[10]

9. This interpretive principle is codified in the concept of ambivalence: if one both wishes for and fears *x*, then whatever appears on the surface can be contradicted beneath it.

10. Freud himself believed differently, of course; he thought that he was describing the nature of dreams, instead of setting forth a methodological proposal for interpreting them. In his *Introductory Lectures*, for instance, he asks precisely the question that we have asked, namely, "Granted that dreams always have a sense, and that that sense can be discovered by the technique of psychoanalysis, why must that sense, all evidence to the contrary, be

"Does this imply, then, that dreams do *not* in fact express wishes or that it is an arbitrary matter whether we believe one way or the other about them?" Not at all. It means only that the interpretation of dreams as wishes—this particular language game—has found a place within the practice of psychoanalysis. It means that this is how the method of psychoanalysis proceeds and that the proposition "Dreams express wishes" belongs among the basic axioms of the theory. But the question whether dreams *actually* express wishes is, in this context at least, no more relevant than the question whether the dreamer *actually* had such and such an image during sleep.[11] (Does "2 + 2" *actually* equal "4"? How do we know?)

2.18   "The dream is a *disguised* wish fulfillment." But whose wish is it that is satisfied in the dream? Not the ego's, since the wish originates in the unconscious and often even contradicts the conscious wishes of the ego. Not that of the unconscious, since what is represented ("hallucinated") in the dream is precisely *not* the fulfillment of the wish but something else (viz., the *disguised* representation of the wish). Not the censor's, since all the censor can do is give things a new form. Hence, according to Wittgenstein, "the dream is not an hallucinated satisfaction of anything" (LC, 47).

---

invariably pushed into the formula of wish-fulfillment? Why should not the sense of this nightly thinking be of as many different kinds as that of daytime thinking?" His answer, however, refers not to a method but to the reality of the dream itself: "My first answer to the question why should not have a variety of meanings in the sense indicated is as usual in such cases: 'I don't know why they shouldn't. I should have no objection. As far as I'm concerned it could be so. There's only one detail in the way of this broader more convenient view of dreams—that it isn't so in reality' " (IL, 222).

11. It is therefore irrelevant to insist, as Wittgenstein does, that there may be many different kinds of dreams and many different ways of interpreting them. In the *Lectures and Conversations*, Wittgenstein says, for example, "Suppose we were to regard a dream as a kind of game which the dreamer played. (And by the way, there is no one cause or one reason why children always play. There is where theories of play generally go wrong.) . . . Compare the question of why we dream and why we write stories. Not everything in the story is allegorical. What would be meant by trying to explain why he has written just that story in just that way?

"There is no one reason why people talk. A small child babbles often just for the pleasure of making noises. This is also one reason why adults talk. And there are countless others" (LC, 49–50; cf. ML, 309, and CV, 68–69).

But, for Freud, it is the stipulation that dreams *are* wish fulfillments that allows them to be interpreted; without this stipulation, there would be no consistent procedure by which to go on. So one wonders what Wittgenstein has in mind here. (There is no point in arguing with the hedonist that some people, at least, do *not* seek pleasure but, say, the fulfillment of duty, since it is part of what the hedonist means by "pleasure" that it encompasses this. Again, it is a grammatical point, not a factual one.)

2.19 "The representation [*Darstellung*] of a wish is, *eo ipso*, the representation of its fulfillment" (RFGB: 64–65). The dream represents a wish; it therefore also represents the wish fulfilled.

2.20 Freud says that the dream satisfies both the conscious and unconscious wish—that is, the wish to sleep and the originating, infantile wish—through the compromise formation of the dream. But note that when we speak of "satisfaction" here we mean something very different in these two instances: for satisfaction of the first, the conscious wish, is a matter of experience, whereas satisfaction of the second, the unconscious wish, is not. (In the latter case, "satisfaction" means something like "discharge of energy.")

2.21 It has often been noted that there is a deep ambiguity in the psychoanalytic correlation of meaning and wish, one that runs through the whole of psychoanalysis, from the interpretation of dreams and the famous case studies, through the metapsychology of repression and the unconscious, and extending even to the theory of culture (sublimation). The very meaning of meaning is ambiguous in Freud.[12]

When Freud writes, for instance, that a dream is "a *form of expression* of impulses" (ID, 614), this seems to suggest that the dream is a kind of text, a symbolic representation, in a different medium, of certain repressed ideational contents; the dream, in other words, seems to present a kind of *text* (the view represented in the hermeneutic and linguistic approaches of Ricoeur and Lacan, respectively). But the same statement can also be taken to mean that the dream is the *product* of unconscious impulses and that it refers to these impulses more in the way that a clue, or directional sign, points toward something. In this reading, the dream is meaningful, not because it expresses or represents a wish—as, for instance, a symbol expresses meaning—but because it can be related to a nexus of mental causes; in other words, the dream is no longer a text but is a *causal effect* (the view of a number of the more empirically minded theorists, e.g., Robert Shope and Adolph Grünbaum). In this latter instance, "meaning" is primarily a matter of *inference* not interpre-

---

12. It was Paul Ricoeur who first insisted that we take this ambiguity seriously, placing it at the very center of his monumental work *Freud and Philosophy: An Essay in Interpretation*, trans. Denis Savage (New Haven: Yale University Press, 1970). My debt to Ricoeur—not only in the discussion of this issue but throughout the entire book—will be evident to anyone familiar with his writings. Indeed, it was my encounter with Ricoeur's work on Freud and psychoanalysis, many years ago now, that convinced me that Freud himself ought to be taken seriously. (Wittgenstein later taught me that while Freud needs to be taken seriously, he should not taken literally.)

tation. How are these two apparently conflicting notions of meaning to be reconciled? What is the meaning of "meaning" here?

2.22   We began with the question, How is the unconscious *known*? and we are looking at Freud's theory of dreams as the paradigmatic instance of "knowing an unconscious thought." Now we find that there are two very different, perhaps even contradictory, accounts of the process of knowing, each based on a different understanding of the concept of wish. For if wish is conceived on the model of a physical force, as a kind of dynamic quantum that produces psychical effects, then the unconscious is correspondingly conceived as the locus of *efficient causes*—described as "thoughts," "ideas," or "representatives" but conceptualized as discreet mental "entities" with dynamic characteristics—that produce certain psychological phenomena (dreams, symptoms, parapraxes, etc.) as their *effects*; hence, by this account, the unconscious is a reality that is *inferred* from its manifest effects in consciousness. Let us call this the causal-empirical model. On the other hand, if we conceive the wish on the model of a symbol and its significance—that is, as something ideational, as having more to do with intention, motivation, meaning, and purpose than with impersonal mental forces of some sort—then the unconscious will likewise be conceived on the analogy of text, a source of hidden meanings whose reality is relative to those hermeneutical procedures by which it is *deciphered*—namely, free association, transference, resistance, and interpretation. This, then, we will call the hermeneutic-linguistic model.

(*Is* a wish a kind of force? Or is it an idea, a symbolic construction of some sort? Surely our first inclination is to say that it is *both*. We are *moved* by wishes, yet we also conceptualize them; we represent them to ourselves.)

This issue lies at the bottom of a number of rather pressing questions concerning the status of psychoanalysis—including, in particular, the question whether it is to be regarded as an observational, clinical, or broadly "empirical" (hypothetico-deductive) science, on the one hand, or a form of hermeneutics, on the other. By way of anticipating the discussion to follow, my suggestion would be that psychoanalysis constitutes a unique form of discourse, one that is irreducible *either* to empirical science, as this is commonly understood, or to hermeneutics, and that both the causal-empirical and the hermeneutic-linguistic models are based on misleading analogies (in one case, the analogy between a wish and a physical force; in the other case, the analogy between a wish and a verbal meaning).

The uniqueness of psychoanalysis consists—and is manifest—in the uniqueness of its grammar and the peculiar logic of its concepts. A large measure of this uniqueness consists precisely in its identification of meaning and causes, in its conception of meanings *as causes* and causes *as meaning*.

2.23   Consider, first, the notion of the dream as a text to be interpreted. The analogy between dreams and language is, of course, an obvious one, for there seems to be a natural affinity between dreams and linguistic symbolism. As Wittgenstein notes in one of his published conversations, "There seems to be something in dream images that has a certain resemblance to the signs of a language," like a series of marks on paper or in the sand might have. "There might be no mark which we recognized as a conventional sign in any alphabet we knew, and yet we might have a strong feeling that they must be a language of some sort: that they mean something. There is a cathedral in Moscow with five spires. On each of these there is a different sort of curving configuration. One gets the strong impression that these different shapes and arrangements must mean something" (LC, 45).

Despite its illogical character, the dream *seems* to say something, it seems to be a communication of some sort, a message. The dream, we think, is like a strange language whose characters and syntax we do not understand, one that invites us to decipher its code. We then conceive interpretation as the process of translation from one language to another—or, better, from one medium of expression (images) to another (words). To interpret a dream is to translate the visual images of the dream—the pictorial representation of wishes—into words and ideas, according to a certain set of procedural rules. Everything rests on the idea that there is an intrinsic similarity, or structural homology, between dreams and language—a common syntax, grammar, and logic. The dream, we might say, is structured "like a language (Lacan)."

2.24   What, then, is the nature of this analogy between dreams and language? How far does it extend?

Dreams have meaning; words have meaning. Our words belong to the symbolism of the language; our dreams, to a universal symbolism of images. But now ask yourself, *How* do words have meaning? and *How* do dreams have meaning? Do both words and dreams mean something in the same way, or are there perhaps very different senses of meaning involved here?

First, with respect to words, we might say something like this: Words have meaning because they belong to the complex rule-governed activity we call "using a language." Meaning is therefore contextual. Words belong to the system of language: the meaning (or signified) of a word (or signifier) is its place within that system, in the grammar of the language. We could also say that the meaning of a word is its *use* in the grammar (i.e., the use as prescribed by the rules of the language). Describe the different uses of the word, and you define its various meanings.

If I ask, then, how do words mean? I am inclined to say that no "how" is involved here. A word is a "word" only *because* it has meaning; there can be no words without meaning, no signifiers without signifieds, for it belongs to what we mean by "word" that it is meaningful. A word without meaning is mere nonsense or noise.

Note, too, that this implies that there is no "gap" between a word and its meaning; if meaning were not intrinsic to the word, if there were not a generally agreed-upon use for the word, *we* could not supply it. (Against deconstructionism.)

2.25 Do dreams have meaning in the same way that words have meaning? In the first place, of course, dreams do not belong to any accepted symbolism (except, perhaps, in a very general way), even when they make use of existing cultural symbols. Dreams are not signifiers as words are signifiers, for their construction is not rule governed in the way that language use is. The relation between a dream and its meaning, signifier and signified, is the relation between a symbolic construction and its interpreted meaning. Dreams are not (generally) immediately meaningful but only *become* meaningful through interpretation. (If, in a dream, I have an image of "a cow walking down a country path," I recognize this as a cow—but, short of interpreting the cow as this or that, I cannot attach any immediate meaning to it.) Or, to be more accurate, we might say that dreams are meaningful but (generally) *nonsensical*: dreams are meaningful to the extent that they represent scenes that can be described ("And then I found myself wandering across wide pasture . . ."), but nonsensical insofar as there is no logical or narrative coherence to the sequence of scenes ("Suddenly, I was in a room with a number of strange people . . ."). But even if this coherence were given, we would still want to know what the narration has to do *with us*, that is, what it signifies for our lives. In this latter sense, then, the dream would still lack meaning, even though it might be perfectly coherent. (That is, the dream may represent a coherent narrative, with no logical gaps or discontinuities, but would still be just an irrelevant story if I could not *connect it* with my life.)

Dreams have meaning not as words have meaning but rather as a cryptic and as yet undeciphered text has meaning: like the text, dreams must be interpreted before they are meaningful.

In dreams, as opposed to words, there is indeed a gap between signifier and signified, manifest image and meaning, that must be bridged by an act of interpretation—a gap that is defined, in part, by the term "the unconscious." (The concept of the unconscious defines the interval between the manifest and latent senses of things.)

2.26 Suppose we say this: "Every dream has a meaning; the meaning of the dream is the wish it expresses (the latent dream thought). The dream is a signifier whose meaning—or signified—is a wish."

What, then, is the relation of signifier to signified? (And again, this is simply another way of asking, How do dreams mean?)

2.27 According to one influential analogy in Freud, the manifest dream—the signifier—stands in relation to the latent dream thoughts—the signified—as a disguised, unintelligible representation of the same semantic text, or, better, as the *translation* of that text into a different mode of expression (words → pictorial images). Freud writes:

> The dream-thoughts and the dream-content are presented to us like two versions of the same subject-matter in two different languages. Or, more properly, the dream-content seems like a transcript of the dream-thoughts into another mode of expression, whose characters and syntactic laws it is our business to discover by comparing the original with the translation. The dream-thoughts are immediately comprehensible, as soon as we have learnt them. The dream-content, on the other hand, is expressed as it were in a pictographic script, the characters of which have to be transposed individually into the language of the dream-thoughts. If we attempt to read these characters according to their pictorial value instead of according to their symbolic relation, we should clearly be led into error. (ID, 278)

Before proceeding, note the strangeness of Freud's way of speaking here. Once interpreted, he says, the dream thoughts are "immediately comprehensible"—which, of course, is true, but hardly informative. The dream thoughts—the interpreted meanings of the dream (e.g., the idea that "I hate *x*")—are comprehensible precisely because they *are* thoughts—that is, ideas like any other. How could they *not* be immediately comprehensible? Insofar as these dream thoughts are reached through the process of free association—a process that, by its nature, can only produce thoughts that are "comprehensible" in this sense—it should come as no surprise to find that the interpreted meaning of the dream, like the meaning of a rebus, is immediately transparent, since, once again, it is built into the method. Here, as so often, Freud's way of putting the matter makes it sound as if he were reporting a *fact* instead of offering a grammatical comment: it serves only to obscure the distinction between what belongs to the object (in this case, the dream) and what belongs to his own particular use of language, or form of representation (the grammar of dream thoughts). (In psychology, as in philosophy, we must learn to distinguish factual from conceptual investigations.)

For Freud, the real problem is not with the interpreted dream thoughts but with the dream content, since the sense of the "pictographic script" of the manifest dream is not, like that of the dream thoughts, immediately accessible. These pictographic characters, Freud tells us, must be deciphered individually, according to their "symbolic relation" rather than their "pictorial value." He then goes on to illustrate his point by comparing the interpretation of a dream to the translation of a rebus. "Suppose I have a picture-puzzle, a rebus, in front of me," he writes.

> It depicts a house with a boat on its roof, a single letter of the alphabet, the figure of a man whose head has been conjured away, and so on. Now I might be misled into raising objections and declaring that the picture as a whole and its component parts are nonsensical. A boat has no business to be on the roof of a house, and a headless man cannot run. Moreover, the man is bigger than the house; and if the whole picture is intended to represent a landscape, letters of the alphabet are out of place in it since such objects do not occur in nature. But obviously we can only form a proper judgment of the rebus if we put aside criticisms such as these of the whole composition and its parts and if, instead, we try to replace each separate element by a syllable or word that can be represented by that element in some way or other. The words which are put together in this way are no longer nonsensical but may form a poetical phrase of the greatest beauty and significance. A dream is a picture-puzzle of this sort and our predecessors in the field of dream-interpretation have made the mistake of treating the rebus as a pictorial composition: and as such it has seemed to them nonsensical and worthless. (ID, 277–78)

In short, the dream is like a puzzle in which pictures, letters, and words are all thrown together, each of which must be individually translated in order to arrive at the hidden meaning behind the apparent nonsense of the whole. The meaning of the dream (the signified) is the unconscious thought for which the manifest dream is merely a "disguised" or "distorted" representation (the signifier). Hence, according to Freud, the dream is indeed like a language, and the process of interpretation is simply one of the substitution of one text, one signifier, for another, according to a particular method of translation.

2.28   Well, *are* dreams picture puzzles of this sort? Are dreams a kind of language in this sense?

Let us look at certain characteristic aspects of both dreams and language, what we might call (1) their semantic *structure*, (2) their symbolic *function*, and (3) their symbolic *character*.

Consider, first, *semantic (or symbolic) structure*. The dream, we think, is a *representation of thoughts* that uses *scenes and pictures*, rather than acoustic (or phonological) images, to convey its meaning. The relation between these pictures and the dream thoughts is *motivated*—that is, there is some kind of natural or internal relation between signifier and signified, a relation that is, for the most part, absent from language. The signifier in the dream is the image; the signified, its interpreted meaning.

But now recall that what gets interpreted in psychoanalysis is *not* the dream as such but the *dream report* and that the "ideas" that are thus interpreted—the dream thoughts—are related to the elements of the dream report not as "thoughts" to "representation" but rather as one meaning to another, that is, as interpreted meaning to manifest meaning. In other words, in the case of dream interpretation, the relation between signifier and signified is not semantic (the relation of a material image to its meaning) but *hermeneutic* (the relation of a latent to a manifest meaning). And this, of course, is very different from what we find in language—so different, in fact, that the very concept of meaning, applied to both cases, seems strained.

To return to Freud's comparison. The rebus is a pictographic representation of an ordinary name, phrase, sentence, or whatever; each pictorial element translates directly into a word, or phoneme, a homonym for a semantically significant element. In the dream, on the other hand, there is no possibility of this kind of direct translation, for it is only *through the dreamer's associations* to the different dream elements—the events, objects, and persons represented in the dream—that any meaning can be found; moreover, these associations are themselves profoundly personal and idiosyncratic, which is to say, completely unsystematic. Thus, the dream is *not* like a language in respect to its semantic, or symbolic, structure.[13]

2.29   Turning now to the question of *function*. For the most part—though not exclusively—language functions to communicate ideas. Language is *intentional*: it says something about something *to* someone. The dream, on the other hand, does not *communicate* ideas; if anything, it *represents* them (albeit in an indirect and distorted manner). The dream, we might say, has a *purpose* (to discharge energy) but no intention.[14] Or: the dream serves only a psychological (i.e., dynamic) function, not a social one.

("What makes *A*, the manifest dream, a representation of *B*, the dream thought?" Compare "What makes this picture a representation of *him*?" Not a likeness, surely, but nonetheless a formal correspondence of some sort.)

2.30   Consider, now, the actual *character* of dreams and language as symbolic constructions. Comparing a dream to a rebus, the first thing one notices is that the rebus is translated according to a *common code* (one based on the possibility of a pictorial representation of phonetic elements): it makes use of an existing, regular symbolism (i.e., the correlation of images to phonetic elements). In the case of dreams, by contrast, there is no such common code for interpretation (except in the rare instances of what Freud calls "symbolism" in the technical sense). It is for this reason, as Wittgenstein observes, translation of the dream can proceed in one direction only:

> Suppose you look on a dream as a kind of language. A way of saying something, or a way of symbolizing something. There

13. Not only are dreams not structurally like a language, but one can even question whether they are a form of representation. As Wittgenstein notes, "If Freud's theory on the interpretation of dreams has anything in it, it shows how *complicated* is the way the human mind represents the facts in pictures.—So complicated, so irregular is the way they are represented that we can *barely* call it representation" (CV, 44).

14. Indeed, Freud goes out of his way to insist that dreams do not "speak," that the dream work does not "think, calculate, or judge," but rather "restricts itself to giving things a new form" (ID, 545). In his 1916–17 lectures, he even suggests that the dream, in contrast to language, is *meant* to be incomprehensible: "It must, of course, be admitted that the system of expression by dreams occupies a far more unfavorable position than any of these ancient languages and scripts. For after all they are fundamentally intended for communication: that is to say, they are always, by whatever method and with whatever assistance, meant to be understood. But precisely this characteristic is absent in dreams. A dream does not want to say anything to anyone. It is not a vehicle for communication; on the contrary, it is meant to remain ununderstood" (IL, 231).

might be a regular symbolism, not necessarily alphabetical—it might be like Chinese, say. We might then find a way of translating this symbolism into the language of ordinary speech, ordinary thoughts. But then the translation ought to be possible both ways. It ought to be possible by employing the same technique to translate ordinary thoughts into dream language. As Freud recognizes, this never is done and cannot be done. So we might question whether dreaming is a way of thinking something, whether it is a language at all. (LC, 48)

Language is systematic and rule governed; dreams—at least, so far as we know, and certainly according to Freud's conception—are not. Apart from instances of symbolism proper, dreams lack a common code of translation; they do not belong to—and cannot be encompassed within—a rule-governed system. In the process of dream interpretation, the translation from manifest to latent meaning, from signifier to signified, is, as it were, "motivated"—and even "*rational*"—but not rule governed.[15]

2.31   Is a dream like a language? The answer, it seems, is no, or least it is no more like a language than, say, a painting or a symphony is "like a language"; that is, once viewed *as a symbol* (i.e., as something to *be* interpreted, a designation that will always remain, in principle, open to question), it participates in the same culturally given system of meanings as any other symbol. (And here one wants to ask why Freud should insist that dreams have only *one* meaning. Why not any number of possible meanings, just as a work of art is open to any number of possible interpretations?)

What *is* like a language—precisely because it is, in fact, purely linguistic—is the content of the dream report (i.e., the various elements to which associations are brought), as well as the procedures by which it is interpreted (i.e., the various associations and the interpreted meaning). But this is simply to call our attention to the obvious.

Why is all this important? Mainly because it relates to the question of what Freud intends by the term "interpretation" and to the sense in which it can be said that dreams "have meaning." (Dreams, we say, are "constructed"; interpretation is "rational.") When we consider the

15. To anticipate, it seems to me the translation is rational in the same way that a convincing interpretation of a painting, a poem, or a piece of music might be called "rational": that is, it reveals certain deep and unsuspected connections between things. Dreams are thus analogous to works of art, and interpretation to aesthetic criticism. For just as art relies on conventions, so dreams make use of both universal and—more often—personal symbolism.

proposition that "dreams have a meaning," we are too much inclined to think of dreams on the analogy of language (as Freud and others after him have done), to regard dreams as a kind of symbolism, and to think of the relation between dreams and their meaning as being like the relation between a word or sentence and its meaning (or between two texts in different languages or two different "modes of expression"). But, in fact, this analogy is—for the most part, at least—false: it misleads us into thinking that we can describe the operations of the unconscious in purely linguistic terms, according to the same categories with which we describe the effects of meaning in language; but what belongs to language was there from the beginning, whereas what belongs to the unconscious can only be found in the specific *procedures* through which it is interpreted and explained.

2.32 This is perhaps the place to offer a brief word about Jacques Lacan and his structural-linguistic revision of Freud. In view of the complexity of the issues involved—not to mention Lacan's own willful obscurity, his insistence on a kind of mimetic linguistics that attempts not merely to describe but, as it were, to imitate the movements of the unconscious—it is understood that this treatment is cursory at best.

Like Freud, Lacan bases the topological distinction between the conscious and the unconscious on the notion of repression; his originality in relation to Freud consists in his attempt to define this distinction in purely linguistic terms, that is, to conceive it as the product of what he calls the "structuring effects" of language, a product that is therefore comprehensible through a description of those effects. "The unconscious is neither primordial nor instinctual," writes Lacan; "what it knows about the elementary is no more than the elements of the signifier."[16] And further: "The unconscious is constituted by the effects of speech on the subject, it is the dimension in which the subject is determined in the development of the effects of speech, consequently the unconscious is structured like a language."[17]

The unconscious, according to Lacan, is established in the radical disjunction between signifier and signified, a division symbolized in the famous algorithm, S/s (signifier over signified), in which the "bar" (/) separating the two symbols represents an irreducible cleavage between the realms of signifier and signified, "a barrier," as he says, "resisting signification."[18] This formula gives a kind of graphic, minimal summary

---

16. Jacques Lacan, *Écrits*, trans. Alan Sheridan (New York: W. W. Norton, 1977), 170.

17. Lacan, *The Four Fundamental Concepts of Psychoanalysis*, ed. Jacques-Alain Miller, trans. Alan Sheridan (New York: W. W. Norton, 1978), 149.

18. Lacan, *Écrits*, 149.

of the Freudian discovery, one that is both linguistic and psychody-
namic; it refers not only to the relative *autonomy of the signifier* in
relation to the process of signification (an autonomy supposedly derived
from a privileging of the global relations between signifiers to the
detriment of the local correspondence of a signifier to a signified) but
also to the *priority of the signifier* in determining the "place" of the
subject (a priority based on the idea that the subject is always only the
subject *as it is represented in language*). For Lacan, moreover, these two
aspects of the theory, linguistic and topographical, are inseparable: as
structural linguistics provides the conceptual frame and terminology for
the theoretical description of the unconscious, so, conversely, does
the topographical thesis inform the revision of linguistic theory along
fundamentally deconstructionist lines (which is to say, toward a kind of
radical semantic skepticism).

Through this reciprocal reinterpretation of linguistics and psychoanalysis, Lacan arrives at the dual thesis that, on the one hand, "language is
the condition of the unconscious" and, on the other, "the unconscious
is the logical implication of language."[19] Implicit in this basic conception
are a number of more or less related and secondary theses, such as

1. that the function of language is exclusively *representational*; that
   language represents the subject and the subject's desire ("a
   signifier is that which represents the subject for another signifier");[20]
2. that desire is the product of language or, more specifically, of
   the acquisition of speech, "an effect in the subject of that
   condition which is imposed on him by the existence of discourse
   to cause his need to pass through the defiles of the signifier";[21]
3. that the constitution of the unconscious—or the "splitting" of
   the subject—is correlative to the subject's entry into language;
   that just as language is determined by the unconscious, so the
   unconscious is constituted through language (the unconscious
   being neither more nor less than the reality that is excluded from
   representation—originally, the object of the mother or breast);
4. that as a being determined by language—through the appropria-
   tion of the grammatical category of the I—the subject is essentially and irremediably *alienated*; that insofar as speech is origi-

19. Lacan, preface to Anika Lemaire, *Jacques Lacan* (London: Routledge and Kegan Paul,
1977), xiii.

20. Lacan, *The Four Fundamental Concepts of Psychoanalysis*, 157.

21. Lacan, *Écrits*, 265.

nally directed to the subject from the Other, it is only there, in the place of the Other, that the subject comes into being;

5. that the unconscious, as the product of the effects of speech on the subject, is itself *structured like a language*, that "a material operates in it according to certain laws, which are the same laws as those discovered in the study of actual languages";[22]

6. that the basic operations of unconscious signification—or the displacement of meaning—can therefore be described in terms of the rhetorical devices of metonymy and metaphor, corresponding to Freud's notions of displacement and condensation, respectively; and

7. that insofar as it both emerges in the locus of the Other and manifests itself in conformity with the basic (grammatical, syntactic, and rhetorical) "laws" of language, the unconscious can be described as the *discourse of the Other*: "The desire of the dream is not assumed by the subject who says 'I' in his speech," writes Lacan. "Articulated, nevertheless, in the locus of the Other, it is discourse—a discourse whose grammar Freud has begun to declare to be such."[23]

2.33   Now whatever its value as a corrective to the more domesticated, revisionist forms of psychoanalysis (neo-Freudianism, egopsychology, self-psychology, etc.), and whatever its rhetorical and literary merits, in the end this kind of exclusively linguistic reinterpretation of Freud is, I believe, consistently trivial, redundant, nonsensical—or just plain wrong.

It is *trivial* if it means to claim that the connections between patent and latent meanings—for example, the connection between the manifest and latent meanings of a dream—are determined by rules of grammar and rhetoric, since, as we have seen, the method of free association guarantees in advance that this will be the case. It is *redundant* if it reduces the unconscious to a fact about language—for example, its opaqueness or indeterminacy—since we did not need Freud to tell us that language is capable of meaning something other than what it says, or saying something other than what it means. It is *nonsensical* if it poses as a theory about the nature, function, and logical conditions of language as whole, since—as Wittgenstein was at pains to show—the propositions of such a theory violate the very conditions they attempt to describe, that is, the grammatical conditions for making sensible

22. Ibid., 237.
23. Ibid., 264.

statements *in* our language. And finally, it is *wrong* if it means to claim that psychical phenomena such as dreams, slips, and symptoms represent a form of language, since such phenomena—at least as they are described by psychoanalysis—have almost none of the distinguishing characteristics of a language (e.g., translatability, regular symbolism, and communicative aim).

In the end, however, what is perhaps most objectionable in Lacanian theory—in part, I admit, because it is in some ways the most seductive—is his insistence on the notion of a "gap" in language, the idea, in other words, that there is something (what?) that intercedes between a signifier and a signified, a word and its meaning, an expression and the wish that lies behind it. Not only is this idea based on a complete misconstrual of Saussure (whose distinction between signifier and signified is, I submit, purely methodological, not philosophical); not only does it reduce Freudianism to absurd metatheoretical speculations about meaning (by reducing the unconscious to a function of language); but, most important, it encourages a naïve and pernicious picture of language, one that invariably leads to the kind of philosophical excesses and rhetorical verbiage that pervade so much of the current literature of poststructuralism.

Once language is viewed as essentially representational, once words are taken as mere signs for something else (be it meaning, intention, desire, or whatever)—there will always be a gap between reality and language, or between our experience and its expression. But, as Wittgenstein shows, it is a mistake to look at language in this way—a mistake and, in its consequences, a misfortune.

2.34   The idea that dreams are a kind of language derives from what we might call the semantic-linguistic analogy: the idea that dreams are to wishes, or latent thoughts, as words are to their meaning. The other and, for Freud himself, more important analogy is that between dream construction and the interaction of physical forces and objects. This is what we might call the causal-empirical analogy: the idea that wishes are to dreams as physical causes are to their effects.

Whatever its proximity to the concepts of meaning and text, the notion of wish fulfillment can never be wholly reduced to semantics alone, for in the end it is not only an idea or intention but also, according to psychoanalysis, a dynamic force, or quantum of energy. It refers not only to the *meaning* of the dream as a kind of hidden, undeciphered text, but also to the *function* of the dream as one of "bonding" or "discharging" unconscious energies.

The dream, according to Freud, is a compromise between the demands of the two different psychical systems, unconscious and preconscious; it is the outcome of the conflict between two dynamic psychical forces, namely, the repressed, unconscious wish and the preconscious wish to maintain sleep undisturbed. The dream, by relieving the pressure of the former, effectively fulfills the latter. Clearly, there is no analogue to this in the notion of a rebus or in language generally. With the introduction of the dynamic function of the dream, Freud leaves hermeneutics for economics.

2.35   This brings us to the third proposition of Freudian theory: "The (repressed) wish is the 'motive for' the dream."

The ambiguity in Freud's conception of meaning is the direct result of the ambiguity in his conception of a "wish" (*Wunsch*). A wish, for Freud, is a compound object, one that lies at the intersection between meaning and force, semantics and energetics. The same ambiguity is also present, of course, in our ordinary language, for we speak of wishes as if they were ideas and imaginings ("I wish my friend would arrive") but also as though they were physical forces, dynamic compulsions possessed of a certain strength ("The wish became an obsession: I couldn't stop thinking about my friend, despite my efforts to remain focused on my work"). In the context of the Freudian dream theory, too, we can think of the wish as an *idea* (e.g., the wishful idea that is represented in the dream), or we can think of a wish as a kind of force, or *drive*, something that causes other things to happen (e.g., the wish that "instigates" the dream, or causes it to occur). Freud thinks of a wish in both of these ways, often simultaneously, while also formalizing the inherent ambiguity of the term in his dynamic conception of the psyche. We thus arrive at what is perhaps the central paradox of psychoanalysis: the idea that, within the human psyche, meanings have force and forces, meaning. (This is what Ricoeur refers to as the problem of "mixed discourse" in psychoanalysis: the fact that Freud uses both the language of the natural sciences [mechanics, hydrology, neurology] and the language of hermeneutics [meaning, motive, purpose, intention] and that his psychological explanations employ these languages interdependently.)

Freud's dynamic theory of the unconscious crystallizes aspects of our ordinary understanding of the term "wish," sharpening its natural ambiguity into paradox.

2.36   In the causal-empirical view, a wish is that which seeks to discharge itself in the dream, that which instigates, or "occasions" (if not actually causes), the dream's occurrence. The dream is like the steam that rushes through a safety valve, thus reducing the pressure inside a container.[24] The dream functions to reduce the pressure of unconscious wishes. From this dynamic point of view, then, the dream is less a "representation" (*Darstellung*) of a wish than it is a "substitute gratification" for it. In its function of controlling unconscious pressure, or "excitation," the dream *stands in place of*, rather than *expresses*, an unconscious impulse: its meaning is therefore relative to, and inseparable from, certain energetic, conflictual dynamics, relations of cause and effect, force and counterforce, within the realm of the psychical.

Based on this analogy between a wish and psychical force, the causal-empirical view leads to the idea that the unconscious is known, not through interpretation or translation, as on the hermeneutic-linguistic conception, but rather through a kind of inference from effect to cause. In this view, unconscious, and unobserved, mental acts are "inferred" from conscious, and observed, ones. The unconscious is thus a reality that is inferred from its manifest effects in consciousness.

2.37 Let us look more closely now at what is at work in this conception. To begin with, of course, everything is based here on the model of empirical causality (as well as, we might add, on the picture of a "cause" as something that pushes or pulls, a directional force of some sort): namely, an observed conjunction of two events (x and y) such that the first event regularly brings about the second (if x, then y). In dreams, for example, the manifest content of a dream, once it has been interpreted, is explained by reference to certain psychical causes (e.g., wishes, residual memories, and censorship) that are held to account for its construction, both as a whole and in respect to its particular features. Based on the assumption of this kind of causal relation, Freud then claims to infer from the conscious ("observed") event of the dream the existence of certain unconscious ("unobservable") psychical processes, that is, to *deduce* them as hidden causes from manifest effects: if this dream x, then these unconscious psychical processes, or events, y.

But now suppose we ask, What kind of causality is supposed to be at work here? Indeed, what does Freud mean by "cause" and "inference" here? The more we think about this question, the more it begins to seem that whatever else Freud intends by the terms "cause," "causality," "inference," and the like, in this context—and it is never quite clear just *what* he means—it bears little resemblance to what we ordinarily mean by the term. For ordinarily the idea of a cause is based on an observed and regular conjunction of two events, one that is at least in principle

<hr>

24. See, e.g., ID, 618.

subject to experimental confirmation. In the case of dreams and other psychical phenomena, however, not only do we *never* observe the originating cause or causes as such (since, of course, they are unconscious and therefore removed from view), but we are also not even in a position to form a coherent, testable hypothesis about them—of the form, if *x*, then *y*—at least according to the terms and criteria that Freud sets out (since *y* is not only hidden from view but *in principle* inaccessible by any direct means). Hence, at least on the standards and criteria of our ordinary practices, there is nothing in this case to warrant our calling it an instance of "causality" and therefore also nothing to justify the supposed inference from conscious effect to unconscious cause. (Consider: it is a matter here, not of inferring unconscious cause from conscious effect, but of *seeing* the conscious act or event *as* the effect of unconscious causes.)

Moreover, even if there were some kind of observed regularity in dream construction, an inference based on this regularity could not lead to the kind of cause that Freud wants to secure. For whatever the actual causes of a dream—and there is every reason to believe that such causes exist, both psychological and neuropsychological—they belong by definition to a different logical category than the "dream thoughts" arrived at through interpretation; in other words, they are not logically or grammatically of such a nature as to be identifiable with, or assimilable to, the *meanings* interpreted through analysis. (Think of the differences between the grammar of "brain" and the grammar of "mind," that is, the differences between the ways we use these two terms; now, consider what we ordinarily understand by "meaning," together with what Freud understands when of he speaks of the meaning of, for instance, a dream.)

"Causes," in the accepted sense of the term, are things that we *infer* on the basis of observed regularities and that we conform through experimentation. Motives are things that we *interpret* and that can only be confirmed through *avowals*. (That is, we ask, "Did you want to. . . ?") In this sense, we can say that psychoanalysis has to do with *motives*, not causes; it is not an observational, or hypothetico-deductive, science but a hermeneutic one; it is not predictive but interpretive.

In psychoanalysis we might say that *meaning precedes explanation*. Whatever their usefulness in making sense of certain psychological occurrences, causal explanations follow from and subserve the procedures of interpretation. They represent, not hypotheses, but post hoc constructions that function to give sense and coherence to various psychical phenomena (dreams, symptoms, etc.) that would otherwise be senseless.

2.38 Again, this is not to say that Freud's use of a causal, naturalistic language is necessarily a mistake, even if it is shown to be confused (what is confused, in fact, is not the use of the expression but the way it is understood, the way it is appropriated and the implications that are drawn from it); nor is it to suggest—as many since Freud, including Wittgenstein, have done—that causal explanations in psychoanalysis can and should be translated into a language of "reasons" or "motives." On the contrary, I would argue that psychoanalysis cannot be compre-hended on the basis of a strict disjunction between reasons and causes—or, still less, through a reduction of the latter to the former. By the very logic of its interpretive method and theoretical framework—and specifically by its commitment to a *dynamic* (conflictual) view of psychi-cal functioning—any truly psychoanalytic description of psychical phe-nomena and their relations entails recourse to what Ricoeur has called, with appropriate ambiguity, quasi-physical metaphors, that is, meta-phors that evoke the qualities of physical objects and causal relations.[25] For it is part of what Freud *means* in calling certain psychical contents and processes "unconscious" that they behave essentially *as objects* and that they can be comprehended, therefore, only through the language of the natural sciences (mechanics, hydrology, etc.).

At the same time, it is also true to say, as Wittgenstein aptly puts it, that "Freud did not in fact give any method of analyzing dreams which was analogous to the rules which will tell you what are the causes of stomach-ache" (ML, 310). There is no question, in other words, that Freud was wrong to insist on the *naturalistic-empirical* nature of his discoveries and wrong to claim that his explanatory theories were strictly derived from observable facts and therefore subject to empirical verification. For "unconscious thoughts" cannot be inferred from dreams or pathological symptoms as fire is inferred from smoke or as rain from certain atmospheric conditions. Explanation in psychoanalysis is, as it were, heuristic rather than inferential.

2.39 Freud claims that the (unconscious) wish is the motive for, or instigator of, the dream. He believes that the wish drives the actual construction of the dream and, indeed, that the dream demands such energy that only a powerful, infantile wish is sufficient to produce it. But why should the production of dreams require energy of this kind? Does daydreaming require energy? Does thinking require energy if, for

25. See Paul Ricoeur, "The Question of Proof in Freud's Writings," in *Hermeneutics and the Social Sciences*, ed. and trans. John Thompson (Cambridge: Cambridge University Press, 1981), 257.

example, I am just walking down the street allowing my mind to wander as it will? Even under conditions of great stress, what kind of energy is required for the normal acts of thinking, cognition, feeling, and the like? Is it the same kind of energy of which the physicist speaks when he talks about the sum of energy required to do a certain amount of work?

Here we may be tempted to say, Yes, of course, thinking requires energy, just as all bodily activity requires energy; intense thinking requires more energy than daydreaming, but it stands to reason that even the latter requires some expenditure of energy. But notice that when we say this we are no longer referring to energy in the sense in which Freud wants to use the term. For what we mean is *physical* energy (which is in fact the only kind of energy with which we are familiar in our everyday dealings with the world), energy that can be measured in quantifiable terms (e.g., calories expended); when Freud speaks of energy, on the other hand, he means *psychical* energy, energy that can be quantified, if at all, only in a very vague and relative way (e.g., in the notion that certain ideational contents are invested, or "cathected," with greater energy than others).

It is obvious, of course, that Freud conceives psychical energy on the analogy of physical energy—but he never specifies exactly how the concept of psychical energy *differs* from the concept of physical energy. Indeed, he proceeds as if the only difference lay in the fact that they belong to separate but parallel spheres, the mental and the somatic, with the "instinct," or "drive" (*Trieb*), mediating between them, acting as a kind of messenger from one to other.

2.40   But why shouldn't it be just as natural, if not more so, to assume that dreams, occurring as they do in sleep, require little or no energy at all? (Just as my next thought, if I do not direct my attention in any particular direction, occurs spontaneously and without effort.) This would be the commonsense view of the matter—but psychoanalysis, as we know, has at best a strained relation to common sense. For psychoanalysis, it is because dreams are to be viewed as the product of conflicting desires, which is to say, as the product of conflicting *forces*, that it must be presumed that the dream only occurs as the product of some instigating force or energy.[26] Any other assumption would be inconsistent with the theory as a whole.

26. In general, Freud always assumes, first, that mental activity demands energy and, second, that the source of this energy can only be *outside* of the mind. As Philip Rieff has noted, this tendency to explain mental activity by reference to a motivation outside of itself aligns Freud with the "psychologizing philosophers," Schopenhauer and Nietzsche, and

Now, ask yourself, What would experiment prove here? Indeed, what kind of experiment could possibly be devised that would either prove or disprove either of these two guiding premises: first, that dreams represent wishes, and second, that it is the wish that produces the dream? The wish is not an observed phenomenon but an interpreted meaning ("motive"), not an inferred cause ("It happened because . . .") but a methodological injunction ("Proceed as if . . ."). In short, it begins to seem that the entire psychoanalytic theory of dreaming—at least as Freud presents it—has nothing whatsoever to do with observation and experimentation or, for that matter, with what goes on in current dream research. (It follows that the neuropsychology of dreams is totally irrelevant to psychoanalysis; at best, it merely contributes other, largely redundant criteria to those already available.) Psychoanalysis is not an empirical theory about dreaming but a method for the interpretation of dreams—whatever Freud himself may suggest.

2.41   Some statements in psychoanalysis—and in the sciences generally, both natural and human—that look like empirical propositions actually tell us less about the object than about how we are to proceed, about what we are to look for and where. We must learn to recognize these statements when we encounter them.

It is not an empirical fact but a rule of grammar that red is a color and that *this* is the color red; it is not an empirical fact but a rule of grammar that a chair is an object; and it is not an empirical fact but a rule of grammar that the unconscious is accessible only through interpretation or that dreams are the expression of wishes. Moreover, we say of rules not that they are "true" or "false" but only that they are "appropriate" or "inappropriate," "useful" or "not useful," or something of the kind.

---

against the idealism of Kant. For Freud, with the exception of sexuality, no thought or feeling is self-explanatory; it must be referred to something earlier and simpler that is being represented. (See Rieff, *Freud: The Mind of the Moralist* [Chicago: University of Chicago Press, 1959], 51.)

3

THE GRAMMAR AND LOGIC
OF DREAM INTERPRETATION

3.1 Returning to the question of how the unconscious is known, suppose we say, "Unconscious thoughts are not properly *inferred* but *interpreted*. The unconscious is something that derives its meaning from the procedures of interpretation: it is a purely interpreted reality. It is, in effect, the sum total of interpreted meanings." Well, now we need to ask, "What does it mean to interpret something in psychoanalysis?" That is, what does Freud call "interpretation"?[1] This is a question about the grammar of "interpretation" in psychoanalysis.

3.2 At the very outset of *The Interpretation of Dreams*, Freud writes, "In the following pages I shall bring forward proof that there is a psychological technique which makes it possible to interpret dreams, and that, if that procedure is employed, every dream reveals itself as a psychical structure [*psychisches Gebild*] which has a meaning and which can be inserted at an assignable point in the mental activities of waking life [*das seelische Treiben des Wachens*]" (ID, 1).

Dreams are meaningful because they can be related, through interpre-

---

1. We should note that the German *Deutung* has no direct equivalent in English, that it can mean "interpretation" or "explanation" or even "clarification," according to the context. In general, for Freud, *Deutung* is closer to "explanation," as when he says that the *Deutung* of a dream consists in determining its *Bedeutung*, or meaning.

tation, to our normal, conscious activities. This, for Freud, is a matter of definition: to say that a dream has a *meaning* is simply to say that *it can be so related*, that it *is* a psychical act. (Once again, Freud's way of speaking tends to confound the issue; in the statement just quoted, the two phrases "has a meaning" and "can be inserted . . . in the mental activities of waking life" are redundant.) To interpret a dream is to ascribe a meaning to it other that the one that is immediately apparent; it is to *replace* the largely unintelligible, manifest dream with an intelligible sense, one that can be situated within the continuum of conscious psychical life and thus related to conscious desires, intentions, purposes, and so forth. "The aim I have set before myself is to show that dreams are capable of being interpreted [*einer Deutung fähig sind*]," Freud writes elsewhere. " 'Interpreting' a dream implies assigning a 'meaning' [*Sinn*] to it—that is, replacing [*ersetzen*] it by something which fits into the chain of our mental acts as a link having a validity and importance equal to the rest" (ID, 128).

3.3 Interpretation is the substitution of one meaning for another; it involves a movement from one meaning, or one level of thought, to another. Thus the distinction between the manifest and the latent content of the dream: the *manifest* content is the dream as it is experienced and remembered, the subject of the dream report; the *latent* content is the interpreted *sense* of the dream, what Freud sometimes describes as the dream thoughts in contrast to the actual, remembered dream.

It is this relation of the manifest to the latent content of the dream, the movement from the one to the other, that defines the process of the "dream work" (*Traumarbeit*). The dream work comprises all the unconscious mechanisms by which the original (repressed) dream thoughts are converted or transcribed into the dream itself: namely, "condensation" (*Verdichtung*), "displacement" (*Verschiebung*), "considerations of representability" (*Rücksicht auf Darstellbarkeit*), and "secondary revision" (*sekundäre Bearbeitung*). It is thus also the work of these mechanisms that accounts for the unintelligibility of the manifest dream, for the fact of "distortion" (*Entstellung*) in dreams.

The latent content of the dream is something psychical, a thought or idea; to say that dreams have a meaning is therefore simply to say that there are "thoughts" concealed beneath the senseless appearance of the dream, thoughts that are not essentially different from those of waking life. We can diagram these relations among the different dream elements as shown in Figure 1 (we call this "the logical structure of dreams").[2]

---

2. It should be regarded as a remarkable thing that *logical* relations can be represented *spatially*. This tells us something important about logic—and also about the possibility of *displaying* logical relations discursively, as in the method of grammar.

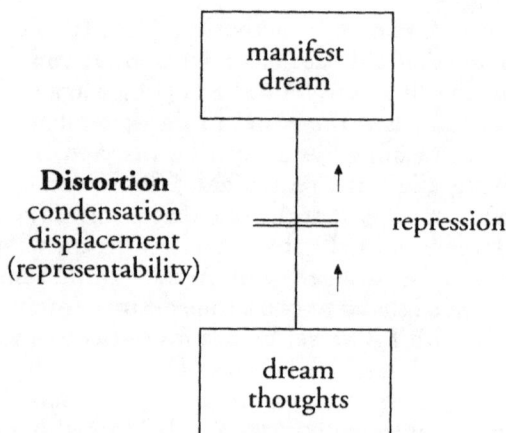

Fig. 1. The logical structure of dreams as symbolic constructions

In moving from the manifest dream to its latent meaning (the dream thoughts), the process of interpretation effectively *reverses* the process of construction: it arrives at the sense of the dream by undoing the distortion in its content and, by implication, deciphering the mechanisms of this distortion. "The work which transforms the latent dream into the manifest one is called the *dream-work*," Freud writes. "The work which proceeds in the contrary direction, which endeavors to arrive at the latent dream from the manifest one, is our *work of interpretation*. This work of interpretation seeks to undo the dream-work"[3] (IL, 170). (The strict parallelism of these two processes, dream work and interpretation, should be kept in mind; eventually we will want to ask about the criteria by which these processes are distinguished; that is, we will want to ask whether Freud's explanatory account, in terms of psychical mechanisms and their causal relations, might not itself be viewed as a reversal of what actually occurs in this process, whether it is not in fact the interpretation of a dream—and, more exactly, the production of meaning through the interpretation—that, in a sense, precedes the explanation of the dream's construction.)

The *rules* of interpretation—the formal procedures by which one moves from manifest to latent meaning—are derived from the theory of *repression*, specified from both an *economic* (quantifying) and a *genetic*

---

3. Similarly, in "On Dreams" Freud writes, "I shall describe the process which transforms the latent into the manifest content of dreams as the 'dream-work.' The counterpart to this activity—one which brings about a transformation in an opposite direction—is already known to us as the work of analysis" (OD, 641).

(historical) perspective. To the extent that they are meaningful, to the extent that they are symbolic, or psychological, entities—which is to say, to the extent that they are *capable* of being interpreted psychoanalytically—dreams, for Freud, are the disguised representations of repressed desires; they are genetically conditioned by ancestral and childhood experiences (as the *repetition* of primitive and childhood experiences) and economically conditioned by the dynamic relations and conflicts of desires (as *substitute gratifications*).

This understanding of dreams in terms of their genesis and economic function, together with Freud's innumerable examples of interpretation ("exemplars"), constitutes a methodological paradigm. Whatever dream is offered for interpretation must be interpreted in conformity with this paradigm; whatever dream occurs can be thus interpreted.[4]

3.4 "We did not interpret dreams . . . because it was discovered that they were meaningful," writes one of Freud's more perceptive critics, "but we insisted that they were meaningful in order that we might interpret them."[5] Yet, how are we to distinguish between "finding" and "inventing" here? Are dreams meaningful "in themselves," or is it we who somehow *impose* meaning on them? By what means are we to decide this question? And what would it mean to say that dreams are meaningful *in themselves*? Are words meaningful "in themselves," or is it we who impose a meaning on them? (Compare "We *use* words to convey meaning.") Is a work of art meaningful "in itself"? (What would *this* mean?)

"What about natural occurrences, like rain, or natural objects, like trees and mountains and rivers? Surely, if there is meaning here, it is only the meaning that we ourselves have introduced." But even this sounds strange, for what are we trying to say when we *deny* that these things are "intrinsically" meaningful? In many cases, it seems to me, it simply seems to make no sense to say either that we discovered meaning or that we insisted on it.

Well, then, perhaps we should ask, Are dreams more like words and works of art (symbols or symbolic constructions), or more like rain

---

4. It is often reported that people in Freudian analysis dream Freudian dreams, whereas people in Jungian analysis dream Jungian dreams, and so forth, as if this were an indication of the powers of therapeutic persuasion. In point of fact, however, there is no such thing as a Freudian or a Jungian dream—only dreams interpreted according to Freudian or Jungian methods.

5. Frank Cioffi, "Freud and the Idea of a Pseudo-Science," in *Explanation and the Behavioural Sciences*, ed. Robert Borger and Frank Cioffi (Cambridge: Cambridge University Press, 1970), 498.

(chance occurrences)? Once again, how do we go about trying to decide this issue? And isn't this in fact the *whole* issue (i.e., that some insist that dreams have only natural causes, like rain, whereas others insist that they are humanly significant, like words and symbols)?

Did Freud *discover* that dreams had meaning, or merely decide to call them meaningful in order to find a place for them in his psychology—that is, in order to construct a unified view of the human psyche? But now ask, How would we make this discovery, if not by procedures like those which Freud himself employed?

3.5   It was Freud's achievement to have extended the range of what is to be regarded as meaningful in psychical life, what is to be regarded as a significant construction, or a symbol, rather than a mere chance occurrence. Freud extended the boundaries of meaning to include things like dreams, slips, forgetting, neurotic symptoms, and so forth. But why should we want to say either that this meaning was *found* or that it was merely *invented*? Is there any difference between "interpreting dreams" and "discovering that they are meaningful," or between "insisting that dreams are meaningful" and actually interpreting them? We do in fact interpret dreams. The question is not *whether* dreams are meaningful but *how* we find them so, that is, according to what procedure and by what logic. Or, the question is not whether dreams are intrinsically meaningful; the question is whether *we* will choose to interpret them.

3.6   With this in mind, let us look at how this meaning comes about, that is, at the actual process of interpretation. The general procedure is familiar enough. The patient begins by recounting the dream as completely as possible. This narrative account of the dream, or the dream report, as Freud calls it, represents the manifest content (A). Proceeding by the method of "free association," the analyst then elicits from the patient whatever ideas occur to him or her in connection with the dream or with particular elements within it ($a1$, $a2$, $a3$, $a4$ . . .), regardless of how intimate or seemingly irrelevant these ideas may seem. Each of these various associations leads, then, to some implicit or unstated idea ($b1$, $b2$, $b3$ . . .), and thus they provide a point of correlation or comparison between the given element of the dream report (A) and this unstated idea. Finally, once all the associations are given—and the ideas abstracted from these associations brought together—the analyst assigns a meaning to the dream as a whole (B); that is, based on the analyst's familiarity with the patient's personality and history, the analyst constructs interpretations aimed at revealing the unconscious thoughts behind the actual recounted dream, the so-called latent dream thoughts.

Now, among these unconscious thoughts, Freud says, there is invariably at least one that is the expression of a wish, most often a wish that is morally repugnant and alien to the waking life of the patient: in short, a *repressed* wish. It is this wish, or "wishful impulse," that is the motive for the dream, that which provides the actual energy for its production. The interpreted dream is the representation of a situation in which this wish is somehow satisfied or fulfilled; hence, according to Freud's famous formula, the dream is "a (disguised) fulfillment of a (suppressed or repressed) wish" (ID, 160).

3.7   Let us look more closely now at the procedure of free association. The dream is recounted, then broken into different elements and episodes (the various elements of the dream content, *A - B - C . . .*). The patient then associates to each of these different elements individually (the associations, *a - b - c . . .*). From these various associations the analyst then constructs an interpretation of the whole, an interpretation that shows the dream to be the representation (expression) of one or more unconscious wishes (e.g., the dream thought, "I wish P. were dead"). We might represent this process as in Figure 2.

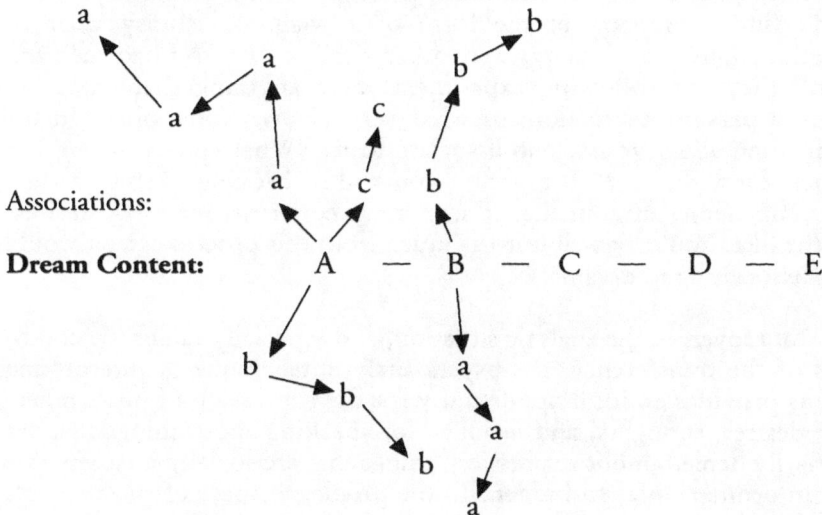

Fig. 2. (Interpreted) dream thought: "I wish P. were dead."

3.8   Let's assume that the dream is mine. Now notice, first, that if the meaning of the dream is to be derived from the associations that I have to the various elements, and if these associations are—as they inevitably must be—ideas concerning my personal interests, problems, emotional attachments, and the like (if they are, in other words, expressions of my conscious preoccupations and concerns), then why should we be surprised that the meaning constructed from these associations is "psychological" or that, as Freud says, it "fits into the chain of our mental acts as a link having a validity and importance equal to the rest" (ID, 96)? For in fact, of course, there is no "fitting" to be done here; the relevance of the (unconscious) dream thoughts to waking life is not something that is discovered through interpretation but rather something that is built into the method. Whatever associations I produce will naturally bear a certain psychological significance for my life—and probably a very important one—simply because they are *my* associations. The meaning interpreted in these associations will doubtless be no less psychologically significant.

Second, it seems to me that there is also no reason to be surprised at the fact that the method of free association leads to a *wish*, for this, too, could have been expected from the method. As Wittgenstein notes, if you are preoccupied with something, with a personal problem of some sort, then no matter where you start from, the process of free association will very likely lead you back to the same theme—and probably more than once (LC, 50–51). It also seems perfectly natural that this problem would find expression in the form of a wish, or fantasy, that is, something like "I *wish* things were otherwise" or "I *wish* I had such and such." (Try the following experiment: take anything that comes to mind—a person, a situation, or whatever—or even some object in the room, then allow yourself to associate to it: "What comes to mind in connection with. . . ?" Inevitably, you will be brought back to certain recurrent themes in your life, to important concerns, interests, desires, and the like. You may well learn as much from this process as you would from associating to dreams.)

3.9   Moreover, in the analytic situation, and especially under the conditions of the transference, the psychoanalytic technique of interpreting dreams provides an ideal opportunity for the expression of one's innermost desires, thoughts, and feelings, for speaking about things that are ordinarily denied public expression, things that are socially unacceptable and, in ordinary life, forbidden. In the privileged space of the analyst's consulting room, dream interpretation allows for a uniquely intimate form of confession. The aura of scientific respectability and detached objectivity, the analyst's professional demeanor, the furnishings and environment (the couch, the lighting, the tastefully selected art works, etc.)—all of these things, too, undoubtably contribute to the sense of security, relaxation, and trust that the analysand needs to speak freely. Under these conditions it is hard to imagine how anyone would *not* end up talking about precisely the kinds of wishes, fantasies, anxieties, and so forth, that are typically attributed to the latent meaning of dreams.

3.10 Taken together, these two facts—that free association tends to converge on our most pressing and personal concerns and that the analytic situation uniquely encourages the expression of these concerns—may also go a long way toward accounting for Freud's belief that sex, or the sexual instincts, are the primary motive behind the formation of dreams and symptoms. If I am preoccupied with certain aspects of my sexual life—or with my erotic relationship with another person—I can begin a train of associations virtually anywhere, and I will soon be led back to the same issues: for example, to the pain and anxiety that attends this relationship, to my concerns about my sexual performance, to guilt over my sexual conduct, to my frustrated emotional and sexual needs. In other words, to the extent that sex is a problem, sex will form the content of the meanings interpreted through this process. If I am personally preoccupied by sex, how could this preoccupation *not* be reflected in my associations—and hence also, as it were, in my dreams? (Does this mean that the dream is *about* sex or that it is motivated by sexual wishes? Well, how would we go about trying to answer this? Where would we *look* for an answer?)

In Freud's time, and among the persons of late bourgeois Western culture, sex was a major preoccupation; today, it seems it is less so.[6] Does this mean that our dreams have changed? (What is it that you are most inclined to deny about yourself? What thoughts or motives are you most likely to disavow? What about yourself do you find most difficult to accept? Through analysis, your dreams will tell you.)

3.11 The great French psychologist Pierre Janet was talking to an enthusiastic student of Freud's about the dream theory. "Last night," he said, "I dreamt that I was standing on a railway station platform—surely that has no sexual significance." "Oh, indeed it has," said the

6. It is now a commonplace that issues of self-esteem and narcissism have displaced sexuality as the major preoccupation of most men and women, as the issue, in other words, that is at once the most personally important and most likely to be socially condemned. Hence, today we have narcissistic disorders and the psychology of self, whereas previously we had hysteria and the psychology of the instincts.

Freudian; "a railway station is a place where trains go to and fro, to and fro, and all to and fro movements are highly suggestive. And what about a railway signal; it can be either up or down, need I say more?"[7] Janet went on to point out that if we allow such freedom in the interpretation of symbolism, every possible content of a dream can be construed along these same lines, and the theory becomes "fact proof": it cannot be refuted by any conceivable occurrence. Whatever the dream, the theory will prove true.

Here we may want to say, "A theory that cannot be disproved by any conceivable experience is without meaning. The Freudian theory of dreams is therefore senseless." Yet it is also important to see that certain statements that look like factual propositions are actually more on the order of grammatical recommendations. They seem to say, "This is how things are," when in fact what they mean is, "Look at things *like this*." "The dream represents repressed sexual needs and desires," "The symptom is the product of certain childhood experiences," "Your unwillingness is a sign of resistance," and so forth—what looks like a statement of fact may actually be a statement of grammar: it does not tell how things are but introduces new criteria for the use of our language. (Compare "There are two men sitting in this room" and "Two plus two equals four.")

3.12   The link between the unconscious thought and its manifestation is—at least in classical psychoanalysis—almost always forged on a few very simple ideas: something is being detached from something (castration), something is moving (copulation), something is hard work (deflowering), something is coming out of something (defecation), and so forth.[8] In Freud, everything becomes a metaphor for something else—and most often, of course, for certain aspects of human sexuality. Thus, as Wittgenstein suggests, it all becomes a matter of finding the right similes (L I, 40).

3.13   Concerning the method of free association, suppose we ask, "How do we know when to stop?" Our first inclination is to say, "Well, at a certain point, the flow of associations just stops. We reach a kind of terminus and nothing more is forthcoming." But why shouldn't this terminus be regarded as a sign of resistance? How do we know that this is truly an *end* and not an indication of repression, defense, or whatever? When do we know that an interpretation is complete? Indeed, why

7. Reported by M. O'C. Drury in *The Danger of Words* (London: Routledge and Kegan Paul, 1973), 16–17.

8. See Frank Cioffi, "Wittgenstein's Freud," in *Studies in the Philosophy of Wittgenstein*, ed. Peter Winch (New York: Humanities Press, 1969), 203–5.

shouldn't interpretation go on *interminably*? (And this is another way of asking, How do we know an interpretation is correct?)

3.14 Just how "free" is the method of free association? It would seem that anyone who chooses to undergo analysis already has a fairly good idea of the kind of associations that the analyst will find important—and even if they don't, they will soon pick up the appropriate cues from the analyst, particularly since the analyst generally intervenes only when the opportunity presents itself for pushing an appropriately Freudian point.[9]

Does this invalidate the method, or show it to be so thoroughly contaminated as to undermine the legitimacy of all appeals to clinical evidence? Freud believed that freedom from external interferences and from the critical interpellations of the patient would allow a flow of associations that were causally determined, and hence allowed certain kinds of etiological inferences; but even if we give up the idea that the validity of the method rests solely on its explanatory capacity, its effectiveness in revealing certain causal connections between ideas and complexes, there is nothing to say that the method may not nonetheless retain a certain curative value. (In fact, there is every reason to believe that the method *can* produce material that is both revealing and therapeutically efficacious.) In any case, there is no reason to assume that the value of the method is strictly tied to its explanatory capacity, at least as this is usually understood.

3.15 Imagine that the interpreted meaning of my dream is the thought "I wish P. were dead," even though P. does not appear in the dream, nor is there any reference to death. It makes sense to ask then, "*Do* I in fact wish P. were dead?" since I have never acted to harm P. in any way, have never been conscious of any desire to harm him, much less to wish him dead; and indeed, so far as I am aware, I don't want any harm to come to him. It will be argued, of course, that desire for P.'s death is real but "unconscious"—but then we must see that this description, while possibly true in one sense, is of a very different kind than the description

---

9. See Sebastiano Timpanaro, *The Freudian Slip: Psychoanalysis and Textual Criticism*, trans. Kate Soper (London: New Left Books, 1976), esp. 49–61. The brilliance of Timpanaro's work lies in his suggestion that the "facts" that Freud adduces as evidence for the existence of an unconscious mind can be explained more economically by certain principles of textual criticism (the tendency toward banalization, omission of words inessential to the context, etc.). In other words, contrary to Lacan and the various linguistic revisionists, Timpanaro claims—correctly, I think—that psychoanalysis rests on pointed ignorance and misunderstanding of linguistic theory and philological methods. He fails to appreciate, however, that this fact alone does not invalidate the practice of psychoanalysis.

I would otherwise give of my intentions. Here again we can speak of two different motives, one conscious and one unconscious, and two different descriptions of my desire, both of them in some sense "correct." The important thing is to see that these descriptions are *not logically commensurable*, that, as Wittgenstein puts it, "the games played with these two motives are utterly different" (LC, 22–23).

Does this mean that there is no conflict between these two descriptions of my desire? The answer to this, I think, is neither a simple yes nor a simple no.

3.16 "I wish P. were dead" and "I do not wish P. were dead": both of these thoughts are *my* thoughts, but in different ways. We can say that one is "unconscious," the other "conscious"—yet the distinction between conscious and unconscious motives is not reducible to the distinction between, say, "hidden" and "concealed," or "seen" and "unseen," causes. For what we mean by these expressions, how we use them, is very different from what their surface grammar suggests. (One way to explore this difference is to ask, "How do I know that. . . ?" another is to ask, "How did I first learn use the expression, 'I had an unconscious wish that. . .'?" or perhaps, "How would I teach the use of this expression to someone else?")

Still, it is quite conceivable that during the course of analysis—or even in the process of interpreting a single dream—I would exchange the one description for the other; in other words, I would be *persuaded* of the truth of the one description over the other. This seems to suggest that the two descriptions are conflicting, after all. (But notice that what is involved here is a very complicated process of coming to see things in a new light, possibly even of changing my entire way of understanding myself: in other words, what is at issue is not a conflict between two factual descriptions, one of which will be judged "true" and the other "false" according to commonly accepted and public criteria, but rather a shift from one way of describing my experience to another. If these two descriptions conflict, then, they do so only one some level other than the factual. [Keep in mind that we do not learn new facts in the course of analysis; rather, we learn *to see the facts differently*.])

3.17 Imagine a people for whom the term "unconscious motive" had no meaning: How would we go about teaching it to them? We would probably begin by trying to show them situations in which there was a contradiction between a person's description of his or her motives and what the situation itself seemed to indicate (e.g., a man who consistently denied any attraction to his sister-in-law yet constantly invented pretexts for spending time with her). In this way we might eventually educate this people to recognize for themselves different instances of unconscious motivation. (And, of course, this is not unlike what goes on in analysis: that is, we gradually learn to recognize certain kinds of behavior as instances of unconscious motivation.)

But now suppose that no matter how many purported instances of unconscious motivation we cited, these people adamantly refused to accept that there was in fact any contradiction between the description the person gives and what the situation itself indicates (there are, in fact, good reasons for the man's spending time with his sister-in-law), or that they explain this discrepancy in other ways (e.g., the man is bewitched or in the grip of a demon of some sort). Can we still justifiably say there are in fact instances of unconscious motivation, even if the people themselves refuse to believe it? Here one wants to say, Of course!—but consider the implications of doing so. (If a group of people refuse to join the game we are playing—if they refuse to abide by the rules of that game—shall we say that they have "lost"?)

Suppose, finally, that these people not only reject the idea of unconscious motivation but that they are incapable of understanding what a description in these terms *means*: Are we still justified in applying the concept to them, in using it to make assessments of *their* lives? Can there be such a thing as an unconscious motive that not only is consistently denied in fact but also cannot be acknowledged *in principle*? (And notice that how we answer this question will depend, once again, on how it is that unconscious motives are known.) Finally, what grounds are there for believing that our description is better, or "truer," than theirs? *Mustn't there be such grounds?*

3.18 Suppose I allow that the dream is in fact an expression of my unconscious wish. What evidence do I have that this wish was active at the time of the dream, that it contributed to—or caused—its formation? Indeed, what *could* count as evidence in this case? To what could we possibly appeal in making this judgment? (Not to anything in the dream report, certainly, since it is an ex post facto construction, or to the dream itself, since we have no access to it.)

"One may discover certain things about oneself by this sort of free association," Wittgenstein notes, "but it does not explain why the dream occurred" (LC, 51). If we say this, however, then why shouldn't we also ask whether it doesn't make sense to say, not that the dream occurred *because* I hated P. (i.e., as a relation of effect to cause), but that the reason I dreamed *this* dream, with this particular unconscious meaning, was *because* I do in fact "hate P" (i.e., as a reason for the dream). The dream, we might say, is *motivated* but not caused, at least not in the usual sense of this term. The dream, then, is not the *effect* of my unconscious feelings but their *expression*, their "vehicle," as it were. (Just as we can distinguish between the vehicle and the tenor of a metaphor.) Thus, it seems that there is nothing to prevent me from saying that the dream represents a wish—even if it makes no sense to say that it is this wish that caused the dream to occur.

3.19 Dreams may have a powerful effect on us, an effect that is still further enhanced by the process of association—that is, the process of relating the various elements in the dream to different aspects of my most personal, intimate life. Furthermore, like all things that effect us deeply, dreams seem to demand an explanation. It may be, however, that an explanation is actually not what is wanted here.

In one of his notebooks, Wittgenstein suggests that finding the *cause* of the dream may be irrelevant to the impression that the dream makes on us (just as, for Wittgenstein, finding a cause is irrelevant to our understanding of religion or religious behavior):

> Recounting a dream, a medley of recollections. These often form a significant and enigmatic whole. They form, as it were, a fragment that makes a *powerful* impression on us (*sometimes* anyway), so that we look for an explanation, for connections.
>
>   But why did just *these* recollections occur now? Who can say?—It may be connected with our present life, and so too with our wishes, fears, etc.—"But do you want to say that this phenomenon can only exist in these particular causal surroundings?"—I want to say that it does not necessarily have to make sense to speak of discovering its cause. (CV, 83)

When something is disturbing, or when it impresses us deeply, we look for an explanation; we want to know why? This is a natural tendency but very often, it seems, a mistaken one (similar to the tendency that leads us to ask about the cause of aesthetic impressions). This kind of mistake has been aptly described as "looking for consummation in the wrong place":[10] we ask about the *cause* of a phenomenon when what we really want is some understanding of the *impression* it makes on us. *Why* does the dream affect us as it does, like an intimation of something mysterious or ominous or beautiful? *Why* does this piece of music or this single phrase move us so profoundly? *Why* do certain

---

10. Frank Cioffi, "Wittgenstein's Freud," 197.

ritual actions inspire dread, or others a deep sense of peace? Whenever we are deeply moved, it is natural and appropriate to ask why. Our mistake is to construe this question too narrowly as a demand for an explanation in terms of causes and conditions. ("The dream is the product of an unfulfilled wish." "Music expresses emotions." "Religion grows out of the anxiety we feel before the immensity of nature." And so forth.) But giving a cause rarely removes our sense of unease, and theoretical explanations are almost always unsatisfying. (This disparity between impression and explanation is part of the reason that the life of the intellect is potentially so fraught; we are constantly seeking an explanation, or "the right theory," to account for our experience, when what is needed is more like an analysis of the impression.)

3.20   Imagine the following language game. You bring me a story that you have read and found interesting. I break the story into different parts and ask you to tell me whatever comes to mind in response to each of these parts. These are your associations to the story. From these associations I then try to construct a second narrative as a kind of subtext to the first. This subtext is what we might call "the-story-as-it-affects-you-personally," and we might say that this is what the story "really means" for you.

It may happen that after this process the original story no longer has the meaning for you that it did before, that what matters to you now, the real significance of the story—at least for you personally—is that which is brought out by your associations. This game, then, gives us a new way of talking about "the meaning" of the story, a new context and use. What Freud does with dreams is similar to this.

3.21   Or imagine the following game. One person, A, has a deck of cards. On each card is a different pictogram, sometimes with accompanying letters, sometimes with fragments of words and sentences. Person A shows individual cards to another person, B. B then responds to each card with whatever it brings to mind—in other words, he brings forward different associations to each of the cards, just as Freud prescribes in relation to different elements of the dream. Imagine, too, that the rules state that B *must* say whatever comes to his mind, regardless how trivial or embarrassing it may be. A then attempts to construct a coherent narrative, based on these associations, first about the meaning of each card (i.e., what it means *for* B) and then about what each card indicates about B himself (his interests and desires, his fears, his character, etc.)—interpretations that B is free either to embrace or to reject. To the extent that B accepts the interpretations offered, we might want to say that these interpreted meanings were previously unconscious and that they were made conscious only by the process of analyzing the pictograms.

This is exactly what Freud does with dreams, only now we see that the actual dream—the private, nocturnal drama—drops out of consideration entirely. (What matters for the process of interpretation is not the content of the dream but the richness of the associations. For it is not *what* the dream means that is important, but what it *might* mean, that is, all of those things that the dream evokes in our minds. So, too, it is not what the man is actually doing with his sister-in-law that is of consequence, but what he *might* be doing.)

3.22   Responding to Freud's comment that after analysis the dream "appears so very logical," Wittgenstein remarks, "And of course it does. You could start with any of the objects on this table—which certainly were not put there through your dream activity—and you could find that they all could be connected in a pattern like that; and the pattern would be logical in the same way" (LC, 51). It seems to me that what Wittgenstein is saying here is that the principles of association are limited and universally applicable. Name any two things you want: there will always be *some* relation between them, and that relation will necessarily be either one of *contiguity* (this appears together with that) or one of *similarity* (this is like that). These, however, are not "laws of the mind," or mechanisms of the dream work, but purely logical and semantic principles; they belong to grammar, not to psychology. (What belongs to psychology I can imagine as other than it is; what belongs to grammar I cannot imagine otherwise. I can imagine the mind being such that different memories would be grouped in different "compartments" according to, perhaps, a principle of perceptual intensity, such that experiences that were particularly intense would produce the most vivid memories and therefore be stored nearest to the "recall center," and so forth. I have no difficulty imagining the mind to be like this, but I can imagine no principle of association between things—two memories, say—other than those of similarity and contiguity.)

3.23   What makes this interpretation the *right* interpretation? How do I know that it is correct? What are the *criteria* for a correct interpretation of the dream?

It seems that if there are no objective criteria for evaluating the correctness of an interpretation, if there are no means by which to distinguish true interpretations from those which we merely find convincing, then interpretation becomes purely a matter of rhetoric, an exercise in persuasion without any objective, or rational, basis. Indeed, it seems as if, unless we can show what makes one interpretation better than another, unless we have some kind of objective criteria for judging the validity of an interpretation, the entire process of analysis becomes arbitrary and gratuitous.[11]

3.24   How is the truth of an interpretation verified? To what do we appeal in making judgments about its truth? What criteria do we use? A number of such criteria have been suggested.

1. An interpretation is correct when *the patient accepts it as such*, or is judged correct on the basis of the sense of conviction that it produces in the patient: "All we have in psychoanalysis is the sense of conviction." This strikes me as inadequate, in part because there are so many different factors that contrive against the accuracy and objectivity of the patient's judgment. There are, first, the patient's own interests (i.e., a need for clarity and coherence, a desire for a successful analysis, an emotional attachment to the analyst [the transference], etc.); second, the patient's general ignorance about psychoanalysis and psychoanalytic interpretation (i.e., a general lack of expertise, the fact that he or she has not been trained to make interpretations or to distinguish true from false interpretations); and third, the patient's typical complacency (i.e., a tendency to accept the interpretation that is most "agreeable" or that causes the least conflict between patient and analyst, even if it is perhaps demeaning or morally repugnant). On the other hand, we might ask, Could an interpretation be "correct" that the patient *never* accepted, even, say, at the conclusion of analysis? Or, still further, could there be unconscious meanings that were *never* recognized or acknowledged—*by anyone*? (This is analogous to Wittgenstein's question about games: "Could there be a game in which all moves were *false*?" [PI, 345].)

2. An interpretation is correct when *the analyst, on the basis of training and experience, judges it so*, or, as we might say, it is correct when it produces a sense of conviction in the analyst. Here we must consider, however, first, the analyst's own interests (i.e., a desire for a successful analysis, a wish to be correct in his or her judgment of the

---

11. Indeed, Wittgenstein himself seems to say this when, after denying Freud's claim to be scientific, he goes on to make the following pronouncement: "He [Freud] speaks of overcoming resistance. One 'instance' is deluded by another 'instance.' The analyst is supposed to be stronger, able to combat and overcome the delusion of the instance. But there is no way of showing that the whole result of analysis may not be 'delusion.' . . . Couldn't the whole thing have been treated differently?" (LC, 44–45). The question is, How do we decide whether "the whole thing could have been treated differently"? (Imagine a man who was told, at the conclusion of an analysis, that it was "all just a joke.")

patient's situation, a general need to be right, a need to be esteemed, a commitment to the truth of psychoanalysis, etc.); second, the analyst's conditioning (i.e., long training in psychoanalysis, both theoretical and practical, a professional identity as an analyst, an attachment to others in the profession and especially—perhaps—to his or her own analyst, etc.); and third, the analyst's inherent limitations (i.e., a lack of familiarity with the patient, an ignorance of other interpretive techniques, a lack of empathy, etc.).

3. An interpretation is correct when *it is consistent with psychoanalytic theory* or when confirmatory associations, affects, or reactions follow. However, the theory is so flexible—and subsequent behavioral and emotional reactions so ambiguous—that within certain very broad thematic parameters (Oedipal, narcissistic, erotic, masochistic, etc.) virtually *any* interpretation can be made to accord with it. Moreover, it can hardly be called a confirmation of the truth of an interpretation just because the interpretation squares with the theory that informs it (like confirming that a whale is a fish by appealing to the accepted theory that all animals that live in the water are fish).

4. An interpretation is correct when *it is therapeutically efficacious*— that is, when it succeeds in lifting the repressions, when it furthers the analytic process, when it leads to self-understanding, and so forth. "The only criterion of the truth of an interpretation is that it deepens and enhances the analytic process." The problem here is, first, that there are no universal standards for therapeutic success, or even for "progress" in analysis; second, that it is in principle extremely difficult—and perhaps impossible—to demonstrate that success is actually linked to the truth of the interpretations proffered (rather than the result, say, of suggestion or the "placebo effect");[12] and third, that if it were actually the case that the truth of an interpretation could only be judged pending the outcome of the analysis, or pending some indication of substantial progress (e.g., in the remission of symptoms, the resolution of resistance, and its productivity in producing new information), the analysis would scarcely be able to begin, much less reach a therapeutically favorable resolution.

In short, each of the proposed criteria is to one degree or another problematic or deficient, and none seems entirely adequate, at least at first glance. But let us look more closely. (We might want to ask here, Is there perhaps something mistaken about the idea of "objectivity" in this context?)

---

12. For a discussion of the so-called placebo effect, see Adolph Grünbaum, *The Foundations of Psychoanalysis: A Philosophical Critique* (Berkeley and Los Angeles: University of California Press, 1984), esp. 178–89.

3.25   In one of his discussions on Freud, Wittgenstein suggests that the correct interpretation is the one the patient is induced to accept. "If you are led by psychoanalysis to say that really you thought so and so or that really your motive was so and so, this is not a matter of discovery," he says, "but of persuasion. In a different way you could have been persuaded of something different" (LC, 27). Elsewhere Wittgenstein proposes that the attraction of psychoanalytic interpretations is the same as that of "mythology" and that people are inclined to accept these interpretations merely because they facilitate certain psychological and emotional adjustments: "When people accept or adopt this, then certain things seem much clearer and easier for them. So it is with the notion of the unconscious also" (LC, 43). And a little later: "[Psychoanalysis] is something which people are inclined to accept and which makes it easier for them to go certain ways: it makes certain ways of behaving and thinking natural for them. They have given up one way of thinking and adopted another" (LC, 44–45).

All of this seems to imply—and it has often been interpreted to mean—that psychoanalytic interpretations are simply ad hoc constructions, or at best "convenient fictions," that the patient is induced to accept either because they are therapeutically beneficial or because they are intrinsically appealing (i.e., relatively comprehensible, coherent, and dramatically compelling),[13] or merely because of an emotional attachment to the analyst ("I want what he expects of me"). But even if there were a demonstrable connection between the patient's acceptance of an interpretation and certain therapeutic effects, it doesn't follow that the truth of the interpretation is a matter of the patient's decision to adopt it or that the patient's acceptance of the interpretation is the "cause" of its therapeutic effects. On the contrary, there is every reason to think that the matter is considerably more complicated than this: that it has less to do with the personal authority of the analyst or "the notorious passivity of neurotics" (Grünbaum) than it does with the whole complex of factors—personal, social, historical, and cultural— that contribute to the patient's *finding* it persuasive, factors that go well beyond the analytic situation to certain fundamental dispositions and forms of life. In other words, whether an interpretation is correct is, it seems to me, not a psychological question at all, but a cultural one. (The patient does not *decide* to accept an interpretation any more than the analyst *decides* what the proper interpretation will be.)

13. As Wittgenstein notes, "It may then be an immense relief if it can be shown that one's life has the pattern . . . of a tragedy—the tragic working out and repetition of a pattern which was determined by the primal scene" (LC, 51).

Even if we grant this, however, we are still left with such questions as Is there any "objective truth" to an interpretation of this sort? Are these factors such as to allow for a "rational" judgment of the truth or falsity of an interpretation? If so, what are the criteria of judgment in this case? Once again, our response to these questions will take the form, not of a yes or no or an explanation of some sort, but of an attempt to clarify the *grounds* on which these questions might be decided. (I want to suggest that these grounds are properly neither philosophical or psychological, but cultural, historical, and, in the broadest sense, aesthetic.)

3.26 The question is, How do I know that the interpreted meaning of a dream is the correct one? One possible answer might be, The correct interpretation is the one that is acknowledged as such. The only test is the test of conviction. "It's like searching for a word when you are writing and then saying: '*That's* it, *that* expresses what I intended!'—Your acceptance certifies the word as having been found and hence as being the one you were looking for" (CV, 68).

It is your acceptance alone that certifies the word as the right one, as the one you were looking for—the Aha! that signals that *this* is what you were seeking. But think now of all the different factors that come into play here—factors of taste, training, education, aptitude, context, timeliness, and so forth. Is it merely a *decision* that determines your accepting this word as the right one? Could you *decide* to choose some other word? Does a poet "decide" that the poem should go this way rather than another? Does a composer "decide" how a musical theme is to be developed?

So, too, in dream interpretation: if I acknowledge this as the correct interpretation of my dream, it is not merely because I have *decided* to accept it, with the implication that another interpretation might do just as well or better. No, I accept the interpretation *because it is right* (even if I may later decide that it was perhaps not "as right" as I had originally thought).

(Keep in mind that this is intended not as an explanation of what happens in dream interpretation but rather as a clarification of what we mean—or what Freud means—by "interpretation" in this context. Again, all I can do here is to offer suggestions and reminders, to draw certain parallels and analogies; what I present is not an argument but, as it were, a recommendation to view things in a particular way.)

3.27 Compare a dream interpretation to a style of music. Is a musical style arbitrary? Can we choose one at will? Can I, if I am really clever, *invent* a new style? Is it merely a question here of what is pleasing and what is not—a question, in other words, of certain psychological reactions? I think not. (Cf. PI, 2:230.)

How do I recognize the dream as the expression of *my* desire? How do I find this symphony exultant, or this painting somber and tragic? Why do I prefer Shakespeare to Harold Robbins, or Brahms to Philip Glass? In psychoanalysis, as in art, one is educated to a certain sensibility; in the striking phrase of one interpreter, one learns to be "psychoanalytically musical."[14] The trained analyst, like the critic, is the one who has an acquired taste and a developed sense of judgment. The patient, too, eventually acquires this taste and judgment—not through the power of suggestion but, we might say, through an *education in sensibility*.

3.28 Of course, it might also be said that interpretation generally—and not only in psychoanalysis—*is* persuasion, that any interpretation recommended by one person to another bears a rhetorical element. It wants to elicit assent. ("Wherever there is persuasion," Kenneth Burke writes, "there is rhetoric and wherever there is 'meaning,' there is 'persuasion.'")[15]

But if I call all interpretation persuasion, then I am in danger of saying at once too much and too little.

3.29 "So you really wanted to say . . ." This expression belongs to persuasion, to rhetoric. "We use this phrase," Wittgenstein tells us, "in order to lead someone from one form of expression to another" (PI, 1:334). In proffering interpretations, the analyst is like the person who gives us the "right words" to express that for which the words were lacking, that which we really wanted to say. But it is important to bear in mind that "various kinds of things may persuade us to give up one expression and adopt another in its place" (PI, 1:334). It may be the case that we merely lacked the right words; it may also happen that, like the person who tries to trisect an angle with a ruler and compass, the solution we really want comes only with the realization that what we thought we wanted is impossible. (We might even say that "consciously" we sought to trisect the angle by this method, while "unconsciously" what we really wanted all along was something that only the demonstration of its impossibility could give.)

14. Peter Homans, from a class lecture, "Kohut and Winnicott on Morality, Culture, and Religion," Divinity School, University of Chicago, fall 1983.

15. Quoted in Samuel Ijsseling, *Rhetoric and Philosophy in Conflict: An Historical Survey* (The Hague: Martinus Nijhoff, 1976), frontispiece.

3.30   The patient must be *convinced* in order to be cured; this means that decision alone is not enough.

3.31   Let us return to our earlier question: Can an interpretation be correct that *in principle* cannot be understood by the person to whom it is offered, a person, say, of a different culture, one for whom the entire notion of unconscious motivation in Freud's sense simply has no meaning? Now, ask yourself, What would be the standard of correctness in *this* case?

3.32   There is this important difference between psychoanalytic and aesthetic interpretation, among many other less significant ones: that whereas the latter is almost infinitely variable with respect to both themes and method, the former is severely restricted. Indeed, a good deal of the appeal of psychoanalysis as a style of interpretation derives from the simplicity and elasticity of its rules, together with its limited—and thus manageable—number of recurrent themes (Oedipal, phallic, narcissistic, etc.). Which is to say, the method of psychoanalytic interpretation is highly repetitive and ultimately, perhaps, not very interesting.

3.33   There is also a uniquely self-justifying quality to many psychoanalytic themes and interpretations, as if their mere statement were sufficient to establish their truth, as if they were utterly transparent to anyone who would look and see. Wittgenstein writes, "There is a strong tendency to say: 'We can't get round the fact that this dream is really such and such.' . . . If someone says: 'Why do you say it is really this? Obviously it is not this at all,' it is in fact difficult to see it as something else" (LC, 24). Certain types of interpretation or interpreted meanings—and especially, it seems, in psychoanalysis—carry a kind of intrinsic conviction: once we learn the rules of the game, they seem utterly self-evident. "Try telling someone who is psychoanalytically oriented that Van Gogh's mutilation of his ear may have had no connection with castration, or that Oedipus' blinding of himself was not a castration substitute and you meet not so much with incredulity as bewilderment," writes Frank Cioffi. "He will have difficulty in giving your statement sense. He behaves as if he had learned the expression 'castration-symbol' ostensively. This is simply what castration-substitute *means*."[16]

With certain games, once we have learned the rules, it no longer even occurs to us that the game might be played differently; we no longer see

16. Cioffi, "Wittgenstein's Freud," 200.

that the rules are, in an important sense, arbitrary (though in another and equally important sense not).

3.34   One still wants to ask, What are the *grounds* for believing that the interpretation is *true*? and by "truth" here we mean some kind of deep correspondence between the dream and its interpreted meaning, one that is not merely incidental but, as it were, internal: *This* is what the dream means! Without such grounds, everything once again seems arbitrary and potentially vicious.

But compare: What are the *grounds* for believing that these are the *right* rules to a game? Why should I believe, for example, that the bishop can only move diagonally in the game of chess? Suppose I wanted to change the rules? Is this purely an arbitrary matter? And if I did introduce a radical change in the rules—if I decided, for instance, that the bishop is allowed to move in any direction and without regard to turns—wouldn't that destroy the whole point of the game and, at the same time, our enjoyment in it? Or suppose we ask, What grounds do we have to justify our preferring this style of painting to some other? Is *this* purely arbitrary? Is it purely a matter of taste? (What do we mean by "taste" here? Surely not something that is purely subjective and personal.)[17] Or: What grounds do we have for believing that James Joyce is a better writer than Norman Mailer? What *kind* of ground do we appeal to in each of these cases? And if there are such grounds (and surely there are), are not these grounds in some very deep sense *rational*?—and therefore also *objective*?

I want to suggest that our judgment concerning the correctness of an interpretation in psychoanalysis is no more arbitrary or subjective—and, conversely, no less motivated—than our judgment of a style of painting or our evaluation of the relative merits of different literary figures. (This should not be taken to mean, however, that it is "purely" aesthetic— whatever *that* might mean!)

3.35   "But is there, then, no connection between an interpretation, on the one hand, and something objective and factual, on the other?" Of course there is—in the same way that there is a connection between an

17. In his *Lectures and Conversations on Aesthetics, Psychology, and Religion*, Wittgenstein argues that the meaning of words like "taste," "appreciation," and so forth, is extremely complicated and that an explanation of that meaning ultimately entails a description of the culture to which these words belong. "What belongs to a language game is a whole culture," he says there—and this is true not only of aesthetic terms but also of moral and psychological ones (LC, 8). In the end, I would submit, such judgments are no more subjective than my judgment that *this* is red.

aesthetic interpretation and its object. The point here is only that this connection is both much more complicated and of a different order than we imagine it to be, and that it is not subject to verification—or falsification—by the standard procedures of the natural sciences. (Ask yourself, How did the game of chess come about? How did we determine the rules? How did we decide that *these* are the correct rules for playing the game? *Did* we decide? Certain rules made the game more interesting than others; by and large, these were the rules that were adopted. The game itself survived because it was found to be interesting—not because any one person enjoyed it.)

An interpretation in psychoanalysis is less like forming a hypothesis than it is like discerning a figure among a mass of lines and shapes; judging an interpretation "correct" is less like judging a proposition to be "true" than it is like judging a musical phrase, or a word, to be "right": in each of these cases, what is at issue is a kind of *seeing*, not a fact or proof.

4

INTERPRETATION, PERSUASION, AND "SEEING AS"

Psychoanalysis and Aesthetics

4.1 "In considering what a dream is," Wittgenstein writes, "it is important to consider what happens to it, the way its aspect changes when it is brought into relation with other things remembered, for instance" (LC, 46). The very process of contextualizing a dream, of remembering it and placing it in relation to other memories, fantasies, fears, and so forth, changes the appearance of the dream, changes its "aspect." Wittgenstein continues:

> On first awakening the dream may impress one in various ways. One may be terrified and anxious; or when one has written the dream down one may have a certain sort of thrill, feel a lively interest in it, feel intrigued by it. If one now remembers certain events in the previous day and connects what is dreamed with these, this already makes a difference, changes the aspect of the dream. If reflecting on the dream then leads one to remember certain things in early childhood, this will give it a different aspect still. And so on. (LC, 46)

When the dream is interpreted, its *aspect changes*, as if it were now dreamed again, but differently. An interpretation not only substitutes one meaning for another, but it very often—and perhaps almost always—has the effect of saying, "Look at things *like this*," or "See things *this* way rather than that." (For a discussion of Wittgenstein's understanding of "seeing as," "seeing an aspect," and "aspect change," see Appendix C, "The Concept of 'Seeing As' in Wittgenstein.")

4.2   "The dream affects us as does an idea pregnant with possible developments" (CV, 69). It is characteristic of dreams that they seem *to demand* an interpretation, that they seem both strangely important and maddeningly incomprehensible (like a painting or a piece of music that both attracts and inspires us). Dreams seem naturally to link up with many different aspects of our lives; they seem to speak to us about our own deepest concerns and fears. By making certain of these connections explicit—and excluding others—psychoanalytic interpretation *changes the sense* of the original dream; it *changes its aspect* (we now "*see* the dream *as* . . ."). When the interpretation of the dream is completed, it is as if to say, Look at things *like this*.

This process, we might say, "still belongs to the dream," for it is as if the dream were now "dreamed over again," as if it were extended in new and unforeseen directions (LC, 46).

4.3   What does it mean "to interpret" something? What kind of conceptual movement is involved in this process? "To interpret" often means something like "to translate." That is, in interpreting, I begin with a certain given phenomenon—a symbolic structure of some sort— and I translate this phenomenon into something else, according to certain rules of method (a "hermeneutics"). Generally speaking, these rules are derived from a comprehensive theory that relates symbolic structures (dreams, works of art, social institutions, etc.), on the one hand, to something more fundamental, some base reality (instinct, energy, material conditions, etc.), on the other. In this case, then, the movement from a manifest to a latent meaning is largely based on constructed analogies between the given symbolic phenomenon (*A*) and paradigmatic expressions of the base reality (*B*), so that the translation runs, "*A* is like—and therefore reducible to—*B*," where *A* is, say, a reported dream image (e.g., a cigar) and *B* an analogous object of infantile sexuality (e.g., the phallus). When I interpret in this sense, I move from one meaning, and level of thought, to another, logically more fundamental one.

4.4   But alongside this notion of interpretation—adjacent to it, as it were—is another kind of conceptual process, one that is perhaps less generally recognized but, it seems to me, at least as important. I am referring here to the process of recontextualization and redescription that often occurs as an effect of interpretation proper. This kind of conceptual change is characterized, not by the (hermeneutic) movement from patent to latent, but rather by what might be described as a reorganization of the patent, a perceptual shift based on the perception of a new congruence—or "internal relation"—between the different elements of the symbol and its various associated meanings: that is, "seeing A as B" (e.g., a cigar *as* a phallus). This kind of shift may be tied to an explicit interpretation, or it may not. The important point is that, regardless of how it is effected, it always involves more than a mere change in our opinion about what something means and more than the relatively simple substitution of one form of expression for another; rather, what occurs here is a basic change in our way of seeing—and hence, also, of conceptualizing—things.

It seems to me that much confusion about what actually occurs in interpretation—not only in psychoanalysis but generally—comes from a failure to distinguish these two different processes.[1]

4.5 Look once more at dream interpretation. Almost everything that occurs in this process—free association, construction of interpretations, transference, resistance, and the like—occurs under the aegis of certain figural equivalences ("A is B") and proceeds by way of redescription ("seeing A as B"). Free association, for example, might be described as nothing more than a process of producing metaphors (in the substitution of one meaning for another); the concepts of overdetermination, condensation, displacement, and transference are all merely ways of describing—and in at least some of their applications, *mis*describing—this process. ("Overdetermination," for instance, is *not*, as we are inclined to think, an intrinsic property of symbolisms but rather a word for describing *what we do with symbols*—that is, the fact that we interpret them in many different ways and according to various associations. Similarly, "condensation" is a word we use to describe one kind of relation between the manifest and the latent, or one kind of substitution of meanings; "displacement" is another. In neither case, however, do we need to appeal to any psychical "mechanisms" to explain how these substitutions occur.)

(Let me emphasize again that none of these descriptions should be in

1. It is a striking feature of Ricoeur's monumental work on Freud that despite its original title—*De l'interpretation*—it never addresses the question of what actually occurs, conceptually, in the process of interpretation. Failing this, it is difficult, if not impossible, to give an account of why we find certain interpretations more compelling than others—unless we adopt Ricoeur's procedure, according to which all matters of truth are finally resolved at the level of dialectics.

the least controversial, that they should appear as statements of obvious, even trivial, facts concerning what we do when we interpret a dream. For indeed, what could we be describing in psychoanalysis—in the models of the mind, the mechanisms of the dream work, and so forth—if not different aspects of the process of interpretation, different features of the actual *practice* of interpretation? What other access do we have to either the mind or the dream? How do we *know*. . . ?)

These substitutions, and the manner by which we arrive at them, not only provide us with new meanings for the dream, they also change the way we see it; put differently, what they offer is not just meaning but a new orientation to meaning—as if what were at stake here were not the truth of this or that interpretation but a kind of *Weltanschauung*.

4.6   Consider the following dream from *The Interpretation of Dreams*: "A hill, on which there was something like an open-air closet: a very long seat with a large hole at the end of it. Its back was thickly covered with small heaps of faeces of all sizes and degrees of freshness. There were bushes behind the seat. I micturated on the seat; a long stream of urine washed everything clean; the lumps of faeces came away easily and fell into the opening. It was as though at the end there was still some left" (ID, 468–69).[2] Freud's procedure is by now quite familiar: first, the dream is broken into fragments, the so-called dream elements; second, associations are improvised on each of these fragments in turn, associations that invariably converge on an unstated x, that is, some theme of personal interest or concern; finally, on the basis of these associations and the several themes that emerge—together, of course, with some knowledge of the dreamer's character and history—the analyst assigns a meaning to the whole. This, then, is the latent meaning of the dream, a meaning that, in keeping with the general theory, expresses some unconscious and typically infantile wish.

This entire process can be represented under the form of a metaphor. Once the interpretation is completed, the interpreted meaning (B) stands in relation to the original dream report (A) precisely as the tenor (the principle subject, or underlying idea) stands to the vehicle (the original idea) in metaphor (A is B). Moreover, if we reverse the interpretive movement—that is, if we read the interpreted dream thoughts *back into* the dream, *seeing* the dream *as* the representation of these thoughts—

2. For an illuminating discussion of this dream, as well as an informed philosophical discussion of Freud's method of interpretation, see Fredric Weiss, "Meaning and Dream Interpretation," in *Freud: A Collection of Critical Essays*, ed. Richard Wollheim (New York: Anchor Books, 1974).

then each individual dream element becomes a metaphor for the different associative themes (unstated *x*s). (This, I take it, is what Wittgenstein refers to as "redreaming" the dream in a new context; for now we *see* it differently.) According to Freud's actual interpretation, the washing away of the excrement in the dream thus becomes Hercules' cleansing of the Augean stables (first metaphor); and I (Freud) *am* Hercules (second metaphor and unstated *x*). The hill and bushes become the scene where my children are at play (first metaphor); and in discovering the etiology of the neuroses, I have saved my children from illness (second metaphor and unstated *x*). The seat becomes a piece of furniture given to me by a grateful patient (first metaphor); and it is a symbol of the honor and esteem that my patients hold for me (second metaphor and unstated *x*). The micturating on the seat becomes Gulliver's extinguishing the great fire in Lilliput (first metaphor), as well as Gargantua's revenge on the Parisians (second metaphor); it is "an unmistakable sign of greatness" (third metaphor and unstated *x*). And so forth.

Having exhausted the associations and translated them into unstated *x*s, having read these *x*s *back into* the dream, Freud then proposes a meaning for the whole based on the recurrent themes among the different associations; the manifest meaning, "I urinate all over, with profound effects," thus becomes—by identification with the urinary feats of Gulliver and Gargantua—the latent thought, "I am a very great man," a conclusion that is, according to Freud, virtually "inevitable."

4.7   But why "inevitable"? How is it, in other words, that we find this interpretation so convincing? Or at least, how is it that *Freud* is convinced that this is the true meaning of the dream? What sort of inevitability is involved here? (Note once again that I am asking, not *whether* the interpretation is true, but *why we might be inclined to find it so*—that is, on what grounds or for what reasons.)

To begin with, it is important to see that what is involved here is clearly *not* some kind of logical demonstration; there is no apparent *logical* relation between the original dream elements and the themes that are extracted from them, or between the dream report as a whole and its interpreted meaning.[3] Indeed, the interpreted meaning is gratuitous in

---

3. Doubtless someone will want to interject here that although this relation is not logical in the "narrow, philosophical sense," it is nonetheless rational insofar as it can be described according to certain figural tropes: metaphor, metonymy, pleonasm, irony, and so forth. The problem with this way of describing things is that it begs the question of *which* particular figure dominates which interpretive movement; that is, how do we know in advance what kind of conceptual relation is being represented in the dream—similarity, contiguity, redundancy, reversal, or whatever?

the sense that it is neither directly indicated by nor deducible from the content of the dream as such. No, what makes the interpretation persuasive is not its intrinsic logic but rather, as Wittgenstein observes, the *connections* it provides between the dream and the life of the dreamer, the way in which it allows us to *see* the dream as the expression—or, if you prefer, "representation"—of matters of deeply personal concern, of intimate problems, interests, desires, and so forth. These connections, moreover, are obviously not things we *observe* (indeed, what could "observation" possibly mean in this context?), nor are they such as can be logically *deduced* from the content of the dream; rather, they are, as it were, woven into in the process of interpretation itself. Through interpretation we come to see these connections as *belonging to* dream, and not as things external to it. It is precisely the perception of these connections that convinces us of the truth of the interpretation. (It does not matter that I am told that there is a symbolic equivalence between an oven and the female uterus; what matters is that I come to see the oven in my dream *as* a uterus. The sense of conviction derives from seeing, not thinking.)

4.8 "But how does this process of metaphorical reduction *change* my way of seeing the dream, and change my attitude toward it? How does this shift come about?" Well, one wants to say, it just does. When I interpret the dream, when I bring it into relation to other aspects of my life, when I begin to find symbols of deep significance, I gradually come to see it *like this*—and this is part of what "interpretation" means in this context. Interpretation *changes* the dream; it adds a dimension of depth and significance. The dream becomes a Rorschach image into which we weave the most intimate and most terrifying aspects of our lives. Interpretation allows us to speak about these things; it allows us to claim them as our own.

"Does the dream actually *mean* thus and so?" "Was all of that actually *in* the dream?" The dream, we might say, is only a reminder. What we find in the dream we find in ourselves—and vice versa.

(In dealing with issues of this kind, we keep wanting to develop a theory instead of simply clarifying different aspects of the problem at hand: to state what we know, without theory or explanation. In grammatical analysis, our *habits*—and perhaps even certain of our needs—are against us.)

4.9 "What, then, does 'seeing' consist in here?"

In one of his notebooks, Wittgenstein compares a dream to a play being enacted on a stage, a play that is sometimes incomprehensible, other times quite intelligible. We might suppose that the plot of this play is written down, torn into fragments, and each of these fragments in turn given a completely new meaning. This is similar to what happens in a psychoanalytic interpretation.

Or, Wittgenstein says, we might think of the dream as a picture drawn on a large sheet of paper that is then folded in various ways so that different parts of the original picture are brought together to form a new picture, one that may or may not make sense. This latter would then correspond to the manifest dream, the original picture to the interpreted dream thoughts. The process of interpretation would then be like unfolding the picture, and we can imagine that someone who watched the picture being unfolded might exclaim, "Yes, that's the solution, that's what I dreamed, minus the gaps and distortions" (CV, 68).

The work of interpretation in psychoanalysis is a process of fragmentation, recontextualization, and reconstruction. Through interpretation, the dream changes aspects. "In Freudian analysis a dream is dismantled [*zersetzt*], as it were," Wittgenstein writes. "It loses its original sense *completely*" (CV, 68). Interpretation then gives the dream a new sense.

Viewed in this way, then, interpretation is much less a matter of *discovery*—of unconscious causes, motives, ideas, and so forth—than it is of *persuasion* (through a reconfiguration of the various dream elements); or, we might say, it is a discovery of a very particular kind, one that consists in seeing *connections* between the dream and our life, or refiguring our life through the dream. For what is involved here is not the disclosing of some hidden or previously unknown fact but, once more, a change in our mode of perception: that is, in our being led to see the dream in *this* way rather than that, and to acknowledge *this* as its meaning.[4]

4.10 What has this to do with finding the *cause* of the dream? Do I discover a cause? "Recounting a dream, a medley of recollections. These often form a significant and enigmatic whole," writes Wittgenstein. "They form, as it were, a fragment that makes a *powerful* impression on us (*sometimes* anyway), so that we look for an explanation, for connections" (CV, 83). Why did just *this* dream occur, in just *this* way? Why does it evoke *these* particular memories, these feelings and fantasies? So strange to dream of so-and-so, or such and such a place;

---

4. Note that if this is true, then Wittgenstein's illustrations are a bit misleading; for in both of the proposed analogies there *is* an original meaning—the original drama or picture—of which the interpreted element is an actual distortion. In contrast to the situation in psychoanalysis, then, what is acknowledged in these two instances has a reality independent of that acknowledgment.

we think there *must* be a cause. But if the dream connects up with my life—my wishes, fears, and so forth—with certain thoughts and imaginings, shall I call *this* the cause? What gives me the right to do so?

"What is intriguing about a dream," Wittgenstein writes elsewhere, "is not its *causal* connection with events in my life, etc., but rather the impression it gives of being a fragment of a story—a very *vivid* fragment to be sure—the rest of which remains obscure" (CV, 68). Interpretation fills out the story, extends the impression in particular directions, personalizes it, allows us to find a place for it in our lives. (The demand for narrative coherence: the correct interpretation knits the fragments into a whole.)

4.11   An interpretation in psychoanalysis is not an inference from agreed upon facts, or a hypothesis that might be demonstrated to be either true or false; nor is it merely the substitution of one (latent) meaning for another (manifest), or a translation from one form of expression to some other; rather, a psychoanalytic interpretation is— very often, or always?—a recommendation to see things *like this* rather than *that*. Interpretation expands and contextualizes; it makes connections. In the process, the dream changes aspects.

(Of course, "seeing" is itself to be understood metaphorically here. What we mean by "seeing" in relation to dream interpretation—that is, in relation to the scenes, events, persons, and so forth, of both dreams and our lives—is *analogous to* what we mean by "seeing" in relation to figures and objects: it is direct, objective, and determinate.)

4.12   Let us distinguish between two kinds of persuasion, or two different situations in which we typically use the term "persuasion": (1) logical or empirical *demonstration*, aimed at assent to the truth of a proposition or theory, and (2) discursive *presentation*, or redescription, aimed at a *changed way of looking at things*. In the case of the former, I am persuaded to accept a particular proposition or thesis as true, or led to a judgment about the truth of *x*, either through induction (example) or deduction (enthymeme). The grounds for persuasion are correspondingly either evidential or logical, and in both cases conviction is based on the recognition of something that was not present before, some kind of new information, whether a new fact or a previously unseen implication.

What is at issue in the second kind of persuasion, on the other hand, is not our judgment about the truth of a proposition (*x* is true) but our way of apprehending conceptual relations; more specifically, it involves either (1) *our seeing something in relation to, or in terms of, something else* (seeing x in terms of y, or using y as a perspective on x, where x and y are not propositions, but things, events, processes, and the like), or (2) *our seeing something as something else* (seeing x *as* y). In this second instance, persuasion proceeds by a kind of pointed redescription, or representation, that orders our conceptual field in such a way as to reveal hitherto unnoticed connections and internal relations. In contrast to logical or empirical demonstration, this kind of presentation conveys no new information but merely rearranges familiar things in a new way; it "places things side by side" so as to reveal new connections between them. In this sense, then, persuasion appeals to things that are *known* but in some sense *unrecognized*.[5]

4.13 Freud repeatedly insists that psychoanalysis has to do with the first, demonstrative kind of persuasion, that it is founded on the positivistic principles of observation, inference, and deduction (or what is sometimes called hypothetico-deductive inductivism), and that it therefore should be counted among the "natural sciences" of man.[6] What I am saying is, on the contrary, that psychoanalysis is primarily concerned with persuasion of the second, redescriptive kind, that what occurs in dream interpretation—and in interpretation generally, as both a hermeneutical and a rhetorical art—has much more in common with aesthetics than it does with either logic or empirical science. (Do not immediately take this to mean that psychoanalytic theory is somehow less true than theories in the natural sciences, or that there are no objective criteria for making judgments about its truth; consider instead that what we mean by "truth," "objectivity," and so forth, may be very different in each case.)

4.14 The line between these two kinds of persuasion is, of course, not a hard and fast one, nor is it always easy to draw in particular instances.

5. There are at least four discursive strategies, or devices, that are common to this kind of persuasion through redescription: (1) the use of *metaphor* (to provoke an intuitive, or imaginative, recognition of similarity in difference); (2) the use of *examples* (to provide concretization); (3) the use of *analogy* (to construct or discover relations of "similarity in difference"); and (4) the use of *perspicuous presentation* (to provide an overview that allows recognition of similarities in differences or of differences in similarities). See Chaim Perelman and L. Olbrechts-Tyteca, *The New Rhetoric: A Treatise on Argumentation*, trans. John Wilkerson and Purcell Weaver (Notre Dame: University of Notre Dame Press, 1969); and Perelman, *The Realm of Rhetoric*, trans. W. Kluback (Notre Dame, Ind.: University of Notre Dame Press, 1982).

6. "Psychology, too, is a natural science," Freud writes. "What else can it be?" (SELP, 283).

Moreover, even in psychoanalysis appeals to evidence and deductive reasoning are not entirely absent (though, as I have noted, the relation between fact and theory is generally indirect, or eccentric). The question, however, is whether they are decisive.

(To paraphrase Wittgenstein's remarks on Frazer: What I see in a dream, for example, is obviously something it acquires in part from evidence, including such evidence as is not directly connected with it—from what I understand of human life, from the strangeness of what I see in myself and in others, from the dim perceptions of my past, and so forth [RFGB, 18]. It is not this evidence that makes the dream true, however; rather, it is the dream that evokes this as evidence.)

4.15   Consider the following example.[7] Imagine that in one room I have a jigsaw puzzle with only one space left and, in another room, six puzzle pieces, only one of which will fit the space. Suppose further that I am allowed to see only half of the space before deciding which of the six pieces will fit it. Now, it makes sense in this situation to call my choice of one of the pieces a *hypothesis* that would then be verified or falsified by its either fitting or not fitting the space in question. The half space that was visible provides a clue to which of the six pieces will fit.

Now, suppose that I am allowed to see the whole space, only very briefly, then asked to spend a day in the other room with the six pieces deciding which of them would fit. Here, too, we might call my choice a hypothesis, one that is subject to certain procedures of verification (viz., try it and see). Still, there is a point when the language of hypothesis, of verification and falsification, would no longer be appropriate. For imagine now that I am sitting directly in front of the puzzle with, say, a large triangular piece—the last piece in the box and the only triangular one—and that the puzzle contains a large triangular space, the only space remaining to be filled. In this case, it would be very odd to speak about hypothesis and proof, since here we would claim to *see directly* what the solution is, without any intervening deliberation or choice. Similarly, in the case where I am allowed to see the whole space but then have to wait for a period of time before choosing the right piece: How long would I have to wait, or how intricate would the fit between the space and the piece have to be, before it would be appropriate to speak of a *hypothesis* rather than an immediate "seeing"? It is clear that we cannot lay down criteria for deciding this in advance.

We can distinguish, then, between forming and testing a hypothesis, on the one hand, and seeing, on the other, but there will always be cases

7. From John Casey, *The Language of Criticism* (London: Methuen, 1966), 20.

that are not obviously either one or the other. The issue turns on whether, and the extent to which, it is legitimate to speak of *testing*—that is, of verifying or falsifying—what we believe to be the case. Where testing is possible, we speak of hypothesis and demonstration; where it makes no sense to talk about testing, we speak of seeing, of arrangement and pattern recognition, of perspicuous presentation and persuasion.

In dreams, we have to do exclusively with the latter, for there is no possibility of testing here—only conviction.

4.16   It is said that Wittgenstein was fascinated by reports that for some Indian mathematicians "Look at this!" was taken as a geometrical proof.[8] In one of his notebooks we find an illustration (Fig. 3) of what is sometimes called "intuitively perceptible proof." "How does this proof convince me?" Wittgenstein asks. "It convinces my eyes"[9]

I want to suggest that much of what goes on in interpretation has just this quality of intuitive perception; it involves neither proof nor demonstration, but a kind of immediate seeing, or recognition. (Why do I believe, for example, that my choice of a wife is conditioned by my relationship with my mother? Why do I think that all forms of self-mutilation are linked to castration? Why do I find traces of sexuality in even the highest and most sublime works of art? Why, if not because seeing things in this way allows me to make sense of certain aspects of human behavior and symbolism that otherwise seem senseless and

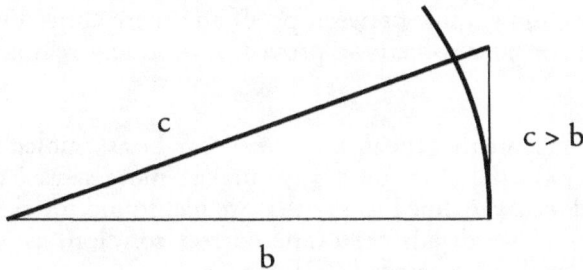

Fig. 3.

8. See PI, 1:144, and Z, 461. For a discussion of the relevant passages in Wittgenstein, see G. P. Baker and P.M.S. Hacker, *Wittgenstein: Understanding and Meaning* (Chicago: University of Chicago Press, 1980), 622–23. As Baker and Hacker point out, Wittgenstein's source for this report is probably Eduard von Hartmann's *Philosophy of the Unconscious*, trans. W. C. Coupland (London: Routledge and Kegan Paul, 1931), 320–22. The general principle of intuitively perceptible proof is set out by Arthur Schopenhauer in *The World as Will and Idea*, vol. 1, trans. R. B. Haldane and J. Kemp (London: Routledge and Kegan Paul, 1883), 90–110.

9. Quoted in Baker and Hacker *Wittgenstein: Understanding and Meaning*, 623.

incomprehensible, because it allows to me to *see* the sense of things, immediately and directly?)

4.17 "But in the case of the jigsaw puzzle there nonetheless remain certain criteria for determining whether my hypothesis is true or not, or whether I am correct in 'seeing' a fit. It is not a matter of my *deciding* that the piece fits; it either fits or it doesn't. This is not the case with dreams." Here, too, however, we cannot always make a clear distinction.

Suppose that there are two pieces of the puzzle left, each of identical shape, and two identical spaces. If you insert the pieces one way, there will be a piece of the cow in the sky and a piece of the sky in the cow; if your insert them another way, everything fits correctly. We might say that this fitting "proves" that the former solution is wrong, the latter correct. But now suppose that we have to move a whole group of pieces to another part of the puzzle or else that the picture, once completed in a certain way, "doesn't make sense." What are the criteria for *this* decision? Is this a matter of hypothesis and proof (demonstration), or of "seeing as" (presentation)? And if you say it is the former, couldn't you also imagine a situation in which it could *only* be the latter? (For what does this "making sense" consist in?) If we are convinced that it is absurd to put a piece of the cow in the sky, isn't this conviction *of the same order* as the conviction that one arrangement of pieces *makes more sense* than some other? And couldn't we say that they are both continuous with the conviction that a particular triangular piece fits the triangular space into which it is about to be inserted?

How do we draw a line between proof and mere conviction? At what point do we consider something proved beyond any reasonable doubt? Can we say?

4.18 Now imagine that the jigsaw puzzle can be assembled in a number of different ways but that some ways make "more sense" than others. When would we be inclined to say that we had found the right solution, and how would we decide this? The correct solution, as Wittgenstein says, is the one that is accepted (CV, 68).

4.19 I am presented with a cluster of dots on a page; suddenly, I see the bearded face of a man. The change will be more or less dramatic in relation to the clarity with which the image is distinguished from background. I can imagine cases in which the fact of my seeing an image could be put in the form of a hypothesis ("*x* is the case"), others in which this would be senseless.

A dream, once set out in the form of a narrative, is analogous to this cluster of dots. Interpretation proceeds by delineating different figures within the cluster of events that constitutes the dream. In considering the process of interpretation, we are constantly tempted to ask, Are the figures *actually present* in the dots, or do we merely *impose* them? But ask yourself, How would we go about deciding this issue? How would we distinguish between what is "intrinsic" and what is "extrinsic" in this case? To what criteria could we appeal?

4.20   Do I actually *see* the face of a man, or merely interpret the dots *as* a face? When this figure shifts from a duck to a rabbit, and back again, do I actually see something different, or merely interpret what I see differently? "To interpret is to think, to do something," Wittgenstein writes; "seeing is a state" (PI, 2:212). Do I *think* when I see the face, or when there is a shift in my perception from duck to rabbit? Do I see the dots and then *decide*, "Yes, this is the face of a bearded man"? I may do something of this sort, but not usually. Usually I go immediately from seeing nothing but a jumble of dots to seeing the face, without any thought whatsoever. Thus, seeing something as something is not the same as interpreting, though I *can* see *according to* an interpretation (as when the text indicates how I am to see the figure of an isometric cube, whether as a glass cube or an open box or a wire frame, etc.).
      Moreover, "interpreting as . . ." is often akin to "forming a hypothesis about . . .": in most situations, it makes sense to ask whether it is true or not; "I see the face of a man," on the other hand, or "Now I see a duck" can no more be verified than the statement "I see red."

4.21   What is it that we perceive when we see something *as* something? Not an object or the property of an object, Wittgenstein tells us, but *an internal relation between objects* (PI, 2:212). I do not see the face of a man, but I see this configuration of dots *as* the face of a man; what I see, in other words, is a relation between these dots and the representation of a face (*x* to *y*). In the example of the duck-rabbit, too, what I see is not the figure of an animal, a duck or a rabbit, but an internal relation between two distinct figures; where I see only one figure, I am seeing the duck or seeing the rabbit, but I am not seeing the form *as* either a duck or a rabbit. What changes in the shift from one to the other is, moreover, not the visual impression (which, of course, remains the same) but the way in which this impression is *organized*.
      In dream interpretation, too, what I "see" when the elements of a dream are brought into relation to other symbols and to various aspects of my life and interests is not so much a new meaning, a kind of subtext

to the dream, but an internal relation between the dream and my life, such that the dream becomes, as it were, a *representation* of my life (or more exactly, for Freud, a representation of my wishes). The dream—which formerly impressed us as "pregnant with possibilities"— is now imbued with deep personal significance. What changes in the process of interpretation is not the dream itself, however, but the way in which the different elements of the dream are *organized*, the meanings and weight we attach to these elements (condensation and displacement are nothing but terms for describing what occurs in the course of this reorganization).

When I interpret a dream, its aspect changes: I *see* it differently. This seeing is not reducible to a change in meaning, though seeing it differently certainly implies that its meaning changes.

4.22   There is a close connection between the experience of "seeing as" and certain kinds of aesthetic experience. At one point in the *Investigations*, in the course of a discussion of what a figure must be like in order to produce the experience of "seeing as," Wittgenstein links the ability to "see an aspect" to the capacity to appreciate *styles* in art: "Could I say what a picture must be like to produce this effect? No. There are, for example, styles of painting which do not convey anything to me in this immediate way, but do to other people" (PI, 2:201). *How* we see the figure is not part of the figure itself, any more than our appreciation for certain styles of art is part of the painting. Moreover, it is often the case in conversation on aesthetic matters that we use expressions related to the concept of "seeing as," or seeing an aspect. We say, for example, "You have to see it like *this*, this is how it is meant," or "You have to hear this bar as an introduction," or "You must attend more to spacial relations than to color,"[10] or "Look at the piece as an extended allegory," and so forth (PI, 2:202). In another place, Wittgenstein suggests that it is primarily from aesthetics that we derive the concept of "seeing as" in the first place: "For how do we arrive at the concept of 'seeing this as that' at all?" he asks. "On what occasions does it get formed, when is there need of it?" And he answers, "(Very frequently in art.) Where, for example, there is a question of phrasing by eye or ear" (Z, 208).

There is, then, a close analogy between the experience of "seeing as" and aesthetic experience, just as there is a similarity between the kinds

10. Later we will want to ask about the nature of this imperative, "You must," as it pertains to aesthetics. Is this a "logical" imperative, or a practical one? And if it is the latter, then what do we mean by "practical" here?

of criteria to which one appeals in making judgments about these experiences. (How do I decide whether this configuration of lines is to be viewed as a face or as a river or as nothing at all?) In both cases, how I experience is necessarily conditioned both by the context (where is the figure found?) and by my previous training and experience (how have I been taught to see such things?); in both cases, the experience *seems* to be something inner, private, and only indirectly accessible (I alone know how I am seeing); and in both cases, *what* I perceive—the content of the experience—must always be described in relational terms ("*x* to *y*"). Many of these same elements are also characteristic of psychoanalysis and of the kind of justification relevant to psychoanalytic interpretations.

4.23   If we want to know why we find dream interpretations convincing, it is useful to compare this to certain problems in aesthetics, and particularly to questions about aesthetic judgments, such as "Why do I find this painting so striking?" "What is it about this musical phrase that seems wrong?" "Why do you think this piece more beautiful than the other?" and so forth. By looking at how judgments are made in aesthetics we learn something about how judgments are made in psychoanalysis—and about the kinds of criteria relevant to such judgments.

Aesthetic criticism, like psychoanalysis, is primarily a matter of persuasion rather than demonstration. In aesthetics we don't generally talk about hypotheses and proofs; rather, we offer descriptions aimed at eliciting assent. We say things like "This particular phrasing seems wrong, doesn't it?" or "Brahms is a greater composer than Tchaikovsky, don't you agree?" or "This poem strikes me as trite and overwrought, what about you?" In aesthetics, as in psychoanalysis, truth is largely a matter of persuasion and agreement; where there is no agreement or consensus, there can be no truth. (The possibility of judgment, we might say, is based here on the fact of agreement.)[11]

4.24   "But here you are implicitly denying the possibility of cross-cultural interpretations, thus ignoring the vast literature of psychoanalytic anthropology that supports—through *empirical evidence*, no less—the idea of a universal symbolism." Not at all. I don't deny the

11. Of course, one might argue that this is true of all judgments of truth—scientific, mathematical, or whatever—but my point is to emphasize the centrality of the role of agreement in aesthetics and psychoanalysis in the actual practice of arriving at such judgments, to say that here, because there are no fixed and well-defined criteria, virtually every judgment we make demands consensual validation.

possibility of a universal symbolism (though it seems to me that this idea demands more clarification than it has received as yet); what I deny—as Freud himself denied—is the possibility of establishing the truth of an interpretation by appealing to this symbolism (i.e., decoding the dream in accordance with a fixed key).

Whether a dream does or does not make use of a universal symbolism is, in any given instance, irrelevant to the question of the truth of the interpretation as such.

(We appeal to the notion of symbolism—or even "universal features of the mind"—as though this were an explanation, when in fact it is only a restatement of the problem in a new form.)

4.25   Similarly, the postulate of a phylogenetic stratum of the mind is not only unnecessary but misleading. Symbols are readily available in the culture; it is hardly surprising that our dreams should make use of them.

4.26   In both psychoanalysis and aesthetics, we say that certain interpretations seem *more reasonable* than others. Why? What does it mean to be "reasonable" here? Why is one response to a work of art considered appropriate, another inappropriate? Why is *this* interpretation of a dream judged to be the correct one? In this latter case, as we have seen, one answer would be "Because it allows us *to make sense* of the dream"—and by this we mean that it allows us to relate the dream to certain aspects of our life. By forging connections between the dream and my life—by relating it to my interests and wishes, to other of my dreams, to patterns in my behavior, and so forth—by inserting new meanings, by filling in the various gaps and incongruities, interpretation seems to resolve the enigma that the dream presents. "I could imagine that someone seeing the unfolded picture might exclaim, 'Yes, that's the solution, that's what I dreamed, minus the gaps and distortions.'" But then it begins to seem that my acceptance of this as the solution is the sole criterion for its correctness, as if there were no other standard of truth here than my accepting it as such, or as if it were only my calling it true that made it so. (We are tempted to think that judgments of truth are either "objective" or "subjective," and to think, further, that objectivity characterizes descriptions of the physical world, the world of the senses, whereas subjectivity characterizes the inner world of feelings, ideas, emotions, and the like. What is objective, we think, is what belongs to the physical sciences, whereas everything else is, to one degree or another, subjective. Behind these convictions—animating them, as it were—is a picture of the world as composed of two mutually exclusive spheres, namely, physical objects, on the one hand, and ideas, feelings, and the like, on the other. This is a very powerful picture.)

4.27   What does it mean to say that the dream is true only because I accept it as such? Does this mean that there are no objective criteria of assessment here? In one sense, yes; in another sense, no.

The fact that the truth of an interpretation seems to rest on the dreamer's endorsement is, in the first instance, related to the particular grammar of terms like "intention," "desire," and so forth. For it belongs to the grammar of the term "intention," for example, that in an important sense *I alone* can know what my intentions actually are. (If *I* don't know what my intentions are, no one can tell me!) "Only you can know if you had that intention," Wittgenstein writes in the *Investigations*. "One might tell someone this when one was explaining the meaning of the word 'intention' to him. For then it means: *that* is how we use it" (PI, 1:247).

Similarly, there is an important sense in which only *I* can decide if this interpretation of my dream is correct, and I do so precisely by recognizing the dream as the expression of *my* (unconscious) intention, *my* (unconscious) wish, and so forth. (Here, however, in contrast to the ordinary uses of the term "intention," it may make sense on occasion to *doubt* whether I actually know my intention; indeed, it is part of the force of the psychoanalytic view to *encourage* this kind of doubt while also providing new methods and terminology for talking about self-deception in regard to intention. We might even speak here of a new use for terms like "intention," "wish," "motive," and so forth, and a new language game in which to use them.)

All of this gives the impression of a "purely subjective" notion of truth.

4.28   "But what really gives conviction to the truth of an interpretation is its systematic coherence and explanatory power, that is, the way it allows us—over an extended period of time and in the context of a single life history—to *explain* certain aspects of the dreamer's behavior that cannot otherwise be accounted for. In other words, the only way to evaluate the truth of an interpretation is in the context of an entire case history, for here one *cannot* say that it is the subject's acceptance of a given interpretation that codifies it as true. On the contrary, Freud would argue that the subject's acceptance of an interpretation is by itself not more conclusive than his rejection would be."

This is true, of course, but it begs the question of the truth of the analysis as a whole and the grounds on which *that* truth is supposed to rest. We might say, for example, that the interpretation of a dream as an expression of a dreamer's hostility toward his father is true—even if the dreamer himself rejects this interpretation—because it fits well into a general pattern of broadly Oedipal themes and, more specifically, because it contributes to the explanation of the dreamer's horse phobia (its origin, function, and significance). (In this case, we might want to speak of the truth of the interpretation as that which the dreamer *would* accept were his judgment not clouded by neurotic fantasies of one sort or another.) Why should I believe in the truth of the analysis as a whole any more than I believe in the truth of any particular interpretation? Because it is systematically coherent? Because it allows me to explain things in a way that is at once comprehensive and compelling? But couldn't the whole thing have been explained *very* differently? Indeed, isn't this exactly what we find in the conflicting accounts among various depth-psychological approaches (Freudian, Jungian, Adlerian, Kohutian, etc.)?

Furthermore, to what extent is this an argument *against* the idea that an interpretation is true because it is accepted? Isn't truth here still a matter of agreement? Can we imagine *any* analysis—not to say a successful one—in which the patient accepted *none* of the analyst's interpretations, or only a very few? Why is this impossible?

4.29   Generally speaking, we are asking here about the *kind of justification* that is proper to psychoanalytic explanations. That is, how do we decide whether such explanations are true? Note, once again, that the question is not "Are these explanations true?" or "On what grounds are they true?" but rather "How do we go about finding out if they are true? by what procedure, and so on?" The former is a question of evidence, the latter a question of grammar. I am suggesting, then, that the kind of justification proper to psychoanalytic explanations (interpretations) is closely analogous to the kind of justifications we use in relation to certain types of aesthetic judgments;[12] that—contrary to

12. With respect to psychoanalysis, it should be understood that the kind of explanation I have in mind here is the kind Freud offers in *The Interpretations of Dreams* (i.e., an explanation *why* this particular dream occurred, an explanation in terms of its psychological function and significance). When I speak, further, of "aesthetic explanations," I mean the kind of statements we make in order to justify, or defend, an aesthetic judgment. Such an explanation is generally offered in response to the question *Why* do you believe that such and such is the case. If I say, for instance, that Brahms's Fourth Symphony is superior to his Tragic Overture or that Dostoyevsky is a greater novelist than Harold Robbins, there are presumably grounds to which I can appeal in justifying these judgments. Citing such grounds is what is commonly meant by "providing an explanation" in aesthetics.

what Freud believed—the justification of psychoanalytic explanations, like aesthetic explanations, is based neither on induction (or statistical evidence) nor on deduction (logical inference), but rather on what might be called *critical persuasion*; and that what we understand by "justification" in both of these contexts is something that rests, finally, not on facts or propositional knowledge ("knowing that") but rather on a kind of immediate, intuitive perception of certain formal relations ("seeing as").

("But isn't this then a *theory* about the nature of explanation in psychoanalysis, or in any case something that goes beyond a mere description of how language is used?" No, for I only want to point out certain similarities between what goes on in psychoanalytic explanations and what goes on in aesthetics, to show how these two activities [language games] are alike and also how they are different. There is nothing hypothetical about this. I am offering a description of the most obvious facts in each case, showing certain similarities and contrasts between them. You may reject this description as inaccurate or irrelevant, but not "false."[13])

4.30   How do we judge the correctness of a person's response to—or judgment of—a work of art? To begin with, I want to say that this is not an arbitrary matter, even if there is a lot of room for disagreement. There are standards for making such judgments, standards that inhere, as it were, in the culture itself. Generally speaking, an appropriate response conforms to certain rules of taste and cultivation, rules that are established, for the most part, by a recognized cultural elite—the so-called experts. Our response to a work of art is judged "correct" or "incorrect," "astute" or "misguided," on the basis of its conformity to these rules.

Where do these rules come from? Here we might say, with Wittgenstein, that the rules express "what certain people want" (LC, 5). The rules of harmony, for example, "expressed the way people wanted chords to follow—their wishes crystallized in these rules" (LC, 6). Rules reflect what people want; once standardized ("crystallized"), they provide the norms and criteria for making aesthetic judgments.[14] Does

13. An amusing story—probably apocryphal—has it that at a conference on Wittgenstein, after a series of fruitless exchanges, one of the participants stood up and exclaimed, in total exasperation, "Surely Wittgenstein must have been wrong about *something!*" Part of what I am insisting on here is that, properly speaking, if one sticks to the method as Wittgenstein describes it, it is *impossible* to be wrong (which, of course, doesn't preclude the possibility of being either lame or stupid).

14. It may be objected that this way of formulating the issue is not very illuminating. For it seems that the statement "The rules are an expression of what certain people want" must either be a tautology ("What is accepted as a rule is what we want, as shown in the fact that we accept

this mean that aesthetics is reduced to psychology, that is, to matters of personal preference? Not at all; for, as Wittgenstein puts it, "the expression of discontent is not the same thing as the expression of discomfort" (LC, 13). Discomfort expresses our personal feelings about something; it is a psychological reaction, one that might be statistically measured, predicted, explained according to its origins and causes, and so forth. Discontent, on the other hand, expresses a judgment in accordance with the dominant aesthetic norms and rules of the culture; it says, in effect, "Make it higher. . . . Too low! . . . Do something to this," and so forth.

Though subject to change over time, these rules are objective, real, and compelling. An aesthetic judgment is "correct" to the extent that it accords with these rules.

4.31 I want to suggest that just as there is a kind of internal relation between a work of art and the appropriate critical and emotional response to it—expressed in the idea of judging in accordance with the rules—so, too, in psychoanalysis there is an internal relation between a dream and its correct interpretation,[15] and that it is for this reason that psychoanalysis, like aesthetic criticism, is *rational*, even if it is not, and cannot be, "scientific" in the more restricted, hypothetico-deductive sense of this term.[16]

---

it") or a psychological explanation ("We accept these rules because they express what we want"). Only the former, of course, is consistent with Wittgenstein's method, but put in this way it *sounds* trivial. Nonetheless, this is not really an objection, since it is precisely the point of the method to bring these trivialities to notice.

15. For an interesting discussion of this point—and its relation to Wittgenstein's notion of following a rule—see Casey, *The Language of Criticism*, 1–34. According to Casey, there are important analogies between the ordinary process of rule following ("How am I able to follow a rule?"), our critical and emotional response to art ("How do I justify an aesthetic judgment?"), and the process, in psychoanalysis, of forming and accepting interpretations ("How do I judge an interpretation 'correct'?"). More specifically, the common denominator among these different instances is a form of justification that is neither inductive nor deductive but can nonetheless be called "rational."

16. Of course, the general applicability of the hypothetico-deductive understanding of science—even within the context of the aims and methods of the so-called hard sciences—has been severely challenged in the more recent literature of the philosophy of science. (See especially Paul Feyerabend, *Against Method: Outline of an Anarchistic Theory of Knowledge* [London: New Left Books, 1975], and Richard Miller, *Fact and Method: Explanation, Confirmation, and Reality in the Natural and the Social Sciences* [Princeton: Princeton University Press, 1987].) Once again, it is not my intention here to defend any particular view of what should or should not be called "scientific," but only to clarify some of the characteristic features of psychoanalytic language and practice. Nor am I necessarily claiming, in most instances, that these features are unique to psychoanalysis; if certain of the points I make about Freud and psychoanalysis are more widely relevant, so much the better.

4.32 What is the relation between aesthetics and psychoanalysis, or, more specifically, between aesthetic judgment and the process of interpretation in psychoanalysis? In what ways is psychoanalysis like aesthetics, and in what ways different?

In the first place, aesthetics and psychoanalysis both involve a type of justification—and a style of reasoning, or explanation—that is neither inductive nor deductive, but what might be called (for lack of a better term) *constructive*.[17] In both cases, justification consists neither in the finding of new facts nor in drawing logical inferences, but rather in the presentation, or description, of certain logical, grammatical, and broadly formal connections, a presentation that results in a changed way of seeing. (Again, however, keep in mind that there is a continuity between hypothetical and aesthetic modes of reasoning and that the line between them cannot always be clearly drawn, even—I am tempted to say, especially—in the single case of psychoanalysis.)

4.33 Second, the acceptance or rejection of an interpretation is, for the most part, not a matter of decision or will. A patient does not "decide" to accept an interpretation of his or her dream, any more than one "decides" to prefer Brahms's symphonies to those of Tchaikovsky, or to see *King Lear* as a tragedy rather than a comedy. An interpretation or judgment is correct, or true, on grounds independent of personal preference, disposition, or psychology; such judgments refer to *features of reality*, not to anything "merely" subjective, or personal; they pertain to standards that inhere in the very fabric of our world. Hence, we are justified in calling these grounds *objective*. (It *makes sense* to call these grounds "objective" against a voluntaristic, subjectivist, or noncognitivist reading of truth in the humanistic disciplines and the human sciences.[18])

4.34 Aesthetic explanations are logically distinct from hypothetical and empirical explanations (e.g., explanations in terms of "brain mechanisms" or neurological responses). Giving a physical, or a neurological, cause cannot resolve our puzzlement over an aesthetic impression, for our puzzlement is not about causes. Appeals to the "physical substrate," or conditions, of an aesthetic impression cannot answer our question about *why* we are thus affected. (For example, an account of the state of

17. "Interpretive" would be an alternative name for this kind of reasoning and discovery, except that what is involved here is a way of seeing and not (always) an interpretation.

18. For an illuminating discussion of these issues in the context of moral theory—the "realism" and "noncognitivism" debate—see Sabina Lovibond, *Realism and Imagination in Ethics* (Minneapolis: University of Minnesota Press, 1983).

the olfactory nerve while we are smelling a rose sheds no light whatsoever on the question why it smells pleasant, nor does a description of brain activity tell me anything about why I find this particular musical piece so moving.) Aesthetic explanations have to do with *reasons*—with the profound "why?" of an impression—not causes (i.e., the mechanisms by which the impression is produced). No amount of neurological research will ever tell us anything about why one thing is called "beautiful," another "ugly."

Similarly, explanations in psychoanalysis, even when they are couched in the language of physics (force, energy, cathexes, etc.), have primarily to do with reasons, not causes. Like aesthetic forms of explanation, the "why" of a psychoanalytic explanation is concerned with the *sense* of phenomena and only secondarily with their origin, genesis, or causal connections.[19] This has to do, in part, with the specific character of interpretation in psychoanalysis, and particularly the role of agreement in this process, for in contrast to the investigation of a cause, which may be carried out experimentally, the investigation of a reason necessarily entails one's agreement with it (L II, 40). In other words, the truth of an interpretation in psychoanalysis, like the correctness of a judgment in aesthetics, is based finally on agreement. Still, there is a strong tendency in psychoanalysis, just as there is in aesthetics, to seek the *causes* of certain psychological impressions and reactions rather than to recognize that what is really wanted is an analysis of the impression—a tendency that is summed up well in Cioffi's provocative phrase "looking for consummation in the wrong place."[20]

4.35   As Cioffi also points out, explanations in psychoanalysis, like explanations in aesthetics, are fundamentally heuristic rather than informative; in both cases, statements that are apparently descriptive of the past—of origins and conditions—actually serve more to orient us toward

19. There is a large and growing literature on the question of the meaning and validity of the distinction between "causes" and "reasons" in psychoanalysis. In the present context, I want merely to point out that Freud uses the term "cause" in many different ways and that his conflation of "cause" and "reason" has at least two very different meanings: on the one hand, it refers to his mistaken conception about the kind of truth involved in psychoanalysis and psychoanalytic interpretation (as one that might be empirically and experimentally verified); on the other hand, it is part of a *model* of mental activity (the psychic "mechanism" and "thinglike" relation between ideas) that is integral to the process of interpretation. When Freud speaks of causes in this latter sense, he is actually referring, not to a mental or physical substrate, but something like the "theoretical conditions for interpretation."

20. Frank Cioffi, "Wittgenstein's Freud," in *Studies in the Philosophy of Wittgenstein*, ed. Peter Winch (New York: Humanities Press, 1969), 197.

a projected future.[21] The right explanation is the one that is accepted, the one that "clicks." What does it mean "to click"? "You might say that the clicking is that I'm satisfied" (LC, 19). In psychoanalysis, as in aesthetics, the right interpretation (explanation) is the one that brings satisfaction, the one that we *find* acceptable, that alleviates our discontent; more specifically, with respect to psychoanalysis, it is that "which people are inclined to accept and which makes it easier for them to go in certain ways: it makes certain ways of behaving and thinking natural for them. They have given up one way of thinking and adopted another" (LC, 44–45). Such explanations are generally of the nature of *redescriptions*; that is, they redescribe the past in a way that gives it new patterns of significance, new weight and meaning, thus orienting their speakers toward a new and different future.

We might compare this with Wittgenstein's example of trying to trisect an angle with a rule and compass. Once we recognize the impossibility of doing what we thought we wanted to do, we also note a disparity between the description we would give of our activity *before* this recognition and the description we give afterward ("What I was trying to do . . ."). Moreover, the retrospective description is completely different from the former one, and once given, it effectively *changes the meaning* of the original situation. We might say, then, "In trying to trisect an angle by this method, I was attempting to do something that now proves to be impossible—I was trying to do something impossible, not realizing that it was such."

Similarly, explanations in psychoanalysis very often redescribe an event in such a way that it changes its original sense completely, refiguring our life through an entirely new set of meanings, beliefs, interests, and so forth. Through psychoanalysis, for example, I may discover that my flunking the entrance exams to law school was an expression of hostility toward my father (though at the time, of course, I believed that it was due to various external factors: my lack of preparation, my tiredness, distractions in my life, etc.). After this discovery, then, the event changes its meaning entirely; everything is now refracted through the prism of the Oedipal, and I will never view it the same way again. This is exactly analogous to the situation in which we are seeking the word, or the expression, that *fits*, the one that sums up the situation exactly.

So, too, in the case of aesthetics, we might say something like, "My discomfort on initially hearing the piece was due to the fact that I experienced this one phrase as a transition rather than a new opening

21. Ibid.

(though at the time it merely struck me as odd)." Or: "I now understand
that the main character lacked credibility and substance (though on first
impression I knew only that the story as a whole was unconvincing)."
Or: "Haydn seemed a second-rate composer—until I came to see the
wealth of harmonic invention in his works."

Generally speaking, these changes do not come about as a result of
acquiring more information; rather, they are due to some perceptual
rearrangement, some reorganization of sense. Explanation here involves
a form of redescription of the original object or situation such that its
sense *changes* and we come to see it differently. ("What I perceive in the
dawning of an aspect is not a property of the object, but an internal
relation between it and other objects.")

4.36   Redescriptions of this sort often take the form of an analogy or a
simile: that is, finding something to which we feel we stand in a similar
relation as to that which puzzles or impresses us. For example, "The
experience of failing my exams was strangely like the time I announced
to my father that I was leaving home." Or: "Being virtuous is at once
like being rewarded and having no need for reward." Or: "This musical
phrase is like a solemn portent of things to come." Or: "This character
is entirely two-dimensional, like a paper doll." Aesthetic criticism is
very often just such a matter drawing analogies, of "giving a good
simile" and of "putting things side by side." To give reasons in aesthetics
is often to provide further descriptions and thus also to make significant
comparisons of some sort. "What is the justification for a feature in a
work of art?" Wittgenstein asks in one of his lectures. "Is it that you are
satisfied, once something is found which removes the difficulty? What
reasons can one give for being satisfied?" These reasons, he says, are
typically of the nature of further descriptions. "Aesthetics is descriptive.
What it does is to *draw one's attention* to certain features, to place
things side by side so as to exhibit these features"[22] (L II, 38).

So, too, we might say that interpretation in psychoanalysis is largely
a matter of finding the proper analogies and similes. "The display of
elements of a dream, for example, a hat (which may mean practically
anything) is a display of similes. As in aesthetics, things are placed side
by side so as to exhibit certain features" (L II, 40). It is this process of
placing things "side by side" that changes the way we look at the dream,
changes its aspect; we might even want to say that these analogies, once
drawn, are "reasons" for the dream. In this sense, however, reasons are
neither things imported from outside nor things discovered hidden

22. Cf. ML, 314–15.

within the dream; rather, they are the result of *seeing* the dream in a particular way, of viewing it in a particular light or from a particular angle (just as we might speak of the reasons for developing a symphonic theme in this way rather than that, even though these reasons were not present in the mind of the composer).

4.37 In both aesthetics and psychoanalysis, the right interpretation is the one that is accepted, the one that *satisfies* us; once again, however, it is important to see that our acceptance or rejection of a particular interpretation is not a psychological matter but, broadly speaking, a *cultural* one.[23] In aesthetics we speak of the role of the "ideal," or "paradigm" (e.g., the ideal Greek profile, the ideal realization of a musical idea, or the ideal American landscape); in psychoanalysis, we talk about the interpretation that perfectly "sums things up," the one that gives us closure and a sense of resolution, the one that allows us to go on.

In aesthetics, we make judgments both about the relative value of different works of art and about the appropriateness of particular elements within a single work. In each case, as Wittgenstein notes, our judgments are based on some conception of an "ideal." For instance, we say that something is "the ideal Greek profile" or that "these changes in rhythm will bring the thing nearer to an ideal" (L II, 36). In other words, if it is true that the essence of art is *order*, whether formal or thematic, our judgments of the relative value of art, or of particular elements within a single work, are based on a conception of an ideal order (expressed in the different kinds of aesthetic *rules*). When we make judgments in aesthetics, we invariably judge what is actual in terms of an imagined, projected paradigm, a model of perfection. Of course, these judgments are generally expressed in the negative, indicating our perception of something as "not quite right." We say, for example, "This strikes me as wrong for some reason," or "This is too. . . ," or "This needs . . ." Implicitly, however, such judgments are made by

23. This way of putting the matter is potentially misleading, since it sounds as if appeals to the concept of "culture" are somehow explanatory, as if in referring these judgments to the cultural realities, we had found the source of their validity (much as a previous generation of theorists attempted to ground aesthetics in psychological realities). (The tendency to use the concept in this way is especially prevalent today in cultural and symbolic anthropology; indeed, it seems to me that the concept of culture is perhaps the most misunderstood and misused concept in the current intellectual scene.) As I use the term here, "culture" is a purely heuristic notion, one that refers to the totality of rule-governed activities and institutions that form—among any given people—a more or less integrated and self-consistent whole. By calling aesthetic judgments "cultural," I mean to call attention to the fact that they are always context bound, rule oriented, and, to one degree or another, objectively compelling.

comparison to an ideal, that is, to something that would strike us as "just right," even if we are not always—and perhaps only rarely—able to say exactly what this ideal would be or able to formulate a clear conception of it.

The important thing is that judgments of this kind are not based on psychological responses or personal experiences of some sort, nor are they translatable into psychological descriptions (e.g., "This makes me feel good," "This is disgusting," "I don't like the part where . . ."). They refer instead to something at once objective and real, something that is not reducible to personal preference, interests, or experience. In musical criticism, for instance, the statement "The bass moves too much" is not an expression of personal preference; indeed, *it is not a statement about human beings at all* but rather, as Wittgenstein puts it, "more like a piece of mathematics" (ML, 314). It refers to certain norms and standards, to an impersonal set of rules and aesthetic relations, and not to anything psychological. In making such judgments, we are not saying that if it moved less, it would be "more agreeable," but rather that its moving less is, as it were, an end in itself: it brings it nearer the ideal. Similarly, when a painter finds his painting unsatisfactory, he is not expressing his personal response to the work (assuming he is a good painter) but simply *seeing it as wrong*, trying to determine *why* it is wrong and *how* to correct it. "The question of aesthetics is not 'Do you like this?'" Wittgenstein observes, "but 'Why do you like it?'" (ML, 314). The former is a matter of personal taste; the latter involves an appeal to a standard. (This is not to deny that enjoyment is part of the aesthetic experience but to insist that the experience is largely irrelevant to the judgment. To return to our chess analogy: whether I enjoyed the game is irrelevant to the question whether I played *well*—though I wouldn't play the game at all if I didn't enjoy it.)

To summarize the discussion to this point: aesthetic judgments are judgments made by reference to impersonal and objective ideals (rules). Aesthetic issues are cultural, not psychological. The question in aesthetics is not "Do you like this?" but "Why do you like this?" and the proper response to this question is not a cause but a reason. In aesthetics, as in psychoanalysis, such reasons are largely of the nature of further descriptions ("Notice this. . . ," "Compare this to that," and so forth). To the extent that they are successful, the effect of these descriptions is, in both cases, a changed way of seeing ("Now, I see . . ."). (We might say that aesthetic judgments, like psychoanalytic interpretations, cannot be falsified, only *corrected*.)

4.38   The notion of the ideal, or paradigm, is crucial here, and easily misunderstood, in part because it runs counter to the current tenor of our thinking on these matters. Let us ask once more, What does it mean to refer our judgments to an ideal? What *kind* of objectivity is involved here?

In making aesthetic judgments, we frequently talk about certain things being "necessary." We say, for example, "The stark contrast between the different shades is *necessary*," "The continuity of tempo is *necessary*," "The repeat is *necessary*," and so forth. In what sense, then, do we speak of necessity here? Well, listen to two recordings of the same piece of music, one that observes a repeat and one that does not, and compare their effects. Notice that only when the repeat is observed do we experience the full force of the theme. Or listen to the difference in delivery, how the one conductor is able to maintain a flexible continuity of tempo, whereas the other seems constantly to be disrupting the natural flow of the music. Here again, notice, too, that it is not our *experience* of these things that counts, but our perception of *rightness* (and wrongness). Our judgment, we might say, refers to something like an "ideal order," a norm of some sort, rather than to a feeling or emotional reaction, as if, in Wittgenstein's words, "a model for this theme already exists in reality and the theme only approaches it, corresponds to it, if this section is repeated" or if this tempo is maintained (CV, 52).

We could say that the model both is and is not separate from the theme, that the paradigm doesn't exist apart from the performance, except as projected in our imagination, but that it *does* exist precisely there, that is, in our imaginative sensibility, in the rhythm of our language and our lives. "And the theme, moreover, is a *new* part of our language; it becomes incorporated into it; we learn a new *gesture*" (CV, 52). This is the wonder of artistic creation: that each new work expands the realm of meaning, that it "interacts with the existing language," building and expanding on it. (Again, this ideal, or paradigm, is not something we can set before us as a blueprint but something we can get at only through certain kinds of descriptions and comparisons.)

4.39 This notion of the ideal as involving a kind of necessity, an aesthetic imperative of some sort, points again to the reality of certain internal but *objectively perceived* relations, both among the various elements of a work of art and between the work and our response to it (to the extent, that is, that our response is appropriate). It points, in other words, toward a kind of objective "order of the world."

4.40   What the ideal is, how it functions within a particular culture, is a complicated question, one that can only be resolved by looking at specific instances in which it is displayed. Wittgenstein comments:

> The various arts have some analogy to each other, and it might be said that this element common to them is the ideal. But this is not the meaning of "the ideal." The ideal is got from a specific game, and can only be explained in some specific connection, e.g., Greek sculpture. There is no way of saying what all have in common, though of course one may be able to say what is common to two sculptures by studying them. In the statement that their beauty is what approaches the ideal, the word "ideal" is not used as is the word "water," which stands for something which can be pointed to. And no aesthetic investigation will supply you with a meaning of the word "ideal" which you did not have before. (L II, 37)

If you want to understand the ideal in Western sculpture, you must study the great, representative pieces of sculpture in Western art. If you want to understand the ideal in Western music, you must study the great, representative works of Western music. The ideal is not something that can be abstracted from its realizations, nor is it something supra-added to these works; rather, it is *manifested in* these works—and especially through our perspicuous *descriptions* of them. (However transcendent it may seem, the ideal is always an ideal *in our life*, and it always pertains to meaning, to language.)

It might be said that the ideal derives from and embodies certain *rules* (although it is perhaps true to say that the really great works of art transcend rules of correctness: here, "entirely different things enter" [LC, 8]). Familiarity with the rules of a particular field of art, or of a particular style in art, leads to a developed sensibility and critical judgment. "If I hadn't learnt the rules, I wouldn't be able to make the aesthetic judgment," Wittgenstein remarks. "In learning rules you get a more and more refined judgment. Learning the rules actually changes your judgment" (LC, 5). Eventually there emerges a class of people who are educated in making aesthetic judgments, people of a distinctively refined sensibility, taste, and critical judgment. Thus, in aesthetics, "we distinguish between a person who knows what he is talking about and a person who doesn't" (LC, 6). (So, too, in psychoanalysis, it makes perfect sense to distinguish those who have been analyzed—and those who actually practice analysis—from those who merely read about it in books, not because the former have some esoteric knowledge but because they have a certain acquired skill and sensibility.)

4.41   The rules and criteria according to which aesthetic judgments are made are intrinsically related to the culture as a whole. To understand the role of aesthetic judgments in a particular historical period or in a particular culture, one must understand the whole of the social and cultural context within which such judgments are made. "The words we call expressions of aesthetic judgment play a very complicated role, but a very definite role, in what we call a culture of a period. To describe their use or to describe what you mean by a cultured taste, you have to describe a culture. What we now call a cultured taste perhaps didn't exist in the Middle Ages. An entirely different game is played in different ages" (LC, 8). To describe a set of aesthetic rules fully, or to explain what aesthetic judgment consists in, one would have to describe the entire culture, for "what belongs to a language-game is a whole culture" (LC, 8). This is why it is not only difficult but impossible to describe what aesthetic appreciation and judgment consists in: "To describe what it consists in we would have to describe the whole environment" (LC, 7).

4.42   In learning aesthetic rules, one acquires a more and more refined judgment: "Learning rules actually changes your judgment" (LC, 5). At the same time, a distinguishing feature of aesthetic *judgment*, as opposed to mere execution, is the capacity to say that something does *not* accord with the rules. "Perhaps the most important thing in connection with aesthetics," says Wittgenstein, "is what may be called aesthetic reactions, e.g., discontent, disgust, discomfort" (LC, 13). I may learn the rules and apply these rules correctly, but in order to make *aesthetic judgments*, I need to develop a feeling for the rules. I need not only to interpret them but also, in a sense, to "inhabit" them (LC, 5). In making an aesthetic judgment, one is doing more than simply applying these rules or even interpreting them as one applies them; with the development of a certain sensibility and taste, one begins *to see* in accordance with these rules.[24] (I don't think about rules when I play chess; I think about strategy. An accomplished pianist doesn't think about how to play the piano or even—if he or she is truly accomplished—how to play the particular piece; rather, the pianist simply plays the piece more or less blindly, as if by instinct.)

4.43   In aesthetics, the ideal is cultural, not psychological. So, too, in psychoanalysis it is culture, not individual psychology of taste, that is

24. Consider once again the relation here between "interpretation" and "seeing an aspect."

the basis for judgment; an interpretation is correct, not because it pleases us, because we like or want to believe it, but because it "clicks," because it fits with the rest of our life. An interpretation is correct because at some deep level it *makes sense*, and this making sense is far from being an arbitrary matter (even if we allow for a certain latitude in the range of possible interpretations that might equally well be called true).

Thus, to say that psychoanalysis is a form of persuasion is *not* to imply that it is simply a matter of "suggestion" or conditioning (i.e., the idea frequently found among critics of psychoanalysis—including Wittgenstein—that the analyst merely *induces* the patient to accept whatever interpretation verifies the analyst's own theory).[25] What *makes* a particular interpretation persuasive has to do with a whole complex of factors—personal, yes, but more to the point, social, historical, and cultural—that contributes to the patient's *finding* it persuasive, factors that go well beyond the analytic situation itself. In this respect, too, a persuasive interpretation in psychoanalysis is like to an aesthetic judgment: the criteria relevant to determining its truth transcend individual taste, need, or preference. (Of course, this does not preclude the possibility that the interpretation may itself refer to matters of taste, need, desire, and so forth. We must distinguish here between the *content* of the interpretation and its *grounds*.)

How, then, do we explain this "fit" between an interpretation and our life? Just as we explain the fit between this poem and our response to it, or between this musical phrase and the significance we attach to it: that is, through a description of the culture of which it is a part, together, perhaps, with an analysis of the impression it makes—the impression of something singular and profound. (Psychoanalysis, then, is not psychology any more than aesthetics is, for the grounds of

---

25. Freud recognized the problem of suggestion—referring to it once as "uncommonly interesting" (IL, 447)—but his manner of dealing with it is singularly inadequate. The following statement—one of the most extensive treatments of the problem—is typical: "Psychoanalytic procedure differs from all methods making use of suggestion, persuasion, etc., in that it does not seek to suppress by means of authority any mental phenomenon that may occur in the patient. It endeavors to trace the causation of the phenomenon and to remove it by bringing about a permanent modification in the conditions that lead to it. In psychoanalysis the suggestive influence which is inevitably exercised by the physician is diverted on to the task assigned to the patient of overcoming his resistances, that is, of carrying forward the curative process. Any danger of falsifying the products of a patient's memory by suggestion can be avoided by prudent handling of the technique; but in general the arousing of resistances is a guarantee against the misleading effects of suggestive influence" (TEA, 250–51). In other words, the fact of resistance—and its "prudent handling"—tells against the possibility of suggestion; as long as the patient denies the truth of the analyst's interpretation, we can safely assume that the analyst is not using his or her authority to manipulate the patient.

psychoanalysis extend beyond individual psychology. This is part of what is involved in characterizing it as a hermeneutics.)

4.44 To a large degree, our misunderstanding of psychoanalysis stems precisely from our failure to appreciate it as an interpretive, or hermeneutic art, one whose standards of truth are very different from those of the natural sciences (though not, once more, any less rational or objective). This failure cuts in two directions: first, when it leads to inappropriate questions about the legitimacy, or "scientific validity," of psychoanalysis (the naïve rejection of many critics); second, when it serves to conceal the rhetorical and aesthetic basis of psychoanalytic explanations (the naïve acceptance of many followers). I have already said something about the first; let me end with a few remarks on the second.

There are many reasons people find psychoanalytic explanations attractive, not least of which has to do with the pointedly reductive style of those explanations. "The attraction of certain kinds of explanation is overwhelming," Wittgenstein observes. "In particular, explanations of the kind 'this is really only this' " (LC, 24). Many of Freud's most influential explanations are explanations of precisely this sort—"this is really only *this*"—and though we may think we resist their charms, most of us nonetheless secretly cherish a nostalgia for the simplicity they embody. Such explanations, however, even when they are set forth as a scientific ideal, typically belong to rhetoric. "Those sentences have the form of persuasion in particular which say 'This is *really* this,' " Wittgenstein tells us (LC, 27). What matters, we think, is that we find something simple beneath the apparent complexity of things; the more complicated the explanation, the less attractive it is.[26]

4.45 It is one of the great virtues of psychoanalytic explanations that, despite occasional appearances to the contrary, they are fundamentally quite simple. Indeed, there are perhaps no simpler explanations of human motivation and symbolism anywhere. For psychoanalysis, everything is an expression of unconscious, wishful impulses; hence, everything is finally reducible to the formula "This is *really* only that." But

---

26. Kenneth Burke notes that this "essentializing strategy" is not peculiar to Freud but linked with an accepted ideal of science: namely, the attempt to explain the complex in terms of the simple. The problem is that successful realization of this ideal invariably exposes its limitations: "When you get through," as Burke points out, "all your opponent need say is: 'But you have explained the complex in terms of the simple—and the simple is precisely what the complex is not' " ("Freud—and the Analysis of Poetry," in *The Philosophy of Literary Form: Studies in Symbolic Action*, rev. ed. [New York: Vintage Books, 1957], 224).

this virtue—if it *is* a virtue—is also a great danger. For if one of the real strengths of psychoanalysis—and surely the outstanding feature of Freud's genius—lies in the capacity to forge ever new sequences of meaning based on analogies between different patterns of behavior and symbolism, the corresponding temptation is to reduce these analogies to identities, that is, to set forth explanations of the form "This is really this" as if they were demonstrably true and beyond any reasonable doubt. In psychoanalysis, as Wittgenstein notes, there is a strong tendency to say, "We can't get round the fact that this dream is really such and such," or "Clinical experience shows that this kind of behavior really comes down to such and such." And when someone challenges this idea and says, "Why do you say it is really this, when obviously it is not this at all?" it may in fact be difficult to see it as something else (LC, 24). To repeat Cioffi's point once more, the psychoanalytically minded interpreter behaves as if he or she had learned the expression "castration symbol" ostensively: *this*, the interpreter insists, is what castration substitute *means*.[27]

4.46   We need to see that psychoanalysis rests on very different grounds from what we had previously thought, or what both Freud and his critics believed. This does not mean, however, that psychoanalysis is *wrong* or that the validity of its interpretations is thereby undermined (though it clearly suggests certain limits to that validity, both logical and cultural). In psychoanalysis, some analogies are, as it were, grammatical (i.e., beyond questions of fact and evidence), and some symbolic correlations paradigmatic. These analogies and symbolic equations belong to the rules of the game, just as we might say that the ideal in aesthetics embodies rules and norms for making judgments in art: as rules, they are neither true nor false, "good" nor "bad," but a necessary condition for playing the game.

It makes no sense to ask, then, whether all forms of self-mutilation are castration substitutes; rather, we accept that this is what castration *means*.[28] This is not something that is demonstrably or factually true but

---

27. Cioffi, "Wittgenstein's Freud," 200.

28. I take this to be comparable to what Donald Spence means when he says that interpretations are fundamentally paradigmatic, having more to do with the future than with the past: "If it is true that many interpretations function as pragmatic statements, it becomes clear that whatever truth value they possess lies more in the future than in the past. By making an interpretation, the analyst hopes to make the patient aware of a new view of his life; if the interpretation is accepted, then it may bring about a reformulation of certain fixed conceptions, allowing the patient to see them more accurately and respond more perceptively; as a result, he will behave differently and experience his world in a rather different manner. To the extent that it brings about a successful experience of this kind, the interpretation becomes true" ("Narrative Persuasion," *Psychoanalysis and Contemporary Thought* 6, no. 3 [1983]: 467). See

something that is paradigmatic for the practice of interpretation in psychoanalysis. Our acceptance or rejection of this equation is not subject to independent verification or grounding of some sort; rather, our acceptance of its truth is the condition for our being able to think psychoanalytically at all. Our mistake—as well as Freud's—has been to believe that this correlation can and must be established by evidence, or by pointing to "the facts" of the matter. Yet now we begin to suspect that the equation "mutilation = castration" is neither more nor less factual, neither more nor less arbitrary, than the equation "2 + 2 = 4" (though this is not to deny, of course, that the logic and use of these equations is *very* different).

The idea that mutilation equals castration functions in psychoanalysis not as a hypothesis but as a *norm of expression*; it is, as it were, a law of symbolization. (And if we find this a *universal* law, this fact says more about our use of language than it does about supposed universal features of the mind or about cross-cultural invariants of some sort. A word for anthropologists.)

also Spence, *Narrative Truth and Historical Truth: Meaning and Interpretation in Psychoanalysis* (New York: W. W. Norton, 1982).

5

DISCOVERY THROUGH RETRODUCTION:

The Grammar of Laws and Hypotheses

5.1   How do I find the "right" word? What kind of process is involved? I am groping for a word. Several come to mind, but I reject them as inappropriate. I go on looking. The word, we say, is "on the tip of my tongue." Then, suddenly, it comes: *"That's* it! That is what I meant!" Now, I can continue. (Cf. BlB, 41; PI, 2:218.)

We might describe this as the experience of finding the right word. The right word is the one on the tip of my tongue or "before my mind's eye," the word that exactly expresses what I wanted to say; it may also be the word that comes along unexpectedly and "sums everything up," the word that makes me suddenly see things in a new light. We might also say that finding the right word in this way represents a kind of discovery, but it is not clear what kind. We talk about discovering new planets or the secret of DNA; but what kind of discovery is represented in finding the "right word"?

Consider the difference between the following two examples.[1]

Two women are trying on hats. One turns to the other with a look of expectation. Then the second one says, "Sorry dear, it looks worse than terrible." Since the first woman vaguely knows this already, the words reveal almost nothing except, perhaps, something about the speaker.

---

1. From John Wisdom, "Philosophy, Metaphysics, and Psychoanalysis," in *Philosophy and Psychoanalysis* (Oxford: Basil Blackwell, 1964), 248.

But now compare: Two women are trying on hats. The first puts one on and studies it in the mirror. There is a pause; then her friend, looking over her shoulder, says, "My dear, the Taj Mahal." Instantly, the look of indecision on the first woman's face disappears. She had sensed that something was wrong all along, but couldn't put her finger on it. Now she suddenly sees what it is: the hat is entirely too grand and imposing, too "monumental," too pretentious. All of this happens, moreover, in spite of the fact that the hat could be seen clearly and completely before the words "Taj Mahal" were uttered.

In contrast to the first example, the second, it seems, represents a kind of discovery. What occurs in this second instance is not simply a confirmation of something we already knew, nor does it involve learning some new information; rather, what is involved here is a kind of aspect change. No facts are discovered, no explanation is given, but *our way of seeing is changed*. How does this change come about? What happens in this process?

5.2   Two people are studying an arrangement of photographs just hung on the wall. A few minor adjustments are made; one picture is tilted down a bit; another shifted slightly to one side. Still, something is wrong. Then one person exclaims to the other, "They just hang there! They don't *move!*" Now minor adjustments are no longer sufficient; now, with the introduction of the idea of "movement," everything changes; the entire arrangement has to be looked at again with a very different eye.

This, too, is an example of an aspect change: things are *seen differently*, though no solution is proposed.

5.3   Now compare this example. Two men are talking together over a drink. The first has recently remarried for the third time and is already complaining of feeling trapped, restless. "All women are the same," he says, and falls silent. Then the other man turns to the first and says, "But, Joe, don't you see: you've married your mother again!" With this there comes a flash of recognition on Joe's face, an expression of both horror and relief: "Of course!" Now, suddenly, everything changes; not only will his wife never look quite the same again, but every woman he meets will be viewed in this new light. We might even say he inhabits a new world.

This last example, while similar to the first two, is also significantly different, for what is involved here is not only a change of aspect—a reorganization of perceptual elements—but a *conceptual* shift. With a shock of recognition, everything suddenly *makes sense* in a new way;

now the past is refigured in new patterns of meaning; a whole complex set of dispositions and behavior suddenly appears in an entirely new light. Things are not only *seen* differently but conceptualized in a radically new way ("Now I understand!"). The sense of this new world is different; things *cohere* in a new way.

5.4   Each of these examples represents a particular kind of discovery, one that consists neither in finding new facts nor in drawing logical implications, but rather in seeing things differently, or in making sense of things in a new way. Following the work of philosopher of science Norwood Hanson, we can call this process of discovery "retroduction" and the reasoning it involves "retroductive reasoning,"[2] thereby distinguishing it from other kinds of discoveries and reasoning. For just as there is a categorical difference between "seeing" and "seeing as," so retroductive reasoning is irreducible to either inductive or deductive reasoning, and the discovery that follows from it is distinct from other kinds of discoveries, both in the sciences and in everyday life.

5.5   Retroduction, we might say, belongs to the logic of discovery, as opposed to the logic of justification:[3] it consists in finding—or inventing—*contexts* within which things previously puzzling or nonsensical are made to appear intelligible. What is discovered through retroduction is not an object or a new piece of information but rather a *new mode of organization*—and thus also, to the extent that it is expressed propositionally, a new *form* for representing a regularity whose existence was already in some sense recognized. (In order for such representation to be possible, there must be regularity in our experience; certain things must *seem* equivalent.)

We use retroductive reasoning constantly, often without any awareness of doing so. It plays an important role in many aspects of our daily lives, as well as in science and, most of all, in aesthetics and aesthetic

2. Norwood Hanson, *Patterns of Discovery: An Inquiry into the Conceptual Foundations of Science* (Cambridge: Cambridge University Press, 1959), 85–92.

3. In keeping with the accepted practice in discussions of the philosophy of science, we can distinguish the "logic of discovery" from the "logic of justification." Generally speaking, the logic of discovery is concerned with the reasons for *suggesting* a hypothesis; the logic of justification, with the reasons for *accepting* it. Retroductive reasoning pertains, then, to the logic of discovery; deductive reasoning, to the logic of justification. It should be emphasized, however, that this distinction is at best a rough one, for much of what goes on in science cannot clearly be assigned to one or the other exclusively. (For example, the fact that a hypothesis offers a plausible explanation of the data can be not only a reason for suggesting it but also a reason for accepting it once it has been suggested. Moreover, as the aesthetic case shows, discovery and justification are sometimes one and the same process.)

criticism. Its importance to psychoanalysis—and its relevance to our understanding of Freud's discovery—will, I think, be obvious.

5.6   Retroductive reasoning is reasoning that forges new connections and contexts, reasoning that consists precisely in *seeing* these connections. This distinction between retroductive and deductive reasoning is related to the earlier distinction between two kinds of persuasion, namely, persuasion based on logical or empirical *demonstration* and persuasion through perspicuous *presentation*. Retroduction, as a kind of conceptual discovery, is the process of creating contexts within which things are made comprehensible—or, as we might say in respect to the natural sciences, the process of finding new forms of representation that allow us to see connections between observed regularities. (Science, we might say, is largely just this attempt to find suitable forms of representation for observed regularities, forms of representation that *connect* these regularities in specific and useful ways. Rhetoric intervenes—in science and as in everyday life—whenever one person induces another to see things according to the contexts and patterns that retroduction has revealed; critical persuasion, as I use the term, is precisely this process by which one person *converts* another to a new way of seeing.)

5.7   Imagine that you and I are looking a work of art—say, a painting. I tell you that I think it is really quite striking; you say that it seems glib and clichéd. How do we resolve our disagreement? Not by appealing to any factual information or by offering explanations of one sort or another; rather, we each *describe* what we see, pointing out especially those features of the work that lead us to the judgment we have made. By this process of description (or "redescription"), I may be led to see things your way, or you to see things my way; or, of course, it may happen that we never come to any agreement about the matter—and that's that. In any case, what is involved is a process of persuasion, of rhetoric. Each of us tries to persuade the other to see things differently.

If, in fact, I change your way of seeing, we can say that I have led you to make a kind of discovery; this is what I am calling "discovery by retroduction."

5.8   What kind of truth is represented in this process? If someone claims to have discovered something, whether in science or in everyday life, we want to know what *justifies* us in agreeing that, yes, something can now be regarded as known that was previously unknown ("I know that *x*"). This justification will often entail citing reasons ("I believe that *x* because . . ."), but it may also take the form of a perspicuous presentation ("Look at things *in terms of*, or *from the perspective of*, *x*"). In this latter case, what is involved is a presentation that *exhibits* grammatical—that is, semantic, logical, and conceptual—relations, rather than proves something deductively. This exhibition, or display, changes our way of seeing; now we say, "Yes, I see that. . . ," and we feel that we could convey this same insight to someone else as well. Then we feel justified in saying, "It is true that . . ." (Can we *prove* the truth of our assertion? What would proof amount to here? How do I prove that this arrangement is wrong?)

5.9   Retroduction, we have said, is closely linked to the experience of "seeing as" and to aspect change. Retroductive reasoning, to the extent that it is persuasive, necessarily entails a change in aspects (since seeing connections and seeing according to particular contexts both involve, by definition, seeing aspects), though not every aspect change is an instance of retroductive reasoning. (Of the three examples cited above, only the third truly represents a form of retroductive reasoning, whereas the first two are relatively straightforward examples of an aspect change.) Retroduction involves an element of *explanation* (though an explanation in terms of reasons, not causes: "Now, things make sense!") and therefore also of something that demands explanation, that is, the recognition of some kind of conceptual problem (e.g., difficulties with one's wife resolved—more or less—by seeing how one's wife becomes one's mother). An aspect change, by contrast, merely marks the shift from one way of looking at things to another (e.g., "duck-rabbit").

5.10   Let us look at another example from the writings of John Wisdom. "Imagine," he proposes "that until now all maps have been drawn on Mercator's projection. Mr. A receives a map of the world on an extraordinary projection," one that he has never seen before and that he therefore cannot decipher. "He takes it to a friend, P, who says immediately: 'But can't you see, its a map of the world!' " It may happen that nothing more is needed, that just these words are enough to change Mr. A's perception, "causing him to see what were formerly a chaos of lines as a representation of the world." But it may also happen that something more is needed, something like a redescription of the thing: for example, "Here is Africa, here Australia," "This is east, that west" (again, just as we might redescribe a work of art to bring certain features into view). The process may then be more gradual, involving a procedure of putting before Mr. A more and more pointed descriptions, each one representing a more radical departure from the familiar Mercator's projection. It may happen, then, at the end of this process, that he suddenly says, "Yes, I can see it now! A map of the world!" With this realization, we say that Mr. A has made a discovery. The question is, once more, What kind of discovery is this?[4] How do we decide?

Again, the first thing to notice is that what is revealed in this process is not a quality or characteristic of an object, nor is it the observation of new phenomena; rather, it is the perception of a hitherto unrecognized relation *between* things (e.g., the correspondence between these different lines and certain geographical regions). Seeing an aspect involves the perception of an internal relation between two or more things; seeing an aspect is seeing things *according to this relation*, whether the relation itself is explicitly recognized or not. For instance, returning to the previous examples, with the words "Taj Mahal," a link is forged between the hat and a monument too grand and imposing; with the pronouncement that pictures "just hang," a connection is established between certain spacial arrangements and a perception of movement; with the pronouncement that Joe has married his mother, an internal—and possibly deeply disturbing—relation is established between his wife and his mother. Such connections, once made, change our way of looking at things, often permanently.

5.11   Now, in psychoanalysis, it seems to me, retroduction occurs at two levels, or in two different contexts: first, at the level of the interpretation of symbolic phenomena (e.g., in seeing dream element *A* as *B*), and second, at the level of theory formation (e.g., in seeing dreams as instances and expressions of repression). These two instances, while distinguishable, are also clearly related, since retroduction at the first, interpretative level (leading to the discovery of latent meanings) is represented discursively at the second, theoretical level (leading to the discovery of an unconscious and of unconscious mechanisms, through which latent meaning is transposed into manifest symbol).

Through analysis, psychoanalytic patients learn to see various phenomena in their lives as instances of psychological conflict, of repression and repetition, and so forth—that is, they come to view their lives in terms of certain theoretical concepts and relations—just as they also learn, through the process of interpretation, to see individual dreams as the expression of their own—repressed and distorted—desires. Virtually the entire process, at both levels, is one of reductive *seeing*, which is to say, seeing induced through pointed redescriptions of one kind or another. (As *The Interpretation of Dreams* has aptly been called the

4. Wisdom, *Philosophy and Psychoanalysis*, 264–65.

quintessential "see-what-I-mean" book, we might describe the whole of psychoanalysis as a distinctively "see-what-I-mean" enterprise.[5])

Having noted how retroduction is similar at both levels, I would also insist on a difference: retroduction at the level of interpretation typically entails seeing previously unnoticed connections between different aspects of one's life and behavior; retroduction at the level of theory, by contrast, entails the construction of new forms of representation, that is, new terminologies, new logical and syntactical sequences, that allow us to forge unsuspected connections between different concepts and conceptual fields, very often through the use of certain grammatical innovations (e.g., the concept of "sexuality" extended to include specific kinds of infantile activity). In this latter instance, then, we speak not only of a changed perception (aspect changes induced through the recognition of new patterns) but of a new *theoretical* understanding, one that typically brings new ways of *explaining* what was formerly inexplicable (changes in one's worldview brought about by new kinds of conceptualization and explanation).

(Freud did not merely interpret dreams, he also *explained* them; he gave us not only a method but a new, comprehensive psychology—and with it a new vision of the human.)

5.12 Through the process of dream interpretation, analyst and analysand—working together, certainly, but under the direction and guidance of the analyst—come to see the dream as something that is at once sensible and rational, something that is integrally related to the analysand's waking life: that is, as the distorted expression of certain repressed wishes and needs (e.g., the dream is the expression of the repressed wish that P should die). So, too, in the broader context of the analysis as a whole, the analyst gradually leads the analysand to view his or her life as whole in an entirely new way: that is, as evincing certain previously unrecognized patterns, as sensible in ways that previously failed to make sense (e.g., to see certain segments of his or her behavior as the expression of hatred toward P, to see *patterns of hatred*). Over time, the

5. See Marshall Edelson, *Hypothesis and Evidence in Psychoanalysis* (Chicago: University of Chicago Press, 1984), 33. Edelson also affirms that this kind of retroductive, or "see-what-I-mean," reasoning plays a more prominent role in the social sciences than in the natural sciences: "Freud's work, in this connection, should be read as in part at least an effort to make it possible to see things differently. His gift for making it possible through his examples and case studies for others to 'see what I mean' is impressive. In fact a great amount of work in the social sciences does not involve hypothesis-testing even when it appears in that guise, but an effort by one or more, through the collection and organization of facts and proposals of explanations of them, to persuade others to see what they see" (32).

analyst's interpretations change the analysand's way of seeing his or her life; if the analysis is successful, the analysand's behavior, experience, and sensibility also change accordingly. (To the extent that this occurs, we may want to call the interpretations "true.") Finally, on a still different level, the analyst appeals to theory to account for the fact that, first, the analysand's dreams *are* the expression of repressed wishes and fantasies, and second, that the analysand's behavior, in both its normal and pathological aspects, manifests certain patterns of repetition (though presumably it is only the neurotic aspects that are dysfunctional and that therefore demand recognition for a favorable therapeutic resolution). Interpretation, construction, theoretical explanation—at every level, retroduction and critical persuasion are at work.

Note once more the distinctive character of this process, what might even be regarded as the hallmark of the psychoanalytic method ("the talking cure"). Without discovering, or introducing, any new facts, without conveying any information whatsoever, the analyst leads the analysand to recognize certain previously unnoticed patterns in his or her life, to assume responsibility for certain actions that previously seemed outside of his or her control. (The concept of the unconscious, far from undermining our personal sense of responsibility, actually extends it; what formerly belonged to chance now becomes an expression of will.)

By the same token, an analysand does not discover, on the basis of new information, that he hates his father, nor does he infer this to be the case; rather, he comes to *see* certain kinds of behavior, previously thought to be beneficent or innocuous, *as* the manifestation of that hatred. He gradually learns to see connections between what he had always thought of as acts of love and what he is now willing to regard as acts of hatred; what he had previously seen as the expression of love comes now to be regarded, at least in part, as the expression of hatred. In this way, he comes to see his whole life in an entirely new light.

The actual discovery of facts, of things hidden or previously unknown, plays almost no role in this process. (Of course, it may happen that new memories are produced in the course of analysis—what Freud describes as the recovery of repressed memories; but when we think about the context in which such memories are brought forth, and recall that their historical veracity is irrelevant, we are much more inclined to see them, too, as retroductive constructions—as the products, in other words, of fantasy—and to regard their role in the overall construction of a life narrative as supplementary rather than definitive.)

5.13   As we have said, retroduction is not confined to psychoanalysis but is now generally recognized as an integral part in the process of discovery in the natural, or physical, sciences as well (though, of course, with important differences). Quite often in the natural sciences one argues from the existence of observed phenomena that are puzzling, to a hypothesis that, if true, explains these phenomena. What is discovered in this process is, once again, not a new fact but the *form* of a regularity whose existence was already in some sense recognized. The theory, we might say, provides a pattern, or framework, within which data appear *intelligible*, a kind of "conceptual gestalt." Thus, it is not that the theory is pieced together from observed phenomena; rather, it is the theory that makes it possible to *see* phenomena as being of a particular sort and as related to other observed phenomena in particular ways. (It frequently happens in this process that there is a redefinition of the phenomena themselves, such that the original conceptual problem is not so much solved as *dissolved*; that is, it simply ceases to pose a puzzle.) Hence, even in the natural sciences, it is less the case that theories are *derived from* phenomena, or inferred on the basis of evidence (though there are certainly instances where one could give sense to this way of putting the matter), than it is that the theory itself determines what observations and phenomena are relevant and how these phenomena are to be described and arranged.

Theories put phenomena into systems, they provide them with a *context*. It is in this sense that we can say that theories in the natural sciences—like theories in the human sciences—are, as it were, constructed "in reverse," which is to say, retroductively. "A theory is a cluster of conclusions in search of a premise," Hanson writes. "From the observed properties of phenomena the physicist reasons his way toward a keystone idea from which the properties are explicable as a matter of course."[6] What distinguishes the natural from the human sciences is, in large measure, merely the *degree* to which this kind of retroductive reasoning is employed. In the natural sciences, it belongs— more or less exclusively—to the logic of discovery and to the initial constitution of conceptual paradigms, prior to the formalization of fixed laws and principles; in the human sciences, it is much more common and widespread, occurring at virtually every stage of description, reasoning, and explanation.

5.14   Consider, for example, the discovery in optical geometry that light travels in straight lines—what is now generally known as "the principle of the rectilinear propagation of light."[7] We begin with various

6. Hanson, *Patterns of Discovery*, 90.
7. The discussion that follows is based on Stephen Toulmin's analysis of this example in *The Philosophy of Science: An Introduction* (New York: Harper and Row, 1953), ch. 2, 17–56.

facts of our common, daily experience of light and shade—of the way light affects and is affected by objects—such as our perception that the length of shadows is relative to the movement of the sun, and the like; with the different practical skills and techniques that have developed out of that experience (our use of sundials, of lamps and lanterns, our construction of shades, etc.); and with the known regularities among optical phenomena (e.g., the consistency with which shadows vary in relation to the source of light). Given these facts, then, how do we move to the conclusion that "light travels in straight lines"? Again, what kind of discovery is this?

"Well," we might say, "it is an inference based on the observation of the behavior of light in different situations. We see the sun move in relation to objects and observe that the shadows of these objects vary in proportion to the angle of the sun. Thus, we infer that the light emanating from the sun moves in a straight light."

But what observation leads us to believe that anything is traveling here? Do we *see* the light move? Indeed, do we see "light"—as something that moves—at all? Clearly not.

Compare the inference that leads, say, from Crusoe's perception of footprints on a beach to his conclusion that a man had been walking there. This, too, might be called a discovery, a discovery that can be stated in the form of the proposition "A man has been walking along the beach." But notice that in this case the truth of the proposition can be confirmed by direct observation; at any moment, we may in fact encounter the man who is responsible for these prints. By contrast, in the case of the inference from the primitive phenomena of light and shade to the conclusion "Light travels in straight lines," *there is no possibility of direct confirmation* (or falsification) of this supposed inference, for there is no observation—or any inference based on observation—that can, in itself, confirm the proposition in question.

Crusoe's discovery is based on applying familiar modes of inference to new data: "Footprint! Footprint means man. Therefore, man." In the optical example, on the other hand, what is novel is not *the data*—that is, the behavior of shadows and light—but precisely *the nature of the inference itself*, for by this inference we are led to look at familiar phenomena in an entirely new way—not, as we might think, at new phenomena in a familiar way.

The discovery that light travels in straight lines does not come about merely as a result of observation (e.g., the observation that where nothing was thought to be, there is in fact something traveling from one point to another, or one way rather than another); rather, it is the discovery that we can in fact speak profitably of something traveling in these circumstances and that, by doing so, we are able to link a number of previously disconnected phenomena (e.g., light from lamps and light from the sun). Once again, however, this discovery is not based on inference or deduction but, like the other examples we have discussed, on *retroductive reasoning*, reasoning *after the fact*. Moreover, in contrast to the Crusoe example, what is involved here is, in part, an *innovation in the use of language*, one that changes the way in which we *see*, and hence also conceptualize, the relevant phenomena. As Toulmin observes, "In Robinson's discovery . . . the language in which the conclusion is expressed . . . is the language of everyday life: there is no question of giving new senses to the words involved, or of using them in a way which is at all out of the ordinary." In the optical discovery, however, the situation is markedly different, for here what is involved is a change in language, a change in the way we actually use words—a change in meaning:

> In the optical case, both the key words in our conclusion— "light" and "travelling"—are given new uses in the very statement of the discovery. Before the discovery is made, the word "light" means to us such things as lamps—the "light" of "Put out the light"; and illuminated areas—the "light" of "The sunlight in the garden." Until the discovery, changes in light and shade, as we ordinarily use the words (i.e., illuminated regions which move as the sun moves), remain things primitive, unexplained, to be accepted for what they are. After the discovery, we see them all as the effects of something, which we also speak of in a new sense as "light," travelling from the sun or lamp to the illuminated objects. A crucial part of the step we are examining is, then, coming to think about shadows and light patches in a new way, and in consequence coming to ask new questions about them, questions like "Where from?", "Where to?" and "How fast?", which are intelligible only if one thinks of the phenomena in this new way.[8]

In other words, to say that "light travels in straight lines" is not merely to sum up the observed facts about shadows and lamps; rather, it is to set forth a new way of looking at these phenomena, one by which we can make sense of the observed facts about lamps and shadows. Furthermore, the introduction of the notion of "light" as something "traveling" is not the straightforward, literal discovery of something

8. Toulmin, *The Philosophy of Science*, 21.

moving, like finding worms in an apple or children in the bushes; rather, it is a grammatical extension of the term "traveling," one that is used in the service of a specific scientific discipline—in this case, optical geometry.

5.15   In answer to the question "What sort of discovery is this?" we can say that it is, at least in part, the discovery that the everyday phenomena of light and shade can be *seen as* the effects of something traveling, or being propagated, from the light source to the surrounding objects. The core of this discovery, then, consists in two things: first, the introduction of new techniques for representing phenomena, techniques that are found to fit a wide range of existing facts and also to establish connections between them; and second, the adoption of a new model, one that allows novel ways of drawing inferences (i.e., the procedures by which it is possible to *exhibit* general relations among natural objects, procedures that are irreducible to induction or deduction). (In the natural sciences, models allow us to explain, represent, and *predict* the behavior of phenomena under investigation; in psychoanalysis—as well as in the human sciences generally—the models allow us to represent and, with certain qualifications, to explain, but only very rarely, and in a limited sense, to predict.)

5.16   The process of retroduction thus involves two indispensable elements: first, looking at things differently (an aspect change), and second, using language differently (a grammatical innovation). In virtually all significant scientific discoveries, we look at familiar phenomena in a new way, not at new phenomena in familiar ways. Such discoveries also—and in consequence—necessarily involve new linguistic usages, particularly the use of familiar words in unexpected and *extended* ways. New terminologies are introduced, new semantics and syntaxes, new rules of grammar.

To repeat: what is discovered in retroduction is not an object or a new fact about the world but a *new form* for the description of regularities within the world (a "paradigm," broadly understood), regularities whose existence was already in a sense recognized but whose sense and significance is now dramatically altered.

5.17   Let us consider one more example from the physical sciences: Newton's discovery of the law of gravity. Again, we begin with certain everyday observations about the behavior of objects: the fact that apples fall to the ground, the seemingly irregular motion of the planets, the rising and falling of the tides, and so forth. What happens, then? We might say that with the discovery of the law of gravity,[9] Newton did a truly remarkable thing, perhaps even two things at once: that is, not only did he connect falling apples to the motion of the planets, but he also found a way of unifying the science of an infinite universe, of, in effect, reconciling the continuity of space with the discontinuity of matter.[10] By "flinging gravity across the void," Newton not only explained the observed motion of bodies that previously seemed inexplicable, he also provided a comprehensive framework within which *all* of the known data became intelligible. Again, however, notice that the law of gravity is not something that can be deductively derived from the phenomena (for we never observe "gravity" as such, nor can we infer it from any observation or group of observations); instead, it is the law that determines which phenomena are relevant—and it does so by defining them, retroductively, *as instances of that law*.

John Wisdom makes this point with characteristic lucidity and wit. "We say that Newton discovered gravity," he writes. "But now what was it he did? After all we didn't need Newton to tell us that apples fall." What is involved here, he continues, is actually an innovation in language, one that allows us to make new connections between familiar things and, in the process, to represent these things in a unified form:

> With the word "gravity," or the word "attraction," *used in a modified way*, Newton connected apples in an orchard with stars in heaven, a mammoth in a pitfall with waves high on the beach. Till he spoke we had no word connecting every incident in nature by thin lines of likeness, thin as the lines of force but stronger than steel.
>
> Unlike one who uses a pattern ready made for him Newton had to cut out a pattern in order to show connections in a whole which no one had ever apprehended as a whole. We now are given the conceptions of gravity and of energy. Newton developed the conception of attraction and with it presented the power of the distant.[11]

By forging "thin lines of likeness," retroduction creates a unified field of inquiry; it shows connections in a whole that had not previously been apprehended *as* a whole.

9. By which I mean the law that states that the force of attraction that every body in the universe exerts over every other is an amount proportional to the product of the masses divided by the square of the distances.

10. See Charles Coulston Gillispie, *The Edge of Objectivity: An Essay in the History of Scientific Ideas* (Princeton: Princeton University Press, 1960), 143–50.

11. Wisdom, *Philosophy and Psychoanalysis*, 253.

5.18   Now, suppose we compare these various examples from the physical sciences to Freud's discovery that certain psychical phenomena (dreams, hypnotic suggestion, parapraxes, etc.) are the effects of unconscious motivations. What can we learn by this?[12]

The concept of the unconscious, like the concept of gravity, connects phenomena in new ways; it, too, draws "thin lines of likeness" where previously there was only difference, and in so doing it allows us to make sense of what had formerly seemed senseless. In psychoanalysis, too, what is involved, for the most part, is retroductive reasoning, not inference; for, despite his claims to the contrary, Freud does not infer the reality of the unconscious from clinical experience or from the observation of particular psychological phenomena; rather, it is the concept of the unconscious that effectively defines—or represents—these phenomena *as instances of unconscious conflict*, that is, of repression, compromise, distortion, and so forth. In other words, the unconscious is inferred *retroductively*, as the condition for certain kinds of explanation in psychoanalysis. Moreover, Freud, like Newton, uses grammatical innovations in order to establish and set forth the theoretical connections between these various phenomena; in the very process of elaborating the theory, he modifies the meanings of various accepted words and phrases (e.g., "pleasure," "energy," "instinct," and "sexuality"), extending the application of these terms to include objects, acts, and events that were previously described very differently (e.g., the notion of "sexual" applied to activities that are neither genital nor related to reproduction). Through these innovations in language come new ways of seeing—and hence, of conceptualizing—familiar phenomena. The result—in psychoanalysis as in physics—is not simply the discovery of a new object ("the unconscious") but the creation of an entirely new field of inquiry, a new form of discourse (i.e., a new set of terms, syntaxes, images, and models), and a new method.[13]

The basic difference between Newton and Freud, it seems to me—and, more generally, between the process of retroduction as it occurs in the natural sciences and in psychoanalysis—is in the strikingly different

12. I am aware, of course, that these examples prove nothing in themselves and also that they are open to conflicting interpretations. I use them merely to suggest what I take to be a useful way of thinking about these issues.

13. Of course, Freud did not regard his description of the unconscious as an innovation in language, nor did he set out to redefine the concepts of sexuality, pleasure, and energy; rather, he *saw* certain phenomena as the expression of unconscious motivation, of unconscious psychical conflict and compromise; he *saw* phenomena as instances of sexuality, of pleasure, or of energetic relations that had not previously been seen in this way. In the course of elaborating his new vision, he created an entirely new set of concepts, a new rationality, and a new way of seeing the world—a new language game.

applications of their respective theories: in the natural sciences, theory is placed in service of prediction and control (corresponding to the discernable regularities within the natural world); in psychoanalysis, by contrast, the function of theory is primarily heuristic and, to the extent that it is placed in service of the aim of achieving mental health, therapeutic (in consequence, we might say, of the rich ambiguity and complexity of the human world). At the risk of oversimplifying, we might put it this way: in the natural sciences, an explanation tells us why certain natural occurrences and events *had to happen* (e.g., why the apple falls to the ground or planets move in elliptical orbits) by appealing to the appropriate physical law (the law of gravity); in psychoanalysis, on the other hand, explanation tells us what certain psychological events and patterns of behavior *mean* (e.g., why men marry—and sometimes do *not* marry—women who resemble their mothers, or why they resent their fathers) by appealing to the appropriate psychological law (in this case, the Oedipus complex). At the same time, of course, what we mean by "law" is very different in these two instances.[14] (The source of the plausibility of Newtonian theory lies in its usefulness in predicting the behavior of objects under certain conditions. The source of the plausibility of Freudian theory lies in the fact that it allows us to *make sense* of certain human activities and patterns of behavior; it provides a coherent, rational account of seemingly irrational behavior and speech.)

5.19   The process of retroduction, in both the natural and the human sciences, involves finding suitable modes of representation for observed regularities or patterns of activity, modes of representation that are generally expressed in the form of "laws" but that, I would like to suggest, are actually more of the order of grammatical recommendations. To see how this is so, let us briefly consider what we mean by "laws" in the physical sciences and, more specifically, what is implied

14. Commenting on Freud's conviction that "determinism applies to the mind as truly as to physical things," Wittgenstein offers the following observation: "This is obscure because when we think of causal laws in physical things we think of *experiments*. We have nothing like this in connection with feelings and motivation. And yet psychologists want to say: 'There *must* be some law'—although no law has been found. (Freud: 'Do you want to say, gentlemen, that changes in mental phenomena are guided by *chance*?') Whereas to me the fact that there *aren't* actually any such laws seems important" (LC, 42). In other words, in psychoanalysis, as in most areas of the human sciences, the data are too vague, the facts too ambiguous and overdetermined, to allow for the kind of prediction and experimentation that characterizes the natural sciences. This, then, is itself an important fact; it tells us something about the nature of human action as contrasted with the motion of objects, that is, about the different *grammars* we use in the description of human action, on the one hand, and the movement of objects, on the other.

in the accepted distinction between "laws" and "principles," on the one side, and "hypotheses," on the other.

As they occur in the natural sciences, laws are a particular kind of grammatical—which is to say, purely formal—statement. Like rules, they tell us, not how things are, but how they *should be*; hence, they cannot properly be called true or false, probable or improbable (any more than the rules of chess are true or false). In themselves, laws tell us nothing about the world; rather, they express the form of certain regularities within it. As Wittgenstein puts it in the *Tractatus*, "The fact that it can be described by Newtonian mechanics tells us nothing about the world, but *this* tells us something, namely, that it can be described in the particular way in which as a matter of fact it is described" (T, 6.342). Laws do not describe the world; rather, they set forth the grammatical and logical *conditions* for such a description (and, to the extent that they are internally consistent and coherent, what might be called "a grammatical system"). These conditions are no more subject to verification—or falsification—than is, say, the metric system of measurement (though, like the metric system, they may or may not be suitable for particular purposes).

5.20   In order to clarify the point, let us look more closely at the way Wittgenstein develops this idea in the *Tractatus*. When Wittgenstein writes that "the law of causality is not a law but the form of a law," I take him to mean that the law of causality sets forth the conditions for a particular description of the world, conditions that are logical and a priori. (T, 6.32). "All such propositions," he writes, "including the principle of sufficient reason, the laws of continuity in nature and of least effort in nature, etc. etc.—all these are *a priori* insights about the forms in which the propositions of science can be cast" (T, 6.34). In other words, such propositions are, as it were, grammatical recommendations; they provide us with rules for the formation of scientific propositions; they tell us what kinds of statements do and do not have sense, what syntactical arrangements are and are not acceptable. Wittgenstein then goes on to elaborate this idea with the help of a now famous illustration, one that pictures the relation of a scientific system to the world as like that of a network of meshes, or screen, to an irregular picture on which it is superimposed. I quote the passage at length:[15]

15. Note that all square-bracketed words and comments as well as all emphases, are my own, not Wittgenstein's.

> Newtonian mechanics . . . imposes a unified form on the description of the world. Let us imagine a white surface with irregular black spots on it. We then say that whatever kind of picture these [spots] make, I can always approximate as closely as I wish to the description of it by covering the surface with a sufficiently fine square mesh, and then saying of every square whether it is black or white. In this way I shall have imposed a *unified form* on the description of the surface. The form is *optional*, since I could have achieved the same result by using a net with a triangular or hexagonal mesh [rather than a square one]. Possibly the triangular mesh would have made the description *simpler*: that is to say, it might be that we could describe the surface more accurately with a coarse triangular mesh than with a fine square mesh (or conversely), and so on.

In other words, it could happen that there would be a greater degree of correspondence between the shape of the spots and the shape of the mesh in the case of the coarse triangular mesh than in that of the fine square one. Wittgenstein continues, "The different meshes correspond to *different systems for describing the world*"—that is, different *grammatical systems* with different prescriptions for how the world is to be described. Continuing from Wittgenstein:

> Mechanics determines one form of description of the world by saying that all propositions used in the description of the world must be obtained in a given way from a given set of propositions—the axioms of mechanics. It thus supplies the bricks for building the edifice of science, and it says, "Any building that you want to erect, whatever it may be, must somehow be constructed with the bricks, and with these alone."
>
> (Just as with the number-system we must be able to write down any number we wish, so with the system of mechanics we must be able to write down any proposition of physics that we wish.) (T, 6.341)

In the construction of a grammatical system, I place a *unified descriptive net* over the world, through which I can bring everything into a *unitary form*. The properties of this net are given a priori; that is, we know in advance for a particular net the form of the description it will produce. The kind of world description will therefore depend on the kind of net I choose, and if I choose various nets, I will produce various world descriptions: some nets will produce relatively "simpler" descriptions than others do, inasmuch as a relatively coarser mesh suffices for a given degree of precision. One world description—one of many possible such descriptions—is Newtonian physics.

Newtonian physics can perhaps best be understood, then, as a grammatical system, analogous to a set of coordinate axes, rather than as a set of substantial assertions about reality. There is an important difference between a statement like "Every body continues in a state of rest or uniform motion in a straight line unless acted on by some external impressed force" and the statement "Water always flows downhill, unless compelled to do otherwise." The latter is an empirical generalization; the former, on the other hand, is a definition of what the terms "body," "action," and "external impressed force" are supposed to *mean*.[16] In contrast to the empirical generalization—which pertains to the behavior of a specific object (i.e., water)—the empirical law sets forth the grammatical conditions for the description of any object whatsoever; it defines what will, according to this system, be called body, action, and so forth.

It would be misleading to say of Newtonian mechanics that it is either true or false, correct or incorrect, since such judgments can properly be made only on the basis of appeals to evidence, or states of affairs. As the *condition* of any possible description of the physical world, the system of Newtonian physics is not itself open to confirmation or disconfirmation through appeals to evidence; on the contrary, it determines what will count as evidence.

Thus, Wittgenstein arrives at the conclusion that Newtonian physics as such tells us nothing about the world—except that it can be described in this way (or, we might say, the world is such that Newtonian physics *has an application*):

> And now we can see the relative position of logic and mechanics. (The net might also consist of more than one kind of mesh: e.g., we could use both triangles and hexagons.) The possibility of describing a picture like the one mentioned above with a net of a given form tells us *nothing* about the picture. (For that is true of all such pictures.) But what *does* characterize the picture is that it can be described *completely* by a particular net with a *particular* size mesh.

> Similarly the possibility of describing the world by means of

16. I borrow this example from Max Black, *A Companion to Wittgenstein's Tractatus* (Ithaca, N.Y.: Cornell University Press, 1964), 347. For further discussion of these general points, see esp. 354–61.

Newtonian mechanics tells us nothing about the world: but what does tell us something about it is the precise *way* in which it is possible to describe it by these means. We are also told something about the world by the fact that it can be described more simply with one system of mechanics than with another. (T, 6.342)

That the world can be so described is important, but the description itself is properly neither true nor false; rather, it is judged useful or not, according to the prevailing standards, interests, and needs of the scientific community. (This becomes a problem, then, not for science or philosophy but for the sociology of science.)

5.21   In science, the problem is always to determine the *scope*, or range of applicability, of a given law, rather than its truth or the conditions under which it can be accepted as true. In this respect, too, a law is like a rule: by setting forth a form for descriptions, a law implicitly sets out certain semantic and syntactical rules; it tells us what can and cannot be done in language; it determines which syntactical and semantic combinations are acceptable and which are not. The only problem, then, is to determine when the law applies and when it doesn't.

Once again, an illustration may be helpful.[17] Suppose there is a rule against walking on the grass in the commons area of the university. One can ask, then, whether this rule applies to everyone equally or only to certain persons—that is, whether it applies to both students and faculty, whether it applies to persons who want to sit for a while rather than merely take a short cut, and so forth. Thus, one can make statements *about* the rule that can properly be judged either true or false (e.g., "The law applies only to students"), but one cannot sensibly ask whether the rule *is itself* true or false. So, too, with scientific laws: one can legitimately ask whether it applies to this particular case, to this event or to that state of affairs, under these conditions, and so forth; but it makes no sense to ask of a rule, Is it true? (Unless, of course, in asking this we really mean to be asking, Does it have an application?)

5.22   We have said that the statement of a law almost always involves grammatical innovations of some sort, changes in linguistic usage that may come either through introducing a new terminology or through the invention of new syntactical and semantic rules. What exactly is involved here? What does it *mean* to say that laws change grammar?

17. I take this example from Toulmin, *The Philosophy of Science*, 79, though I have changed it slightly.

In the first place, laws typically introduce *new terms* into the language of science, terms that may themselves become subjects for further research. Indeed, much of what goes under the name of "observation," in both the natural and the human sciences, is often simply a working out of the grammatical implications of these terminological innovations, an exploiting of the grammatical resources of the language set forth in the form of observational statements or factual propositions. Second, to the extent that they are accepted, laws set forth new rules of grammar; that is, not only do they introduce new technical terms for scientific descriptions, they also set forth new rules for the use of previously existing terms and phrases—what Stephen Toulmin has described as a language shift.[18] Thus, the development of geometrical optics required a movement from regarding light and shade as primitive phenomena, things to be accepted and left unexplained, to seeing them as common effects of something else, namely, light, but "light" now defined and understood in a new way, as traveling from the sun to the objects lit by it. As Toulmin notes, "This step involves learning to speak and think about phenomena in a new way, asking questions which before would have been unintelligible, and using all the words in our explanations— 'light,' 'travel,' 'propagated,' 'intercept' and the rest—in quite novel and unexpected senses."[19] Later, of course, we come to accept these grammatical extensions as natural, perhaps even to the extent of forgetting that they ever had to be made.[20]

18. See Toulmin, *The Philosophy of Science*, esp. 12–13, 35–36, and 43. In the course of his discussion of the notion of a language shift, Toulmin recounts the following illustration from Wittgenstein: "Suppose . . . that a physicist tells you that he has at last discovered how to see what people look like in the dark, which no one had ever known before. Then you should not be surprised. If he goes on to explain to you that he has discovered how to photograph by infra-red rays, then you have a right to be surprised if you feel like it. But then it is a different kind of surprise, not just a mental whirl. Before he reveals to you the discovery of infra-red photography, you should not just gape at him; you should say, 'I do not know what you mean' " (13–14). For a highly intelligent criticism of this general approach to the question how laws function in science, see Ernest Nagel's review of Toulmin's book in *Mind* 63 (1954): 403–12.

19. Toulmin, *The Philosophy of Science*, 36.

20. In *The Structure of Scientific Revolutions* (Chicago: University of Chicago Press, 1962), Thomas Kuhn makes roughly the same point, arguing that conversion to a new paradigm is largely a matter of adopting "a new way of speaking." He notes, for example, that those who called Copernicus mad because he proclaimed that the earth moved were in fact not entirely wrong, for indeed part of what they meant by "earth" was fixed position. Their earth, at least, could not be moved. Correspondingly, Copernicus's innovation was not simply to move the earth. Rather, it was a whole new way of regarding the problems of physics and astronomy, one that necessarily changed the meaning of both "earth" and "motion." (See *The Structure of Scientific Revolutions*, 149–50.)

Laws change grammar: they not only provide a new conceptual terminology for the description and representation of phenomena, they also—at least implicitly—set forth new rules for how language is to be used. When we accept a law as true, we effectively extend the boundaries of meaning in language.

5.23 Laws function as *modes of representation*, not as premises from which deductions are made. It is for this reason that what counts as a discovery in the natural sciences is generally *not* the detection of a previously unknown regularity but the construction of a "new form" for interpreting and representing relations between already familiar things (although such a new form will, of course, very often bring new things to notice).

Laws allow us to represent observed regularities among phenomena; they provide conceptual patterns in which phenomena appear intelligible. Laws are thus *internal* to the form of representation, not something that is imposed on phenomena from without. As Wittgenstein puts it, "The laws of nature are not outside phenomena. They are part of language and of our way of describing things; you cannot discuss them apart from their physical manifestation" (L II, 79). Laws are not a yardstick we lay against the world; rather they are the system of measurement through which the world has height, length, and breadth. Laws are manifested through the description of phenomena; they are *shown* in the form of representation.

5.24 We may distinguish laws in science from both *principles* and *hypotheses*. Like laws, principles are internal to the logic of a particular mode of representation. Principles, too, belong to grammar and not to the world.

In the logical hierarchy of a science, principles belong to the lowest, or most fundamental, level; laws belong to the middle level; and hypotheses belong to the upper level. Principles are foundational for the practice of a science; a challenge to a principle is, therefore, much more radical than a challenge to a law. Abandoning Snell's law, for example, would amount to a major change in the practice of geometric optics; but abandoning the principle of the rectilinear propagation of light would

---

It is interesting to note that Wittgenstein uses the same example to make a similar point in one of his lectures: "Sometimes a scientific language produces an obsession and a new language rids us of it. . . . Something may play a predominant role in our language and suddenly be removed by science, e.g., the word 'earth' lost its importance in the new Copernican notation. Where the old notation had given the earth a unique position, the new notation put lots of planets on the same level" (L II, 98).

be, in effect, to abandon geometric optics altogether. Because it is itself *grammatical* rather than factual, there is no body of theory against which the proposition "Light travels in straight lines" can be set; rather, it is, as it were, *built into* the mode of representation. "The place of Snell's law is *within* geometrical optics. It holds a fairly fundamental place there, but nonetheless it is still inside the discipline. The principle ᵗhat light travels in straight lines, however, is *not* within geometrical optics, save in a very special sense. The principle is, rather, *built into* the very geometrical mode of representing optical phenomena."[21] Hence, in contrast to a law, a principle stands or falls with the field of inquiry that it at once defines and undergirds; both the principle and the practice must be accepted or rejected *as a whole*. (The same point can be made about certain foundational statements within the human sciences, and particularly about the basic principles of psychoanalysis.)

5.25   In contrast to both laws and principles, *hypotheses* are empirical, or factual, propositions, statements that are subject to verification. They are statements about the ways, the situations, and the circumstances in which laws are to be applied. Hypotheses will be judged either true or false, correct or incorrect, according to the facts.

The distinction between laws and hypotheses, while both real and important, is nonetheless a fluid one. In practice, it may happen that hypotheses, once demonstrated to be fruitful, become laws; in other words, under certain conditions, an empirical proposition may become a rule of grammar. For example, as Toulmin writes, "We might ask 'Is Snell's *hypothesis* true or false?', meaning 'Have any limitations been found to the application of his formula?' But very soon—indeed as soon as its fruitfulness has been established—the formula in our hypothesis can be treated as a *law*, i.e. as something of which we can ask not 'Is it true?' but 'When does it hold?' "[22] When this happens, the hypothesis becomes part of the framework of optical theory; it is no longer subject to verification but rather is treated as a standard, a norm of expression.

How do we decide what kind of statement we are dealing with? In one of his lectures, Wittgenstein points out that our choice between calling a particular statement a law and calling it a hypothesis is, in a sense, arbitrary:

> Suppose that a planet which according to a certain hypothesis describes an ellipse does in fact not do so. We should then say

21. Norwood Hanson, *Perception and Discovery: An Introduction to Scientific Inquiry*, ed. Willard C. Humphreys (San Francisco: Freeman, Cooper, 1969), 337.
22. Toulmin, *The Philosophy of Science*, 79.

that there must be another planet, unseen, acting on it. It is arbitrary whether we say our laws of orbit are right, that we merely do not see the planet acting on it, or that they are wrong. Here we have a transition between a hypothesis and a grammatical rule. If we say that whatever observations we make there is a planet nearby, we are laying this down as a rule of grammar; it describes no experience. We may then be forced to make a queer alteration. We would have to model everything else to account for it.[23] (YB, 70)

Nonetheless, a distinction can and should be made between the *hypothetical* and *established* parts of a given scientific discipline, one that bears on the fact that all scientific theory is "logically stratified," or shows a logically hierarchical structure. Thus, statements at one logical level have a meaning only within the scope of statements, already accepted as established, at the level below.[24] (For example, in geometrical optics, questions about the validity of certain terms [e.g., "refractive index"] will only have meaning in the context of the law to which they ultimately refer [e.g., Snell's law].)

The terms "established" and "hypothetical" are thus understood by reference to the (logical) distinction between those parts of a science which are *taken for granted* in order to state working problems and those which are *actually being put into question*. Of the former, established statements, there are, moreover, two different kinds: first, general laws of nature, and second, statements about the scope and conditions of these laws. Both of these kinds of statements may be legitimately called empirical.

5.26   Laws, principles, and the grammatical systems they set forth are, as it were, antecedent to truth. Generally speaking, those which are found practical are retained, whereas those which are impractical are rejected (usually with the mistaken judgment that they are "false"). In fact, however, the rejection of a grammatical system is like the rejection

23. Think of Freud's theory of unconscious thoughts as the conceptual equivalent of the unseen planet in this example, that is, as phenomena postulated according to a grammatical rule rather than based on observation. But notice, too, that there is this one important difference: the idea of "unconscious thoughts" represents a grammatical innovation, whereas that of "unseen planet" does not. (Recall the disanalogy between "seen" and "unseen" cause, on the one side, and "conscious" and "unconscious" thought, on the other.)

24. See Toulmin, *The Philosophy of Science*, 84, and Hanson, *Perception and Discovery*, 331–44.

of a standard of length; it makes no sense to call this standard true or false, but only practical or impractical.[25]

5.27   This distinction between empirical propositions, or hypotheses, on the one hand, and accepted grammatical statements, on the other, is illustrated beautifully in Wittgenstein's famous metaphor of the river and the riverbed in *On Certainty*:

> It might be imagined that some propositions, of the form of empirical propositions, were hardened and functioned as channels for such empirical propositions as were not hardened but fluid; and that this relation altered with time, in that fluid propositions hardened, and hard ones became fluid.
>
> The mythology may change back into a state of flux, the river-bed of thoughts may shift. But I distinguish between the movement of the waters on the river-bed and the shift of the bed itself; though there is not a sharp division of the one from the other.
>
> But if someone were to say "So logic is an empirical science" he would be wrong. Yet this is right: the same proposition may get treated at one time as something to test by experience, at another as a rule of testing.
>
> And the bank of that river consists partly of hard rock, subject to no alteration or only an imperceptible one, partly of sand, which now in one place now in another gets washed away, or deposited. (OC, 96–99)

There are, in particular, two aspects of this metaphor to be noted: first, that grammatical propositions "channel" empirical propositions (i.e., they determine what is and is not empirically possible), and second, that grammatical propositions are essential to—or "internal to"—the formation of concepts. "The limit of the empirical," as Wittgenstein says elsewhere, "is *concept-formation*" (RFM, 237).

5.28   The attempt to justify grammatical conventions or a grammatical system by an appeal to facts or to experience is inevitably circular, since

25. This, of course, is generally characterized as the "instrumentalist," as opposed to the "realist," conception of scientific theory, and I adopt it here for a specific purpose. At the same time, I don't deny that it is possible to give sense to the opposite, realist account—for what we have here, it seems to me, is not two conflicting theories about how concepts function in science but two grammatically incommensurable accounts of that function (comparable to the old debate between realism and idealism in philosophy).

what is represented is itself determined by grammar. "Grammatical conventions cannot be justified by what is represented," Wittgenstein writes in *Philosophical Remarks*, for "any such description already presupposes the grammatical rules" (PR, 9). As he puts it in "The Yellow Book," "We cannot say of a grammatical rule that it conforms to or contradicts a fact. The rules of grammar are independent of the facts we describe in our language." And he adds, "To say that a grammatical rule is independent of facts is merely to remind us of something we might forget" (YB, 65).

5.29   It belongs *essentially* to science—which is to say, it belongs to the *logic* of scientific inquiry—that certain things are not and cannot be legitimately doubted, for it is only our acceptance of certain truths as both unquestioned and unquestion*able* that allows us to judge other things as true or false, correct or incorrect. "If I want the door to turn," Wittgenstein writes, "the hinges must stay put" (OC, 343).

5.30   So, too, in psychoanalysis certain propositions are foundational; such propositions cannot be justified by appeals to facts but must simply be accepted. Some of these propositions belong to common experience and conventional grammar (viz., general propositions about human behavior and symbolism, about the mind, about the nature of human drives and motivations, etc.—propositions, in other words, that are really no more than extensions of a commonsense psychology); other propositions, however, are peculiar to psychoanalysis and constitutive of its grammar (e.g., propositions about unconscious psychical contents and intrapsychical conflicts and propositions that relate contemporary psychical acts to infantile prototypes). These propositions are not subject to verification or falsification; they are neither true nor false, but remain nonetheless indispensable.

For psychoanalysis, these propositions are the hinges on which the door must turn.

5.31   Of course, there are hypotheses in psychoanalysis, statements that can properly be judged true or false, among which the most important are generalizations based on more or less common explanations of individual behavior, especially in the ascription of motives. One might say, for example, that P acted out of hatred for his father or that Q acted out of jealousy; on the basis of repeated instances, one might also hypothesize that most men in circumstances similar to P's, who behave as P behaved, are likewise motivated by hatred for their fathers; or one might go on to hypothesize, again on the basis of repeated instances, that certain fantasies are associated with the different motives, that there are, for example, typical themes that might be described as Oedipal that generally accompany these motives. All of these statements are subject to verification or falsification and can therefore legitimately be called hypotheses. (Note, however, that even at the level of hypothesis, psychoanalytic statements are not based on observation, for whether a particular instance of behavior is motivated by hatred is, finally, something that cannot be determined by observation, but only by avowal and interpretation.)

5.32 Similarly, if I say that Freud extends the meaning of the term "sexual" in his description of childhood sexuality, this is certainly true, but this fact alone does not exhaust the nature of his discovery, for there is also a sense in which children *really are* far more sexual than we formerly believed—that is, before Freud taught us to recognize sexual behavior in children. (But now suppose we ask, How do we distinguish here between what belongs to language and what belongs to fact? How do we *know* that children are sexual? How do we go about trying to answer this question?)

It is not the fact that Freud extends the meaning of particular words that is important, but rather that, in doing so, he *makes connections* that change our way of looking at things. Freud extends the meaning of "sexuality" to include activities that were not previously thought to be sexual; in the process, he establishes a *continuity* between early infantile sexual activities (sucking, biting, defecating, etc.) and later mature ones (kissing, caressing, etc.). By expanding the meaning of sexuality, Freud is able to find a common explanatory basis for both infantile and adult—as well as normal and pathological—sexual activity; in other words, as he himself puts it, "this enlargement [is] rewarded by the new possibility of grasping infantile, normal and perverse sexual life *as a single whole*" (TEA, 243–44). This changes how we look at things, changes our conception of what certain kinds of behavior and symbolism *mean*. (Psychoanalysis is largely a matter of drawing just such analogies.)

Now, suppose we ask, What is the nature of this connection? Is it true? and so forth. The answer to these questions is deeply embedded in the way we actually use language, which is to say, in our linguistic practices, in what we *do* with words. (The important thing is that when Freud claims that psychoanalysis has demonstrated that children are sexual or that sexuality is different from genitality, we need to ask, How, exactly, did it do this?)

5.33 The transition from *hypothesis* to *law* in psychoanalysis corresponds roughly to the movement from statements about unconscious motives ("*P* unconsciously hated his father")—and explanations in terms of unconscious motives ("*P* dreamed of killing *X* because . . .")—to statements about the supposed psychical mechanisms that render these motivations unrecognizable, that is, explanations in terms of mechanisms of distortion. (Recall, however, that the distinction between hypothesis and law is not exact and is constantly subject to change; it might be argued, for example, that the Oedipus complex, which now effectively functions as a law, was once a hypothesis.)

Finally, *principles* in psychoanalysis are represented primarily in the statements of the metapsychology, in those statements, in other words, that describe the necessary conditions for the practice of psychoanalysis as such, that is, the general class of propositions that refer to the structure, function, and properties of the mind, including (1) the proposition that all psychical acts are purposive; (2) those propositions that refer to or describe a *dynamic* unconscious; (3) those propositions that refer to or describe the distinction between primary and secondary processes; (4) propositions about the general nature of the drives, or instincts; (5) propositions descriptive of intrapsychical conflict; and (6) those propositions that refer contemporary psychical acts and events to infantile prototypes. These statements are, as it were, the *metalanguage* of psychoanalysis; they are grammatical and paradigmatic: statements that are axiomatic rather than factual, statements whose only function is to provide a form of representation—or grammatical system—for the description of facts.

(Abandoning Freud's seduction theory would doubtless amount to a major change in the practice of psychoanalysis; but abandoning the principle that all psychical acts are purposive, or that certain acts are unconsciously motivated, would be, in effect, to abandon psychoanalysis altogether.)

5.34   None of this is meant to imply, then, that "facts" and the accumulation of evidence are irrelevant to judgments concerning the truth of psychoanalytic theories (any more than facts are irrelevant to the theory of evolution—or, in a different way, to musical theory); but in psychoanalysis the relation between fact and theory is far more tenuous, more "eccentric," and, in consequence, much less decisive than it is in the natural sciences.[26]

26. Consider, for example, the question whether there is a causal relation between one's experience of toilet training and one's character. One wants to say that empirical studies ought to yield a confirmation or refutation of the theory. The problem is, however, that the correlation that Freud suggests is too loose and ambiguous to allow decisive testing. (For instance, although strict toilet training might lead to an anal character, it might also lead to the opposite; there is no way to determine in advance which will be the case). Moreover, given the

(Did Freud demonstrate the pervasiveness and strength of libidinal drives, or merely teach us to see certain kinds of behavior—previously believed to be unrelated to sexuality—as libidinally motivated? How would we decide this question? To what "facts" could we appeal? It is not that facts are irrelevant here; it is only that they are highly ambiguous and context dependent. We cannot deal with facts until we have clarified the grammar of the language in which those facts are set forth.)

5.35   In every case, we need to ask, What kind of verification are we seeking when we ask of psychoanalytic statements that they be shown to be "true"? (There are different kinds of verification, just as there are different kinds of truth.)

---

complexity of causal factors involved, no single cause can ever be sufficiently isolated to allow any accurate evaluation of its etiological significance.

6

EXPLANATION AND GRAMMATICAL INNOVATION IN PSYCHOANALYSIS:

The Metapsychology of Dreams

6.1 Returning to the Freudian theory of dreams, we are now ready to consider the proposition "The unconscious is a necessary assumption for the explanation (interpretation) of dreams." What does this statement mean? With this question, we move to the very core of psychoanalysis and of the significance of Freud's discovery.

"We have constructed our theory of dreams on the assumption that the dream-wish which provides the motive power invariably originates from the unconscious," Freud writes in *The Interpretation of Dreams*, "an assumption which, as I myself am ready to admit, cannot be proved to hold generally, though neither can it be disproved" (ID, 598). At first glance, this statement seems odd. Certainly, insofar as dreams are obviously not conscious constructions, it is hardly an assumption to say that they are produced unconsciously, or that they "originate from the unconscious." Where else could they come from? Indeed, it is part of what we mean by the term "dream" that it refers to something we do not consciously create or control. Moreover, if the statement is meant to refer to the meaning of a dream, this meaning, too, can only be "unconscious." For if the dream is in fact a psychical construction, if it is a phenomenon of mental life *capable of being interpreted*, then once again it must be the product of something other than the conscious mind (since its meaning, in *this* sense, is obviously not immediately transparent).

But suppose we allow, for the moment, that Freud's real point lies elsewhere, that it lies not in the descriptive distinction between what is conscious and what is unconscious but rather in the dynamic relation between what he conceives as two distinct spheres of psychical activity, *the* conscious and *the* unconscious. Suppose, in other words, his point is really *explanatory* rather than descriptive. What matters, then, is not that the dream wish is merely unconscious (which is true by definition) but that it is unconscious *and active*, that it both provides the "motive power" for the dream and behaves according to laws that are discontinuous with those of conscious psychical life. Understood in this way, what is "unconscious" is not only "outside conscious control" but also *qualitatively different from* consciousness; it is governed by an entirely different set of principles. It would then make sense to ask about the character and implications of *this* distinction.

Ernest Jones was perhaps the first to point out that Freud's real discovery is not the unconscious as such but rather the systematic distinction between "primary" and "secondary" processes, from which the notion of the unconscious *as an explanatory category* is subsequently derived:

> Careful students have perceived that Freud's revolutionary contribution to psychology was not so much his demonstrating the existence of an unconscious, and perhaps not even his exploration of its contents, as his proposition that there are two fundamentally different kinds of mental processes, which he termed primary and secondary respectively, together with his description of them. The laws applicable to the two groups are so widely different that any description of the earlier one must call up a picture of the more bizarre types of insanity.[1]

When Freud claims that the dream wish "belongs to" or "arises from" the unconscious, what he means is that the formation of dreams must be described in terms of a certain logic—a set of rational or metarational

---

1. Ernest Jones, *The Life and Work of Sigmund Freud* (New York: Basic Books, 1953), 1:397–98. The discovery of this basic dichotomy between primary and wish-fulfilling processes of thought, on the one hand, and secondary, rational processes, on the other, is contemporaneous with Freud's first formulation of his theories of dreams and neurotic symptoms. In a letter to Wilhelm Fliess (February 19, 1899), he writes, "Reality—wish fulfillment—it is from these opposites that our mental life springs" (*The Complete Letters of Sigmund Freud to Wilhelm Fliess, 1887–1904*, trans. and ed. Jeffrey M. Masson [Cambridge: Harvard University Press, 1985], 345). Nor is this surprising, since the theory of two types of mental functioning is built into the method of interpretation itself (where it appears in the distinction between patent and latent).

principles—which is entirely different from that of our ordinary, every-day consciousness, and that it is only by postulating two irreducibly heterogeneous sets of psychical processes, each governed by radically different laws, that we can actually *explain* the dream work, that is, the process of the "distortion" or "transposition" (*Entstellung*) of the dream thoughts into the manifest content. In other words, the description of the different mechanisms of the dream work (condensation, displace-ment, etc.) proceeds from the assumption that these operations belong to a second, logically irreducible system of thought, one that cannot be immediately assimilated to any of the known functions of consciousness. "The dream-work is not simply more careless, more irrational, more forgetful and more incomplete than waking thought," Freud writes elsewhere; *"it is completely different from it qualitatively* and for that reason not immediately comparable with it" (ID, 507). "Conscious" and "unconscious" are thus *systematic*, rather than purely descriptive, designations.

Before proceeding, consider a few preliminary questions: First, do we really *need* a "mechanism" to explain the formation of dreams? Couldn't dreams be explained very differently, according to principles other than those of physics, hydraulics, and so forth? (For example, we might explain them, as Lacan does, in terms of certain linguistic functions, or according to principles of communications theory, or whatever.) Sec-ond, why do we need to *explain* the formation of dreams at all? Does the explanation of dreams—their origin, function, and so forth—contribute to our ability to *interpret* them? (Here I find myself wanting to say both No! and Of course! as if both of these possibilities made some sense. If we didn't know what dreams were, how would we know how to interpret them?) Third, and perhaps most important, how do we know that this description of two different systems of thought actually refers to something "in the mind," or "psyche"?[2] That is, couldn't it be the case that the various processes Freud describes here as belonging to "an unconscious mind" are in fact merely aspects of his own interpretive procedures—that they are, in other words, simply ways of *representing* those procedures and their conditions—and that the distinction between "primary" and "secondary" processes can be best conceived, therefore, not as a substantive division between two separate spheres of psychical activity, but rather as a kind of methodological recommendation, a statement about the way in which dreams, as irrational phenomena, are

2. Should "mind" and "psyche" be distinguished here? Does the psyche, like the mind, have a "within"? (Again, I am grateful to Judith van Herik for making me aware of this as an important but still too neglected issue.)

rendered rational? For how can we distinguish here between what belongs to the mind and what belongs to the method? By what criteria can we differentiate "internal" from "external," "psychical" from "methodological"? *Is* the unconscious mind something internal? (Is the unconscious internal in the same way that my organs are internal? If not, then how?)

6.2 It is this disjunction between two radically different kinds of psychical processes, primary and secondary, that requires the movement from a purely descriptive to a systematic understanding of the unconscious, one that allows the possibility of explaining dreams as the products of *intrapsychical conflict*. It is this movement that constitutes Freud's true conceptual innovation in the field of psychology. For it is in the use of the term "*the* unconscious," as a noun designating a psychic locality in which "ideas" or "representatives" reside, that Freud goes beyond ordinary usage to invent a new psychological terminology and, with this terminology, a new way of conceptualizing human behavior and experience.[3]

The unconscious is a necessary assumption for the interpretation of dreams, according to Freud, because it is only by means of this assumption that we can account for the fact of "distortion" in dreams, because it is only by perceiving the mind as a system of dynamically interrelated

---

3. Freud himself was well aware of the distinctiveness of his theory, even if he was perhaps misled about its nature and implications. Comparing his own conception of the unconscious to that of other psychologists and philosophers before him, Freud writes: "The new discovery we have been taught by the analysis of psychopathological structures and of the first member of that class—the dream—lies in the fact that the unconscious (that is, psychical) is found as a function of *two separate systems* and that this is the case in normal as well as in pathological life. Thus there are two kinds of unconscious, which have not yet been distinguished by psychologists. Both of them are unconscious in the [purely descriptive] sense used by psychology; but in our [dynamic] sense one of them, which we term the *Ucs.* is also *inadmissible to consciousness*, while we term the other the *Pcs.* [the system 'preconscious'] because its excitations . . . are able to reach consciousness" (ID, 614–15). In other words, what is unconscious for Freud is not simply latent but dynamic; it has real, discernible effects in consciousness. Thus, from a systematic point of view, "the unconscious" (used as a substantive) is specifically conceived as an explanatory concept; it refers to those mental contents—wishes, affects, ideas, and so forth—that are not only absent from consciousness but actively repudiated, or *repressed*. It is repression that establishes a *barrier* to consciousness and thereby defines the topological division of the psychical into two systems of thought, conscious (*Cs.*) and unconscious (*Ucs.*)—each with its own particular characteristics, functions, and laws of operation—conceived metaphorically as hierarchically differentiated "regions" within the mental apparatus. Hence, as Freud later expressed it, "in the descriptive sense there are two kinds of unconscious, but in the dynamic sense only one" (EI, 15). The word "dynamic" here refers to the basic modes of conflict by which not only dreams but all other so-called pathological phenomena are produced.

forces that dreams and related phenomena become "scientifically" comprehensible. The language of the unconscious, of repression and its cognate terms, is essentially a language descriptive of these relations.

6.3   Understood in this way, the unconscious is more than just a "connecting term," something that allows us to interpolate hidden processes and meanings; it is also—and more significantly—a category of explanation. It refers to an entire system of forces and meanings within which particular psychological phenomena or events have sense, one that is not only structural but temporal. The unconscious effectively internalizes origins; it creates a space in the mind where all the antecedents that have an explanatory function are located. The concept of the unconscious is a way of accounting for the fact that these antecedents are at once unknown and yet simultaneously present. In the simplest possible terms, we might say that it explains both the manner and the sense in which "things are not what they seem" in our inner life (in particular, that we are far more motivated by infantile wishes and fantasies than we are inclined to think).

6.4   "Should we say, then, that the unconscious really does exist, after all? that there is something external to which this word corresponds?" Of course, we *can* say this, but we may not want to.[4] In any case, we should be aware of the distinctive sense in which we use "exist" here. For it sounds as if, in stating, "The unconscious exists," we were setting forth a factual proposition, something that might be judged "true" or "false" according to the facts, whereas I want to say that this and similar propositions are *internal to the logic* of psychoanalytic theory and that they are not, in principle, subject to independent confirmation or falsification.

To repeat: it belongs to the logic of psychoanalysis that this and related propositions must be accepted; such acceptance is the condition for engaging in the practice that psychoanalysis represents. (Or we might say, The unconscious is not a fact, but a form of notation, something that belongs intrinsically to our method of representation, something that allows us to organize a number of disparate facts. Does a form of notation "exist"? To answer either yes or no is equally misleading.)

Statements that no observation or experience will refute are statements of grammar. We might say, In order for dreams to be interpretable

4. "Say what you choose, so long as it does not prevent you from seeing the facts," Wittgenstein writes. "And when you see them there is a good deal you will not say" (PI, 1:79).

according to the Freudian method, there *must* be an unconscious such as Freud describes. But this "must" is a logical must, not an empirical one, in the same way that gravity *must* exert a force proportional to the mass of the object or light *must* travel in straight lines or time *must* be irreversible. "What looks as if it *had* to exist, is part of the language," Wittgenstein writes in the *Investigations*. "It is a paradigm in our language-game; something by which comparison is made. And this may be an important observation; but it is none the less an observation concerning our language-game—our method of representation" (PI, 1:50).

The statement "The unconscious exists" is, as it were, paradigmatic, not factual: it expresses a *rule* for the use of language (saying, in effect, that the term "the unconscious" has an application), rather than describe an object.

6.5   Hertz argued that if some object did not obey his laws, there must be "invisible masses" to account for this fact. Similarly, Freud claims that the construction of dreams and other psychological phenomena can only be explained by reference to "unconscious psychical processes." Both statements have an identical function and status: namely, they provide norms of expression that allow us to construct certain kinds of explanations. As Wittgenstein puts it, "They enter into language and enable us to say there *must* be causes" (L II, 16). Whenever we say that something *must* be the case, we are using a norm of expression, laying down a rule of grammar—"as if one were to say 'Everybody is really going to Paris. True, some don't get there, but all their movements are preliminary' " (L II, 16).

"Dreams are the product of unconscious psychical conflicts": this is exactly equivalent to saying, "Everyone is really going to Paris, but only a few are aware of this fact."

6.6   At one point in the *Investigations*, Wittgenstein talks about the philosopher who holds certain views about privacy of experience, the reality of sense data, and so forth, and he compares this to the discovery of what he calls the "visual room," that is, the room that *only I* can see, the actual "content" of my visual experience. "When I look around me, when I *see* the objects in this room: I see THIS, and THIS is mine and mine alone." But what does it mean to say this? In what sense do I *possess* what I am talking about here? Indeed, what are these words *for*? For if it is *logically* impossible for someone else to have this, then what sense does it make to claim that it is mine?

The "visual room" is the one that has no owner. I can as little
own it as I can walk about it, or look at it, or point to it.
Inasmuch as it cannot be anyone else's it is not mine either. In
other words, it does not belong to me *because* I want to use the
same form of expression about it as about the material room in
which I sit. The description of the latter need not mention any
owner, in fact it need not have any owner. But then the visual
room *cannot* have any owner. "For"—one might say—"it has
no master, outside or in." (PI, 1:398)

This idea of the visual room, as it is described—and perhaps even
experienced—by the philosopher, might well be called a "discovery";
that is, it might be regarded as the result of finding something that was
previously hidden, or unknown. What one discovers in this case,
however, is not a new fact about the world but rather, in Wittgenstein's
words, "a new way of speaking, a new comparison; it might even be
called a new sensation" (PI, 1:400). The typical mistake—the philosopher's mistake, as well our own when we try to think abstractly about
these things—is to believe that one's discovery here is not a conceptual
and grammatical, but factual, equivalent to the discovery of a new,
quasi-empirical object of some sort.

You have a new conception and interpret it as seeing a new
object. You interpret a grammatical movement made by yourself
as a quasi-physical phenomenon which you are observing.
(Think for example of the question: "Are sense-data the material
of which the universe is made?")
   But there is an objection to my saying that you have made a
"grammatical" movement. What you have primarily discovered
is a new way of looking at things. As if you have invented a new
way of painting; or, again, a new meter, or a new kind of song.
(PI, 1:401)

We invent a new mode of expression, a new concept and syntax, yet we
think we are observing an object; only by clarifying our use of language
can we distinguish what belongs to grammar from what belongs to facts,
and how much of both is a product of our way of looking at things.

6.7   With this in mind, look once more at Freud's various descriptions
of the unconscious: in virtually every case, he sounds as if he were
observing an objective phenomenon, as if he were describing "a quasi-
physical object" and not simply setting forth a new concept and a

form of representation. But the discovery of the unconscious, like the discovery of the visual room, is far more grammatical than factual, a product less of observation than of construction—a new way of seeing; like a new style in painting or a new song, *it redefines the boundaries of sense, but without altering the facts of the world.* (Reading Freud—looking at things from a metapsychological perspective—is like looking at images in a mirror: everything is inverted and just slightly distorted, so we never quite know what direction we are facing.)

6.8 Paraphrasing Wittgenstein, we might say that those who deny the existence of the unconscious attack a form of expression as if they were attacking a factual statement; those who affirm it do so as if they were stating an empirical fact, something demonstrably real with tangible efects (PI, 1:402).[5] Both, however, are equally confused.

6.9 "But *isn't* the unconscious an object? Doesn't Freud intend that we should conceptualize the unconscious *as an object* and, further, that his explanations are intelligible only insofar as we are capable of thus conceptualizing it?" With these questions, we are in danger of reentering the circle. In order to escape, we need to ask again, What *kind* of an object is it? and to recognize that the answer to *this* question can only be found in grammar.

6.10 In his more theoretical writings, Freud frequently recurs to such expressions as "psychoanalysis shows us . . ." or "experience has taught us . . ." or "in psychoanalysis there is no choice but to assert that . . ." and so forth; what follows these expressions, however, is almost invariably not a statement of fact, as Freud would have us believe, but a *grammatical remark.* Freud writes, for example, "We have learnt from psychoanalysis that the essence of the process of repression lies, not in putting an end to . . . the idea which represents an instinct, but in preventing it from becoming consciousness" (U, 166). This is, however, not a hypothetical statement but a definition: it tells us what the term "repression" *means.* Or: "[The physician] . . . learns that the conscious effect is only a remote physical result of the unconscious process . . . and moreover that the latter was present and operative even without betraying its existence in any way to consciousness" (ID, 612). But how does the physician "learn" this? Is there anything in nature of his or her experience that directly conveys this fact? anything that *demands* that he or she infer it? No, statements about unconscious ideas, affects,

5. Cf. BlB, 57–58.

intentions, and the like, are not based on—nor do they refer to—any objective, independently verifiable facts; rather, they set forth certain *grammatical rules* ("a thought is called 'unconscious' when . . ."); and rules, as I have said, need no demonstration.

"Experience shows that it is so." But how does experience do that? For the statement to which it points itself belongs to a particular *interpretation* of that experience.[6] Wittgenstein asks, "Does experience tell us that a straight line is possible between any two points? Or that two different colors cannot be in at the same place?" (RFM, 224). (We almost want to say, *imagination* tells us these things.)

Does experience teach us that repression consists in keeping an idea from consciousness? Or even that repression occurs, as Freud describes it? No, the role of such statements is paradigmatic, rather than hypothetical; they belong to *the means of representation*, not to the object represented. We do not observe repression; rather, we interpret in accord with—or in terms of—the concept of repression; that is, we *see* certain kinds of behavior and symbolism *as* instances of repression.[7] (To repeat: grammatical conventions cannot be justified by describing what is represented, since any such description already presupposes the relevant grammatical rules; thus, to appeal to the fact of repression as evidence for the existence of the unconscious is like pointing to a red object as evidence for the existence of the color "red.")

6.11   Asked by what methods and means an instinct is brought under the control of the ego, Freud responds, "We can only say: '*So muss denn doch die Hexe dran*!' ['We must call the witch to our help after all!']"[8]— the Witch Metapsychology. Without metapsychological speculation and theorizing—I had almost said 'fantasizing'—we shall not get another step forward" (ATI, 225). If grammar is, as Wittgenstein defines it, "a battle against the bewitchment of our intelligence by means of language [*ein Kampf gegen die Verhexung unsres verstandes durch die Mittel unserer Sprache*]" (PI, 1:109), then the metapsychology is indeed the "witch" of psychoanalysis, for the metapsychology is, as it were, the

6. Cf. OC, 130, 145.

7. This does not mean that observation plays no role in psychoanalysis; we might say that the analyst "observes" repression, resistance, unconscious compulsions, and the like, no less than the physicist "observes" the effects of gravity. But the analyst, like the physicist, sees from a particular perspective and according to a particular theoretical framework, and we can no more appeal to these observations as evidence for the truth of the existence of the unconscious than the physicist can appeal to the fact of falling bodies as evidence for the truth of the law of gravity.

8. Goethe, *Faust*, part I, scene 6.

philosophical underpinning of psychoanalytic theory, its logical and conceptual foundation, and hence prone to all sorts of misconceptions and false imaginations. But these imaginings are merely the shadow play of our words; properly understood, the metapsychology is no more mysterious, no more "bewitched," than the method on which it is based.

6.12   To begin with, it should be clear by now that the metapsychology is not a description of an empirical entity, a mental apparatus, or a mechanism of some sort; rather, it is, or should be, *a description—in a mental, or psychological, idiom—of the conditions necessary for the possibility of interpretation.* In other words, the metapsychology describes the mind as it *must be* in order for dreams, parapraxes, symptoms, and so forth, to have meaning, that is, in order for these phenomena *to be interpretable* along the basic lines that Freud sets out.[9] ("But if the interpretation is *true,* aren't we justified in claiming that the mind is like this *in fact*?" Of course! But then we are back to the question "What makes an interpretation true?" And to this question there is no one good answer. Once again we are in danger here of appealing to the theory itself to prove the theory true.)

Freud says, in effect, If I interpret *x,* I get *y.* The question of metapsychology is, then, What must the mind be like to secure this relation between *x* and *y*? And the answer will take the form of a statement about the formal and grammatical conditions for interpretation, set forth in the language of psychology. For example, in order for dreams to be meaningful in the way that Freud describes, the following minimal conditions must be met:

9. In more technical language, we might say that the metapsychology is the elaboration of the a priori—but *contingent*—conceptual conditions for the possibility of a certain kind of intelligibility. Once again, as an a priori construction, no "fact," no experience of any sort, can possibly disconfirm, or provide a counterinstance to, the propositions by which it is constituted. These propositions are paradigmatic, not hypothetical. (What Kant intends by the notion of "synthetic a priori judgments" is analogous to what Wittgenstein means by "statements of grammatical rules," or paradigmatic propositions. In both cases, the function of these propositions is to provide a "system," or general conceptual framework, wherein certain facts, or certain kinds of experience, are possible.)

In broad terms, I think my point here is consistent with the statement by Marshall Edelson that the metapsychology is not "a set of propositions about the world" but "*a set of proposals for building theory.*" Edelson adds, "These proposals prescribe primarily which theoretical concepts should be chosen to specify just those properties and relations of entities in the domain of interest to psychoanalysis that are used to explain the facts psychoanalysis is committed to explain" (Edelson, *Hypothesis and Evidence in Psychoanalysis* [Chicago: University of Chicago Press, 1984], 79).

1. There must also be some place within the mind where memories, ideas, feelings, and the like, are, in a sense, "stored."
2. There must be something that counteracts the tendency of a thought—especially a wish or wishful fantasy—to become conscious, something like what Freud describes as "repression."
3. There must be something in the mind that prohibits the direct expression of wishes in dreams—namely, the censor.
4. Since a dream is clearly not the conscious creation of the dreamer, we must attribute its creation to some other agency, one that is unconscious yet retains causal efficacy in relation to consciousness.
5. Since it seems that I sometimes act under the compulsion of desires or wishes that are not recognizably "my own"—desires, in other words, that I disavow—it is reasonable to presume that it is the same unconscious agency that is active in both waking and dreams. (But now notice: if I attempt to describe my experience of this compulsion—or my observation of a similar compulsion in others—as being like a second, unconscious will of some sort, it makes no sense to turn around and ask whether this will actually *exists*.)

The metapsychology, we might say, is not a matter of speculation but of *deduction*, albeit a deduction that is, as it were, a priori and transcendental rather than causally inferential; that is, it is a deduction from the method of interpretation toward its *conditions*, rather than from a given phenomenon to its causes. The sum total of these propositions, once deduced and systematized into a more or less coherent whole, constitutes a form of representation, or "grammatical system."

The metapsychology is a theoretical description of the basic elements of the psychoanalytic form of representation.

6.13   But now look at how Freud approaches this question. In the famous chapter 7 of *The Interpretation of Dreams*, where—after more than five hundred pages of text—he finally confronts the necessity of setting forth a theoretical description of the psychology of the dream processes, Freud begins with the following pronouncement (and I choose this passage almost at random):

> Before starting off along this new path, it will be well to pause and look around, to see whether in the course of our journey up to this point we have overlooked anything of importance. For it must be clearly understood that the easy and agreeable portion

of our journey lies behind us. Hitherto, unless I am greatly mistaken, all the paths along which we have travelled have led us toward the light—towards elucidation and fuller understanding. But as soon as we endeavor to penetrate more deeply into the mental process involved in dreaming, every path will end in darkness. (ID, 511)

Now, what kind of explanation could Freud possibly be looking for here? What is this "mental process" that Freud wants to bring to light? How do we know about it? Where should we locate it? If what is involved in describing the psychology of dreams is, as I am suggesting, simply the elaboration of a model to account for their construction, then why all the poetic images and rhetorical flourishes? Why the allusions to long, difficult journeys, to a descent from light into darkness, and so forth? Again, what can Freud have in mind here, if not a certain *picture* that his own use of language suggests to him, a picture that reiterates itself each time he attempts to describe the shifting image of the psyche that plays before him? (I want to show that certain aspects of Freud's theory cannot be coherently applied, or, put differently, that a certain picture of the unconscious cannot be coherently applied.)

To repeat: the proper question of the metapsychology is, What must the psyche be like in order for dreams to be meaningful in the way that psychoanalysis describes? The answer, then, will take the form of a statement of "the conditions for the possibility of . . ." Freud, however, makes two basic mistakes in dealing with this question: the one philosophical, the other methodological. First, instead of asking about the conditions for interpretation and attempting to define them, Freud asks, in effect, What is the mind—or psyche—*really like*? as if it were something that was available for description independent of those methods and procedures he uses to explore it; he then succumbs to all sorts of metaphysical and skeptical temptations (e.g., describing the unconscious as the essence of the psyche, as something deep and inaccessible, as the real but unknowable psychical reality, as a cauldron of seething excitements). Second, having framed the question in this way, Freud then proceeds to try to answer it as if it were a factual and empirical issue rather than—as it must be—a grammatical one; hence, he constantly appeals to certain kinds of evidence, or inferential reasoning, when these are actually quite beside the point. (Freud thinks of the mind on the analogy of the brain; but the mind is not an empirical entity, and it is not subject to the same laws that apply to empirical, or physical, objects. The grammar of "mind," in other words, is very different from the grammar of "brain.")

6.14   Freud takes propositions such as "There is an unconscious" and "Repression plays an etiological role in the formation of neurosis" and "Sexual drives and their transformation determine character type" as factual, when they are actually grammatical; that is, they express, not empirical facts, but rules for the use of language.

6.15   "Does this mean that these propositions are not empirical?" No, it seems to me that it makes sense to say that these propositions are empirical, though not factual; that is, they refer to objective, empirical realities, but their role is such that they are not subject to confirmation or falsification (similar, in this respect, to the statement "This is my hand" or "Time is irreversible," but with a more restricted application). The fact that I can easily imagine alternative descriptions of psychological realities suggests that metapsychological propositions are not grammatical in the way that, say, certain mathematical propositions are grammatical; but they are nonetheless *paradigmatic* for the practice of psychoanalysis. (If you want to play *this* game, *these* are the rules.)

If I say of a proposition that "this can be imagined otherwise," this ascribes the role of an empirical proposition to it; a proposition that cannot be *imagined* other than as true has a different function from one for which this is not the case.

6.16   In the application he makes of the metapsychology, Freud repeats what Wittgenstein regards as the fundamental error of metaphysical philosophy: namely, he imagines himself to be stating a matter of fact, or describing a state of affairs, when he is in fact introducing *new grammatical rules* and *a new way of seeing* psychological realities. (What distinguishes metapsychology from metaphysics is its usefulness in representing the *conditions* of a particular practice.)

6.17   Freud conveys the impression that he is describing an object (viz., the psychical apparatus, or the unconscious), when he is actually setting out a form of representation. He gives us the idea that he is actually *observing* these various psychical agencies and processes and attempting to find an adequate description of their true nature and relations. After a time, we think we see them, too. (The situation is similar to that of an optical illusion, only here the illusion is conceptual rather than optical; to paraphrase Wittgenstein: we construe our own grammatical movement as a quasi-physical object that we are observing.)

6.18   Freud typically confuses *norms of representation* with the *objects represented*. (We say that an empirical statement may become a norm for description. Is there also a point at which the rule may become a factual proposition? That is, if I adopt the psychoanalytic way of seeing, would it be correct to say that realities such as the unconscious, repression, and defense may actually become things I perceive—just as the physicist perceives motion as the effect of gravity? Why should we want to insist that Freud's way of expressing himself is "wrong"?)

6.19   In what sense is it correct to say that psychoanalytic—and especially metapsychological—propositions are descriptive of mental states, and in what sense is it not correct? To answer this, we would need to look at what we ordinarily mean by "mental states" and to compare this to what Freud intends in his descriptions of the mind, or psyche. This quickly becomes a very complicated business. For although it is doubtless true that much of what Freud describes has to do with mental states in the usual sense of the term (e.g., the notions of pleasure, pain, sensation, and affect), much else clearly does not (e.g., the notions of unconscious pleasure, unconscious pain, and unconscious affect). It seems that there is no direct correlation between the ideas of pleasure and pain, on the one side, and those of unconscious pleasure and unconscious pain, on the other; but, then, neither is there a complete disjunction. (If unconscious pleasure could not eventually be traced to our commonsense notion of pleasure, and indeed to the *experience* of pleasure, then the term would lose all meaning.)

Here we come back to the idea that such statements are "eccentrically" related to experience; there is no direct route from the grammar of first-person experiential statements to the grammar of unconscious mental events, but there *must* be some connection, however distant or oblique. (Ask yourself, At what point does the idea of unconscious pleasure translate into something you can actually experience? What if this translation *never* occurred?)

6.20   In constructing scientific theories—particularly in the human sciences—we are like the little children Wittgenstein describes in one of his notes: we scribble marks on a piece of paper at random and then want to know "What's that?" "It happened like this," Wittgenstein writes; "the grown-up had drawn pictures for the child several times and said: 'this is a man,' 'this is a house,' etc. And then the child makes some marks too and asks: what's *this* then?" (CV, 17).

We invent terms like "unconscious pleasure" and connect them in various and complicated ways to other parts of our theory without seeing clearly what *kind* of application they have or indeed whether they have an coherent application at all.

The problem here is largely due to our failure to comprehend grammatical differences between different disciplines and modes of inquiry and especially, perhaps, to our fascination with the ideals and methods of the natural sciences. In psychoanalysis, we are trying to construct a more or less comprehensive explanation of human motivation, but even our conception of what an explanation is—not to mention the terminology we use to set forth such explanations—derives primarily from the natural sciences. Hence, we are constantly coming up with expressions whose meaning and applications we do not fully understand. We say, for example, that a dream is caused by a wish, but we fail to notice the profound differences between our use of the concept of "cause" here and other uses (e.g., rain is caused by certain atmospheric conditions, or the wind caused the door to swing shut). Again, it is not that our formulation is "wrong" but rather that we do not comprehend its grammar. Thus, we are inevitably led to draw the wrong kinds of inferences from it.

We have to see that the language of ideas and motivations, or the description of human action, has a very different grammar from the language of physical causes and effects, or the description of the natural world, and that we have yet to devise an adequate way of translating from one language to another.[10] (This, of course, is a very old problem,

10. It is striking that some critics of the humanistic (hermeneutical) approach to psychoanalysis—for example, Adolph Grünbaum—have the idea that those who advocate this approach are somehow "ideologically motivated," that, as Grünbaum puts it, they are trying to insulate the study of human ideation from "the evidential burdens of the standard empirical sciences" ("Précis of *The Foundations of Psychoanalysis: A Philosophical Critique*, ed. Peter Clark and Crispin Wright [Oxford: Basil Blackwell, 1988], 9). It seems to me, on the contrary, that proponents of the humanistic approaches—for example, Ricoeur and Habermas—are simply more sensitive to the grammatical difficulties that attend the effort to conjoin ideas, motivations, emotions, and so forth, on the one hand, and accepted scientific languages, styles of thinking, and practices, on the other. At the very outset of the Freud book, Ricoeur frames the problem precisely in terms of our inability to construct "a comprehensive philosophy of language," one that would allow us "to account for the multiple functions of the human act of signifying and their interrelationships." Continuing, he writes, "We have at our disposal a symbolic logic, an exegetical science, an anthropology, and a psychoanalysis and, perhaps for the first time, we are able to encompass in a single question the problem of the unification of human discourse. The very progress of the aforementioned disparate disciplines has both revealed and intensified the dismemberment of that discourse. Today the unity of human language poses a problem" (*Freud and Philosophy: An Essay in Interpretation*, trans. Denis Savage [New Haven: Yale University Press, 1974], 3–4). Although one may resist Ricoeur's proposed solution to this problem—in the subordination of all of other forms of discourse to speculative philosophy—one can scarcely fault his definition of it. (For Ricoeur's most extended attempt at a constructive philosophical resolution of this problem, see *The Rule of Metaphor: Multi-Disciplinary Studies in the Creation of Meaning*, trans. Robert Czerny [Toronto: University of Toronto Press, 1977], esp. "Study 8: Metaphor and Philosophical Discourse," 257–313.)

dating at least from the methodological inquiries of Durkheim and Weber; yet it sometimes seems that we are no nearer a solution now than they were.)

6.21   Freud observes various common phenomena (dreams, symptoms, certain kinds of irrational behavior, etc.), sees a relation between them, and then attempts to formulate an explanation of these phenomena in terms of a single explanatory category. The question then becomes, for Freud, how to construct a theory that will encompass *all* of these phenomena within a *single* mode of explanation. How to organize, in a single, unified conceptual framework, the perception of these many different relations.

In trying to answer this question, Freud used the language that was most familiar, most generally respected, and most immediately available to him: namely, the language of Newtonian physics, hydraulics, and so forth. Freud *believed* that in doing this he was simply transposing Newtonian mechanics—in the form of contemporary neurology—from the physical to the mental realm, on the assumption that the laws that apply to relations between objects must apply equally to relations between ideas and affects.[11] In fact, however, what Freud did in this process was to create an entirely new form of description and representation, a new set of grammatical prescriptions for bringing the description of "the psyche" into a unified form.

6.22   In one of his lectures Wittgenstein comments at some length on the foundational role of the notion of causality in what he calls the Newtonian "style of thinking":

> Physicists . . . can't deduce their axioms from causality, but think it may be done some time. There is nothing extraordinary in this, but they never really dream of causality in this sense. Yet, in a different way, causality is at the bottom of what they do. It is really a description of their *style of thinking*. Causality stands with the physicist for a style of thinking. Compare in religion the postulate of a creator. In a sense it seems to be an explanation, yet in another it does not explain at all. Compare a workman who finishes something off with a spiral. He can do it so it ends in a knob or tapers off to a point. So with creation.

11. Nothing is more instructive in this regard than a close reading of the "Project for a Scientific Psychology," *Standard Edition* 1:295–397. Freud was not trying to construct a hermeneutics or critical theory; he was trying to construct a natural science of the mind.

God is one style; the nebula another. A style gives us satisfaction; but one style is not more rational than another. Remarks about science have nothing to do with the progress of science. They rather are a style, which gives satisfaction. "Rational" is a word whose use is similar. (L I, 103–4; emphasis added)

One style of thinking is neither more nor less rational than any other, not because any form of rationality is as good as any other, but rather, because what we mean by "rational" is less foundational than the style of thinking. Like physics, psychoanalysis, as a style of thinking, represents a comprehensive way of organizing our experience and perceptions—in this case, our *inner, personal experience*—comparable to the way in which Newtonian physics organized our experience of the *outer, physical world*. The concept of "repression" is the analogue, in Freudian psychology, to the concept of "causality" in Newtonian physics; it both belongs to that conceptual style and, in an important sense, defines it. Moreover, as a new mode of thinking, a new style of introspection in Western culture, psychoanalysis cannot really be judged either more or less rational than other, conceivable and actual alternative styles of thinking; the most we can say about it is that "it gives satisfaction." (Although there is some sense to this idea, it still *sounds* wrong.)

6.23   One game is neither more nor less rational than another: checkers is no more rational than bowling; chess is no more rational than croquet or golf (well, maybe golf). So, too, one language game is neither more nor less rational than another; indeed, in the case of a language game, the very concept of rationality seems not to apply. "You must bear in mind that the language-game is so to say something unpredictable," Wittgenstein writes. "I mean: it is not based on grounds. It is not reasonable (or unreasonable). It is there—like our life" (OC, 559). And elsewhere: "Something new (spontaneous, 'specific') is always a language-game" (PI, 2:224). Each language game has its own distinct set of rules, its own criteria for what is and what is not allowed. To call these rules "rational" would be to set up a realm of metarules by which the operative rules were themselves to be judged (as if you needed a rule to tell you when the rules applied).

6.24   Metapsychological concepts function to organize a certain domain of intelligibility in psychology and, by the same process, to extend the range of psychical facts. Their coherence is inseparable from a strategy of *objectification* that makes them irreducible to any description of conscious experience or, more generally, to first person descriptions of any kind.

"The more we seek to win our way to a metapsychological view of mental life, the more we must learn to emancipate ourselves from the importance of the symptom of 'being conscious,' " Freud writes, in his famous essay on the unconscious (U, 193). For psychoanalysis, the principle of coherence in psychical life exceeds the limitations of any given conscious—intentional or reflexive—perspective; it is in this sense *transcendental*. (Hence, the metapsychology cannot be assimilated to a psychology of consciousness.)

(I am trying to sketch out a new perspective on some of the long-standing conceptual problems that psychoanalysis generates; yet I continually find myself slipping back into the old perspective, asking the same tired questions and coming up with the same tired answers. It is as if the rut were so deeply driven into the road that one could only get out for moments at a time and then, with a bump and a jerk, fall into it once more.)

6.25   We should distinguish in psychoanalysis between what belongs to the form of representation and what belongs to a causal explanation, as it is usually understood. It is one thing to say, for instance, that dreams can be conceptualized as the product of a conflict between different psychical forces (providing a principle of intelligibility), another thing entirely to claim to have demonstrated what *causes* dreams (setting forth a hypothesis). The former will be accepted or rejected on grounds *other than* its correspondence to known or observable facts about dreams, grounds such as its usefulness, its simplicity, its internal coherence and symmetry; the latter, by contrast, refers to actual facts about dreams and the process of dream formation and therefore ought to be subject to certain (experimental) procedures of verification or falsification.

6.26   What Freud says about dreams has nothing whatsoever to do with the actual process of their construction, or their hypothetical causes, but only with their *meaning*. Freud does not explain why the dream occurred but proposes certain reasons, sets forth certain grounds, for its psychological relevance (which is part of why it is the dream *report* and not the dream itself, which is the object of analysis).

6.27   For better or worse, dream research is utterly irrelevant to the truth of the basic psychoanalytic claims. Psychoanalysis is not a theory about dreaming but a method for the interpretation of dreams. Moreover, it cannot be shown that dreams are meaningful, only that they are *interpretable* according to the method that Freud describes—and this because we do in fact interpret them!

6.28   What has the psyche, as Freud conceives it, to do with neurology? Does psychoanalysis *need* a neurological basis? What would be gained by it? Suppose such a basis were found, what then? Would psychoanalysis be *more true* than before? (With physiological data, one simply introduces another criterion for determining questions of truth.)

6.29   If the statements of the metapsychology are not factual but grammatical, then to deny the reality of the unconscious or to dispute the relevance of the metapsychology to the practice of psychoanalysis is not to disagree with Freud's view about certain matters of fact but instead to show ignorance of the meaning of the terms involved.

6.30   On the basis of the discussion to this point, let us now set out what might be called the representational structure of psychoanalysis (see Fig. 4, based on my earlier diagram of "the logical structure of

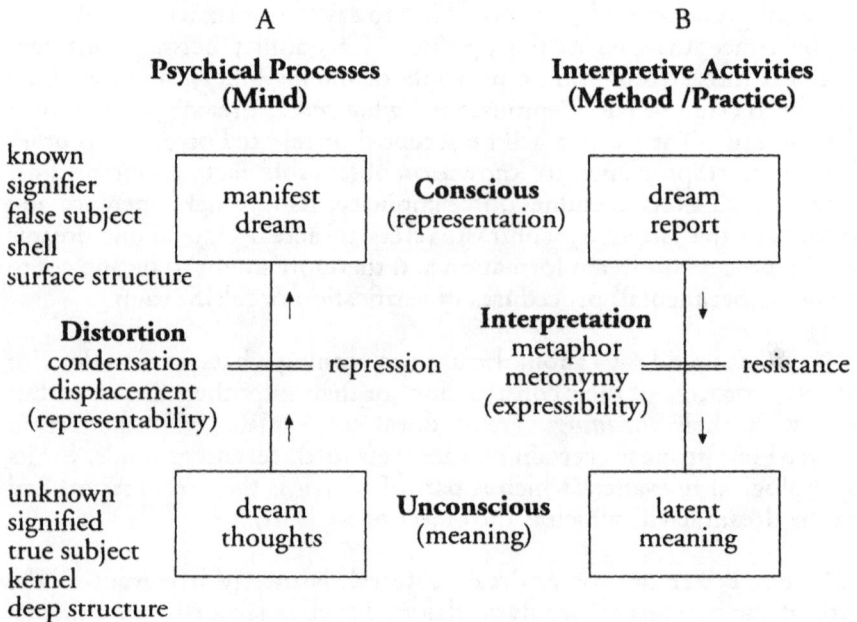

	A		**B**
	Psychical Processes (Mind)		**Interpretive Activities (Method /Practice)**

known
signifier
false subject
shell
surface structure — **manifest dream** — **Conscious** (representation) — **dream report**

Distortion
condensation
displacement
(representability) === repression === **Interpretation** metaphor metonymy (expressibility) === resistance

unknown
signified
true subject
kernel
deep structure — **dream thoughts** — **Unconscious** (meaning) — **latent meaning**

Fig. 4. Representational structure of psychoanalysis

dreams"). The general sense of the diagram should be more or less self-evident. On the left (axis A) is a depiction of the psychical processes involved in the Freudian theory of dream construction: the transformation of the latent dream thoughts into the manifest content of the dream via the various mechanisms of distortion, what Freud calls the dream work; on the right (axis B) is a depiction of the process of interpretation, one that, in Freud's view, is strictly parallel to the process of dream construction (interpretation *reverses* the dream work): the movement from the recounted dream (dream report) to its latent meaning through the various procedures of interpretation (i.e., free association, resistance, transference, etc.).

The two parallel axes, A and B, are intended to convey a reciprocal correlation between the different terms on each axis and, taken as a whole, between psychical processes, on the one side, and interpretive activities (speech acts), on the other; for example, what is described as condensation on axis A appears as metaphor on axis B, and so forth.

On the far left are various other theoretical correlates of the fundamental division between conscious representation and unconscious meaning in psychoanalysis. At the manifest (or conscious) level, for example, is the signifier, symmetrically opposed at the latent (or unconscious) level by the signified. (Of course, the terms correlated are not necessarily synonymous or interchangeable: for example, the concepts "known" and "unknown"—or "unknowable"—are not assimilable to the psychoanalytic distinction between consciousness and the unconscious.)

Finally, it should be emphasized that what the diagram depicts is a *representational* theory of mind or meaning; the dream, as a symbolic construction, or "psychical structure," *represents* a meaning. The dream is the signifier of a particular signified, and it is only for this reason that it is *meaningful*, that is, something that can be interpreted.

My question then is this: If the basic sense of the psychoanalytic theory of dreams can be laid out in terms of these two parallel processes, how, in fact, do we distinguish the one from the other? That is, how do we distinguish what belongs to the psychology of dreaming from what belongs to the method by which dreams are interpreted? If Freud tells us nothing about the actual process of dream formation or about events contemporaneous with the construction of the dream—its causes, conditions, mechanisms, and so forth—*which are independent of the process of interpretation,* then how can we even begin to answer this question? If the metapsychology is, as I am suggesting, grammatical rather than factual, then there are no criteria for distinguishing between what belongs to interpretation and what belongs to the actual process of dream construction, or between what belongs to the method and what belongs to certain mechanisms of the mind. *This distinction is itself, therefore, purely heuristic and methodological;* it belongs to the method of representation and not to anything factual or, in the usual sense, "objective."

This being so, there are two basic points to be stressed. First, this representational structure—the form of representation that is depicted spatially here—is internal to the logic of all specifically psychoanalytic statements about the nature of mind and meaning; it expresses the set of grammatical rules that define the sense and coherence of such statements; it establishes the logical, semantic, and syntactical possibilities within this particular discourse. (The statement "I cannot *know* the unconscious directly," for example, like the statement, "I cannot *know* your pain," expresses a grammatical impossibility, not a physical one; it tells us nothing about the facts of the matter, but only about how the term "the unconscious" is to be *used*.)

Second, there is in psychoanalysis—or among those who theorize about psychoanalysis—a persistent, almost compulsive tendency to ascribe certain properties, events, and causal relations to an "interior" aspect of the mind, or psyche (axis A), that more properly belong to the "external" activities of psychoanalytic practice itself (axis B). In other words, there is a tendency to conceive psychoanalysis on the model of the physical sciences and their relation to the objective world, and to picture the relation of method to object in terms of a naïve empiricism that has long since been displaced even in the natural sciences: to regard psychoanalysis as a positivistic science, with a definable method and a body of knowledge, whose distinctive object is the unconscious mind, just as the object of the physical sciences is the empirical world. By contrast, what I am saying here is that in psychoanalysis *there is no such clear separation of method and object* and that what psychoanalysis sets forth is not a hypothesis about the existence of subterranean mental activities, or the essence of the psychical, but a form for the representation of certain complicated relations between human needs, motivations, and intentions, on the one hand, and their symbolic expression, on the other.

We might say, What psychoanalysis describes as a mind, or psyche, is really *only its own interpretive procedures once more,* viewed, as it were, from a different level of theoretical abstraction—its own linguistic and rhetorical devices (especially metaphor and analogy) and specific aspects of the dialogical situation of analysis itself (especially the transference).[12]

12. It seems to me that Ricoeur is making a similar point when he writes the following: "Freud always tends to reverse the relations between theory, on the one hand, and experience

6.31   Freud wants to ground interpretation in the metapsychology, and the metapsychology in observable facts. But the metapsychology is actually derived ("deduced") from the practice of interpretation, and the validity of interpretation cannot be confirmed by appeals to observable evidence.

6.32   Ricoeur remarks on a number of occasions that it is the notion of *resistance* that makes psychoanalysis a *work* and prevents a characterization of the method as one of simple interpretation, or a "merely intellectual" understanding of the meaning of symptoms and other pathological phenomena. It is because we *want* to believe certain things about ourselves that the truth is so difficult to see and accept. But this does not mean that we are *fundamentally* deceived about ourselves or that distortion belongs *essentially* to the mechanisms of the mind. Nor is there any reason that we are forced to have recourse to a *picture* to explain why we find it hard to admit certain things about ourselves. (On the other hand, there is no reason we can't fashion such a picture, provided that we keep in mind that it *is* a picture.)[13]

In psychoanalysis, the mind is represented both as a text to be interpreted and as a system of forces to be manipulated. The former refers to the process of interpretation, the movement from manifest to latent meaning; the latter refers to the process of persuasion, the overcoming of resistances. As the work of interpretation is the inverse of the dream work, so the struggle against resistances is the inverse of repression.

What is described from one perspective as belonging to the *method* can be described from the other perspective as belonging to the *form of representation:* and if we reject the one, we also reject the other.

---

and practice, on the other, and to reconstruct the work of interpretation on the basis of theoretical models that have become autonomous. He thus loses sight of the fact that the language of the theory is narrower than that in which the technique is described. Next, he tends to construct his theoretical models in the positivist, naturalistic, and materialistic spirit of the sciences of his day" ("The Question of Proof in Freud's Writings," in *Hermeneutics and the Human Sciences*, ed. and trans. John Thompson [Cambridge: Cambridge University Press, 1981], 259).

13. Ricoeur argues, in defense of the economic model, that "man's alienation from himself is such that mental functioning does actually resemble the functioning of a thing" ("The Question of Proof in Freud's Writings," 261). Now, in one sense, of course, this is true, but the resemblance of such alienation to the "functioning of a thing" cannot be attributed to some independent source of evidence (e.g., the nature of mental functioning or the mind) but must be ascribed to the fact that *that* is how we do indeed construe it; for what would "actually" *mean* in this context? Again, the idea to be resisted is the notion that there are mental or psychical "facts" that transcend the language in which we express them and that adjudicate the correctness of our forms of expression.

6.33   One could say that dreams and symptoms, after analysis, invariably have reference to experiences of early childhood; but one could also say that the procedure of free association naturally leads the patient to recount memories and fantasies of early childhood (irrespective of the actual content of the dream or symptom). Similarly, one could say either that dreams and symptoms express sexual wishes or that the procedure or free association allows the patient to give free rein to sexual fantasies. Now ask yourself, To what could we possibly appeal in trying to decide which of these two ways of looking at things is the more correct one? How can we distinguish what belongs to the phenomenon as such from what belongs to the method?

6.34   To repeat: I am not saying that the metapsychology is "wrong," nor, more particularly, am I proposing any *revision* of Freudian language. For what would it mean to say that the metapsychological theory was "wrong" or "inadequate?" (What it clearly would *not* mean, first of all, is that Freud's metapsychological descriptions fail to correspond to the mind as we "know" it, for we have no access to a mind independent of some such description. The mind is not something we observe but the condition of our observations; the word "mind" refers not to a thing but to an organized system of habits, dispositions, capacities, tendencies, skills, and so forth.)[14]

   No, if we say that Freud's theory is inadequate, we can only mean that it is inadequate *to the analytic experience,* or to what we understand about ourselves through psychoanalysis, about those interests and motivations that psychoanalysis discloses. Well, then, is there anything in the analytic experience that cannot be accounted for in terms of the metapsychology? Now, ask, What would such a thing look like?

6.35   "In regard to *fundamental* discoveries," Freud remarked in 1917, "I have hitherto found nothing to alter" (IL, 246). Of course not! For regarding the *fundamental* discoveries there *can be* nothing to alter. The core concepts of the theory—that is, the notion of unconscious psychical processes, of resistance and repression, of infantile sexuality and the Oedipus complex, and so forth—are not subject to refutation or revision on the basis of further investigation. They do not rest on factually empirical grounds; they express, not facts, but *rules of representation,* rules of *grammar.*

   14. This applies as well to the notion of the psyche, though here the matter may prove more complicated (to the extent that the psyche, unlike the mind, is not confined to the sphere of the mental). In any case, it remains that "an 'inner process' stands in need of outward criteria" (PI, 1:580).

It is this—and not Freud's extraordinary genius—that explains why the metapsychology has never been superseded: it cannot be superseded because it is, in principle, unsurpassable. The theory might be judged inadequate only if we mistakenly believed that it ought to refer to *facts* rather than to the *conditions* of facts. (Of course, this is not to deny that an entirely *new* psychology might be devised, with different models and modes of explanation, different theoretical assumptions, interpretive methods, and so forth; but then we would be talking no longer about psychoanalysis but about something else.)

6.36   Instead of seeing condensation, displacement, and so forth, as laws governing unconscious processes, we can now view them as names for different interpretive strategies or as general categories for describing the ways in which an interpreted meaning deviates from the original text; instead of regarding them as the mechanisms by which the dream is constructed, we see them now as rules for the production of meaning.[15]

"Then Freud was wrong after all, at least to the extent that he thought he had *explained* the actual psychical processes by which dreams are constructed." Yes, this is true; but notice that it is not so much that the theory itself is wrong (though some aspects of that theory almost certainly are) as it is that Freud was wrong in the *implications* he derived from that theory. There is no reason for us to doubt, on the basis of this analysis, that the theory *works,* that it actually *does* give coherence and meaning to a large number of psychological and cultural phenomena; what we can—and should—doubt are certain of the implications Freud drew from his theory (e.g., about the nature and function of dreaming and about the relation of dreams to waking life), together with his own understanding of the significance of his discoveries (e.g., that dreams reveal our true wishes and desires and that dreams are structurally and functionally analogous to forms of cutural symbolism).

6.37   We might say, It is not so much that Freud is *wrong* in what he says as it is that *he puts things in the wrong light* (like the philosopher Moore when he says, "I *know* that that's a tree").

---

15. In general terms, as Kenneth Burke puts it, "condensation . . . deals with the respects in which house in a dream may be more than house, or house plus. And displacement deals with the way in which house may be other than house, or house minus. (Perhaps we should say, more accurately, minus house.)" (Burke, "Freud—and the Analysis of Poetry," in *The Philosophy of Literary Form: Studies in Symbolic Action,* rev. ed. [New York: Vintage Books, 1957], 233.) To this we might add that displacement operates by a principle of *contiguity* (or proximity); psychical intensity is displaced from one object or event to another by a principle of contiguity rather than similarity. Condensation operates by a principle of *substitution on the basis of similarity.* (Note that similarity is not *likeness* but a formal or thematic correspondence of some sort.)

6.38 We ascribe to the thing that which belongs to the method and means of representation: statements about the unconscious can be fully resolved into statements about the method of interpretation and the intrinsic limitations of pictorial representation (e.g., the impossibility of representing certain logical relations). In psychoanalysis, everything is fully displayed on the "surface," as it were—in the procedures it employs, in the activities it involves. There are no substrate occurrences. *Nothing is hidden.*

6.39 We may even want to say what Freud really discovered was a *method*, not a mind. The concept of "the unconscious" is a kind of summary designation for the different aspects of this method and its various procedures; it defines the interval between manifest and latent meaning, or—what amounts to the same thing—the interpretive procedures that lead from the former to the latter. The unconscious is a form of notation for the sum of these activities, their effects and their significance. (The unconscious, in other words, has primarily to do with meaning—and especially with the ways in which we now, in contemporary Western culture, go about the business of constructing meaning, of imparting meaning to our personal lives.)

(Yet if I say that the unconscious is, as it were, a purely functional concept, and not a substantive one, then it seems again that I am *contradicting* Freudian theory instead of clarifying its conditions.)

6.40 Freud frequently describes psychological phenomena that are perfectly familiar (perception, critical judgment, sexual attraction, guilt, etc.) in metapsychological terms (i.e., according to certain psychical agencies and mechanisms); then he turns around and uses the metapsychology to *explain* these phenomena. But the idea that the metapsychology *proves* anything about the nature and dynamics of these psychical processes is sheer nonsense; the notion of unconscious psychical processes and mechanisms—as a form of representation—is *deduced from* the procedure of interpretation; it cannot explain any more than is already built into it. (What would a model of planetary motions *explain* about these motions themselves? What does the diagrammatic representation of the principle of the rectilinear propagation of light *explain* about the intrinsic qualities of light?)

6.41 It is a commonplace among contemporary philosophers of science that language affects observation, that the nature of our grammatical system (terminology, syntax, logical relations) affects the nature of what we see; what is less generally recognized is the fact that much of what goes under the name of "observation" in science is actually a matter of drawing out the implicit resources of its grammar, that supposed observations are often merely extensions of terminology. This is especially true in the case of psychoanalysis, as Kenneth Burke has shown.[16] In fact, it is quite possible to "deduce" many of the key elements in Freudian theory, without any appeal to evidence or observation, merely by tracing out the grammatical implications of its basic terms.

Take, for example, the idea of "repressing," of "repression" (understood as a process, a gerund). If there is an activity of repressing, it follows that there must be something that acts as a *repressive agent*. This becomes what Freud calls censorship and, later, the ego. That is, the idea of "a repressive agent," or something that represses, belongs logically to the notion of repressing; it is implicit in the grammar of the concept of repression. (Freud says, in effect, There *must* be something that represses; but this "must" can only be a *logical* necessity, not an empirical fact.) Furthermore, if there is a repressive agent (something active), then there must be *something that is repressed* (something passive): these are the unconscious ideas, emotions, affects. Then, of course, there must also be a *scene*, or *situation*, in which "the repressing of the repressed by a repressor" occurs; this will be the boundary between consciousness and the unconscious—and so forth.

Or consider, once more, the term of "the unconscious" (understood as a place, a noun). To begin with, of course, the term "the unconscious" implies a direct counterpart, "the *conscious*." Then, since any pair of antithetical terms suggests the possibility of an intermediate term, it follows that there must be something like the *preconscious*. With three terms there arises the possibility of a spacial representation; instead of saying merely that repression *is* unconscious, we can situate the entire process *in* "the" unconscious, thus figuratively defining the unconscious *as a place*, or *scene* (the topographic unconscious). Next, by a logical extension of this spacial metaphor, we are bound to ask how unconscious processes can be brought *into* the realm of consciousness, that is, how a psychical content (idea, feeling, etc.) moves from one locale to the other. Then, because we believe that all such processes must finally be rooted in organic realities, we are led to believe that these elements, unconscious and organic, must be somehow related, or *associated* (though we will doubtless find it very difficult to explain just *how* they are related). (Or,

16. In two early essays, "Terministic Screens" and "Mind, Body, and the Unconscious," both included in *Language as Symbolic Action: Essays on Life, Literature, and Method* (Berkeley and Los Angeles: University of California Press, 1968). The analysis that follows is largely just a summary of Burke's major points.

we may be led to insist that they are, on the contrary, *disassociated*.) And so on.

Finally, note that it is because repression designates a *process* and the unconscious a *content* that *both* are required for the generation of the full range of psychoanalytic concepts. (It is for this reason—and *not* as a result of Freud's personal preference—that the Freudian terminology must be generated from *two* originating terms rather than one). See how far we are now from supposing that the fact of repression *proves* the existence of the unconscious or that the unconscious is *inferred* from its effects in consciousness!

6.42   Every statement about the unconscious—to the extent that it is meaningful—can be translated into a statement about the method of interpretation. We might even formulate this as a rule: A statement about the unconscious has meaning if, and only if, it can be translated into a coherent statement about the procedures of interpretation. (Note that this is, once again, a modification of the verification principle; it says that the meaning of certain kinds of theoretical concepts is equivalent to the method by which the object, or referent, of these concepts is *known*.)

To take an example, according to Freud, the unconscious system—or primary-process thinking—can be defined according to four distinctive characteristics: (1) it admits of no degrees of certainty or doubt and no forms of contradiction (the unconscious knows nothing of logic); (2) it is not temporally organized (the unconscious knows nothing of time); (3) it is regulated exclusively by the pleasure principle (the unconscious knows nothing of external reality); and (4) the libidinal energies that constitute it have relatively free mobility by comparison to conscious and preconscious wishes (in the unconscious, energy is not bound but free). Now, consider each of these statements in turn.

1. *In the unconscious there is no negation* (the unconscious knows nothing of logic). This means, roughly, there are no *logical* restrictions on the process of free association; the material uncovered in the course of an analysis—the ideas, wishes, fantasies, motives, and the like, produced in the process of free association and interpretation—may be mutually contradictory. (We are subject to conflicting motivations.)

2. *The unconscious is atemporal* (the unconscious knows nothing of time). This means there are no temporal restrictions on the process of association; the material uncovered in the course of an analysis may be very old, going back to the earliest days of

childhood. (We are subject to childish and infantile motivations.)

3. *The unconscious is regulated exclusively by the pleasure principle* (the unconscious knows nothing of external reality). This means there are no moral or external restrictions on the process of association; interpretation leads to wishes. (We are subject to wishful fantasies.)

4. *The unconscious is composed of free libidinal energies* (in the unconscious, energy moves freely). This means association and interpretation lead to multiple and mutually displaceable interests; as an object of erotic desire, virtually anything can be replaced by virtually anything else. (We are subject to changing desires.)

Similarly, with respect to practically all of the core tenets of psychoanalysis: to the extent that they are meaningful, they refer to some aspect of the method of interpretation, not to the observed behavior of autonomous psychical realities. The notion of "psychic determinism"—that is, the idea that every psychic event has a cause—can be translated into something like "All symbolic formations are capable of being interpreted." (And notice that if we say that every psychical act or event *must* be motivated, this is a statement of grammar, not an assertion of fact. Adducing examples avails nothing.) Or, to say that the meaning of a dream or some other symbolic construction is "overdetermined" means simply that there are any number of associations that can be made to each element within the dream and any number of interpreted meanings to be derived from the whole; interpretation is open-ended. And so on.

In short, whenever Freud makes a statement about the physical object, this statement should in principle be translatable into a statement about the method by which this object is supposedly known. If we cannot make such a translation (as in the case of many of Freud's statements about the construction of dreams), then the statement is at best misleading—and very probably irrelevant or meaningless.

6.43 Other of Freud's statements seem to confuse, not object and method, but representation and meaning. Ask yourself, for instance, How many of those features that Freud describes as belonging to the mode of representation in dreams or to primary-process thinking are actually characteristic of any attempt to represent ideas and logical relations pictorially? (E.g.: "There is no function of negation, or qualification, in dreams," or "The unconscious is comprised of purely images.")

There is no negation in dreams, not because of any quality intrinsic to dreams, but merely because negation is not something that can be pictorially represented; these specific features and limitations are not distinctive of primary-process thinking (thinking in images) but *belong to any form of pictorial representation*.

6.44   It has become popular among commentators to say that Freud's metapsychological descriptions are not literal descriptions of the mind but *metaphorical* ones. According to this reading, repression—the notion of "placing ideas at a distance"—is generally taken as the central metaphor around which various others are organized; thus, we have *textual* metaphors (e.g., translation, substitution, and overdetermination) interwoven with *energy* metaphors (e.g., repressing proper, cathexis, and displacement) to produce other, *mixed* metaphors (such as disguise and censorship), all thrown together to produce this wonderful fiction called psychoanalysis. In short, everything in Freud is metaphorical, and thus "outside of science"—including, and perhaps especially, the notion of the unconscious.

But it makes no sense to characterize a whole class of descriptions as "metaphorical" unless we can specify what a "literal" description would look like. What is it that we mean to deny when we say that Freudian language is "merely metaphorical"? If there is any sense at all to this claim, perhaps it is in marking the *grammatical* fact that descriptions of mind are not assimilable to descriptions of physical processes. But why should we ever think otherwise? Moreover, even if I say that what I mean by "energy" as applied to mentalistic, or psychological, concepts is significantly different from what I mean when it is applied to physicalistic ones, there is still no compelling reason to characterize the former as "metaphorical" and the latter as "literal." The real point is simply that we *use the terms differently in these two contexts*, though this does not mean that either use is more "proper" or more "literal" than the other.

6.45   Freud uses old words in new ways. We think, "He is using chess pieces and a chess board to play, not chess, but a game of his own." But the analogy is misleading. For Freud is playing not only a new game with the old pieces but *an entirely new form of game*, one in which both the *rules* and the constitution of the game are substantially different (like chess and checkers).

When Freud speaks of "unconscious ideas," for instance, is the word "idea" the same as our ordinary word? Does it *mean* the same thing?

Well, yes and no. It seems as if its meaning is *similar* to, but not identical with, what we ordinarily understand by the term.[17] (If the present work shows anything, it should show just how difficult it is to describe what this similarity consists in.)

6.46 "Do we really need a *mechanism* to explain the construction of dreams?" (Of course, we may just *want* such a mechanism, for reasons having to do with our own personal needs and habits. As Wittgenstein notes, whenever we encounter something puzzling, our first response is often to seek some mechanism behind it, some kind of comprehensible cause or nexus of causes.) Or, we might ask, In what sense, if any, does Freud actually *explain* dreams?

Well, suppose we begin by asking, What does it mean generally "to explain" something? There are, of course, many different theories about what an explanation really is and what a proper explanation ought to look like: for example, some would say that an explanation should tell us the *purpose* of things; others, that it should be given in terms of *laws of nature*; others, again, that it is really only a particular way of describing things; and still others, that genuine explanation must go beyond description to a general theory. For some, the aim of explanation is understanding; for others, it is the ability to predict and control. All of these differences of opinion reflect a dispute about what explanation "really" is, about what a "real" explanation ought to be, or about what we should call "an explanation."

Philosophical disputes of this kind are rarely fruitful, for we never seem to find the proper grounds for resolving them. How do we decide what an explanation *should be*, in advance of all other considerations? Instead of arguing about whether something is a real x, it is better to begin by asking what the word "real" means in this context. Is margarine *really* butter? Is the acorn *really* an oak? Is a brown bear *really* a grizzly? Is this substance, x, *really* a gas? or a liquid? Whether a is to be called a real x will usually depend on what one intends, or wants to achieve, by calling it so. The designation "real" or "actual" is most often used to mark things off that are in many respects like other things, but in important ways different.

---

17. In his essay on paradox and discovery, Wisdom describes three different reactions to statements such as those in psychoanalysis about the reality and effects of unconscious mental events—what he calls eccentric, or boundary-breaking, statements—none of which, he says, are adequate: (1) "It's impossible" (or "It *cannot* be true"); (2) "It's purely speculative and hence unprovable"; and (3) "It's only a new way of describing well-known phenomena." It would be possible to examine each of these alternatives with an eye to the ways in which they are correct and also incorrect (Wisdom, *Paradox and Discovery* [New York: Philosophical Library, 1965], 125).

Why should there only be *one* real, or legitimate, kind of explanation? Or only one legitimate use for the term "explanation"? Why not many? And isn't it in fact the case that we use the word "explanation" to describe many different activities and expressions. (I may explain the behavior of electrons under certain conditions, or I may explain to my best friend why I am depressed. These two kinds of explanations will be *very* different from each other—but why should either be viewed as "more correct" than the other?)

With respect to the question of the status of psychoanalytic explanations, the issue is not to argue whether such explanations are "real" explanations; rather, it is to discover the facts about differences between psychoanalytic and other kinds of explanation—assuming that there *are* differences—and then to determine how important these differences actually are in terms of their consequences. In other words, the point is not to provide a theory of explanation or to establish a standard definition but to look at what Freud *calls* "giving an explanation," to note the similarities and differences between this and other uses of the term. (The grammar of "explanation" in Freud: it is often said that psychoanalysis *explains* nothing, that it merely teaches us to *describe* differently. But everything turns here on what we mean by "explanation," or "giving an explanation," and this is not something that is decided in advance. Think of all the situations in which we use the term "explanation" with reference to things very different from scientific or hypothetical explanations!)

6.47 "Perhaps psychoanalysis is less a matter of *explaining* behavior than a matter of giving an order and representation to what we already, in some sense, know. In other words, it is a matter of making certain connections, drawing certain analogies, and so forth. (We adopt a psychoanalytic explanation not because it is demonstrably *true* but because it allows us to *make sense* of things; it responds to our need for rationality, sense, and coherence.)"

But even this seems too narrow. Why shouldn't we say that Freud does in fact explain dreams, parapraxes, symptoms—and even cultural institutions, like art and religion? The real point, however, is to see both the validity and the *limits* of those explanations. (There is no question, however, that much of what Freud puts forward under the guise of explanation is really only a restatement, in a language of occult events, of what we commonly observe and take to be characteristic forms of human behavior.)

6.48 Freud undoubtably possessed a certain genius for constructing unfalsifiable explanations, one that finds expression in both the economic and the genetic aspects of his theory. The concept of "ambiva-lence," for instance, effectively codifies any given interpretation *and* its opposite (a symptom or symbolic construction may be explained by reference to either conscious motive *a* or its unconscious opposite *b* or by any combination of the two, according the economic valence of each). Similarly, the concept of "the plasticity of the libido" is little more than the theoretical counterpart of the extreme flexibility of interpretation (anything can be a displacement for anything else).[18] In respect to the genetic aspect of the theory, the insistence on the etiological role of unconscious fantasy and phylogenetic inheritance in genesis of neurosis nullifies any attempt to ground explanation in an actual event (if event *a*, the efficient cause of the neurosis, did not actually occur, then the unconscious fantasy of the event, itself geneti-cally inherited, is sufficient to account for its occurrence). In other words, whatever meaning is acknowledged in the course of interpreta-tion can be provided with an explanatory basis (one that is situated, of course, in the unconscious), whether economic or genetic or both at once.

6.49   According to Freud, if the conflicts associated with the Oedipus complex are not resolved in childhood, they will return later in adult life. And if they do not return? Well, then Freud has only to claim that they have been resolved in the natural course of development, since such conflicts are, in his view, an indispensable part of the unconscious experience of every child. But on what, then, does the claim to universal-ity rest? Not on the memory of adults, since the experience is uncon-scious, or on evidence of certain psychological conflicts, since they may or may not emerge. No, when Freud claims that Oedipal conflicts *must* be part of every child's experience, this "must" is not based on any actual biographical or clinical data; it is not a generalization based on evidence, but, once more, a grammatical prescription. The Oedipal configuration is built into the theory as an essential and indispensable component; it serves to determine what meanings will emerge in the course of analysis and which of these interpreted meanings will be counted as relevant. ("Does this mean that the Oedipal problematic is *not* an essential part of Western culture?" Not at all: it means only that

18. To this we might add the tendency of the dream work to represent things by their opposites. Freud writes, "As a result of the fact that in the dream-work contraries coalesce, it is always left undetermined whether a particular element is to be understood in its positive or its negative sense—as itself or as its contrary." He then adds, frankly, "Here is a fresh opportunity for the interpreter to exercise an arbitrary choice" (IL, 228).

this question will be decided on grounds other than those which psychoanalysis itself can adduce.)

6.50 In psychoanalysis, "to explain" very often means "to contextualize," or "to place in context of a coherent narrative." To explain a dream, for example, is to situate within the life of the dreamer, to give it a place in the history of the dreamer and the dreamer's wishes, fantasies, anxieties, and so forth (a process of contextualization that follows quite naturally from the procedures of free association and interpretation). So, too, with neurotic symptoms: to explain a symptom is to give a sense in the context of the life history of the patient, to situate it in relation to certain antecedent events and fantasies. This is what Michael Sherwood describes as the *narrative commitment* in psychoanalysis: that is, the fact that even the designation of causes involves a logical commitment to a theoretical framework, or narrative, within which phenomena are considered no longer as independent entities but as "interrelated parts of a single unified process or sequence of events."[19]

Psychoanalytic explanations are narrative explanations to the extent that even generalizations based on causal connections contribute to the coherent narrative of the individual analysand, or the case study. Indeed, in the words of Paul Ricoeur, "all truth claims of psychoanalysis are ultimately summed up in the narrative structure of psychoanalytic facts."[20] (The process of analysis is essentially one of reconstructing a new and more adequate life history on the basis of the meanings interpreted through free association and the transference, a process in which both analysand and analyst are coparticipants.)

6.51 We might want to say that the Oedipal family romance is, as it were, the core narrative of Western culture. If so, then we might also say that the theory of the Oedipus complex is "true" insofar as it helps us to contextualize and to *make sense* of many actions that might otherwise seem senseless. When we say this, however, we mean that the theory of the Oedipus complex is true, not in the same way that the principle of the rectilinear propagation of light is true, but more as the myth of Oedipus itself is true (or as any number of other enduring myths are true): that is, it sums up something essential about ourselves in the story that it relates. Similarly, although the theory of repression is, like the

---

19. Michael Sherwood, *The Logic of Explanation in Psychoanalysis* (New York: Academic Press, 1969), 169.

20. Ricoeur, "The Question of Proof in Freud's Writings," 268.

theory of gravity, axiomatic and grammatical rather than hypothetical, its truth is of a very different kind; for the law of gravity provides the condition for conceptual coherence in the field of Newtonian physics, whereas the theory of repression provides the condition for a kind of *narrative* coherence in the construction of a life story. (The theory of repression functions to explain the disparity between the life story that one brings into analysis and the one that is constructed in the course of that analysis.)

We might call these aspects of Freudian theory "true," while recognizing that they are *not* true in the same way that theories in the natural sciences are true (just as the myth of Oedipus is true—and perhaps even true to the facts—but not *factually true*).

6.52 "Give me any dream—or any slip of the tongue, or whatever— and I can show you the underlying motivation. The fact that this is so demonstrates the basic truth of the theory." That we can always find a motive (through process of free association) says something important about the method, but nothing at all about the truth of theory as such. All dreams provoke associations but tell us nothing about how they are caused, their function, and so forth. (Proponents of psychoanalysis have not realized that the accumulation of confirmatory instances does nothing to prove the truth of psychoanalytic generalizations, just as opponents of the theory have not realized that counterinstances are irrelevant and that falsification criteria are, at best, of only limited use in judging the validity of the theory as a whole.)

"Does this mean that we have no right to expect psychoanalysis to conform to the accepted criteria of the scientific method?" Yes, if by "scientific method" we mean that method as it has evolved in the natural sciences; no, if we mean that by sacrificing this method we give up all standards for evaluation or appraisal. (It is as if we were to say that art was useless because we have no strict standards for determining its value or for making judgments about the relative value of different works of art. The demand for a *single* standard, a single ideal of truth—most often one modeled on the natural sciences—is not only irrelevant in this context but profoundly misleading.)

6.53 What are the effects of the kind of grammatical analysis that we have engaged in here? First, we recognize the relativity of metapsychological propositions, both intrinsic and extrinsic; these propositions are paradigmatic *for the practice of psychoanalysis*; we accept the truth of these propositions as the condition for engaging in psychoanalysis and psychoanalytic interpretation. At the same time, we acknowledge that their application beyond the actual practice of psychoanalysis—in the construction of a general theory of human behavior or development, a general semiotics, a comprehensive theory of culture, and so forth—is, at best, problematic. Second, we recognize that the metapsychology and the procedures of interpretation are strictly correlative and that the validity of metapsychological propositions is coextensive with the validity of psychoanalytic interpretation itself; it can only be evaluated relative to the truth of the meanings thus interpreted (and this is a *very* complicated business).

6.54   How, finally, should we characterize Freud's achievement? There is, of course, no simple answer to this question, and whatever answer we propose is apt to be misleading in one respect or another. Perhaps, however, we might say this: Freud's distinctive achievement was to have forged *connections of meaning* among what we had previously regarded as disparate, unconnected, and even meaningless phenomena. "What is remarkable about Freud is," as Wittgenstein says, "the enormous field of psychical facts which he arranges" (ML, 310). After Freud, we can sensibly speak of many more of our psychical acts as *motivated*, and hence *meaningful* in the specific sense that psychoanalysis gives to this term. By extending the area of motivated behavior, Freud extends the realm of the psychical; by extending the realm of the psychical, he extends the realm of meaning and interpretation.[21] Psychoanalysis unifies a wide range of symbolic phenomena and instances of behavior in a single hermeneutic field; it links these phenomena together through the common denominator of the unconscious.

"The hypothesis of there being unconscious [psychical] processes paves the way to a decisive new orientation in the world and in science," Freud writes (IL, 22). The concept of the unconscious is the basic principle of this organization in psychoanalysis, one that constitutes a new domain of intelligibility, a new form of consciousness, a new kind of interiority. The justification for this concept consists, finally, in its usefulness, that is, precisely in the way it serves to establish the psychical, in both its normal and pathological forms, *as a whole* and to provide a form for its coherent representation. "The division of the psychical into what is conscious and what is unconscious is the fundamental premiss of psychoanalysis," Freud proclaims; "and it alone makes it possible for psychoanalysis to understand the pathological processes in

---

21. In the *Introductory Lectures,* Freud writes, "We have made a quite considerable extension to the world of psychical phenomena which were not reckoned earlier as belonging to it" (IL, 60).

mental life [*Seelenleben*], which are as common as they are important, and to find a place for them in the framework of science" (EI, 13). In this, at least, he was entirely correct.

But, if we say that the unconscious is the distinctive domain of psychoanalysis, its privileged object, so to speak, we must also recognize that this domain is constituted relative to a specific and limited point of view, the position of which determines, but cannot be encompassed within, the field that it organizes. (Think of this on the analogy of the eye and its visual field.) This perspective is itself properly neither "true" nor "false"; rather, it provides the terms and criteria for making particular kinds of comparisons, for drawing certain analogies, for seeing things *this way* rather than that. Hence, we might say Freud's achievement is indeed, as he himself believed, comparable to that of a Copernicus or a Darwin, but only in the rather exceptional sense in which Wittgenstein understands it: namely, it lies in the discovery, not of a true theory, but of "a fertile point of view [*eines fruchtbaren Aspekts*]" (CV, 18).

6.55 It is hard to see oneself with any degree of objectivity. Psychoanalysis, as a form of therapy, allows us to see ourselves with the help of another—not only through a painstaking recollection and arrangement of the significant details of our lives but also through the reenactments of the transference. By this process we become aware of our tendency toward self-deception, how we construct selective narratives according to particular needs and desires, usually unconscious. In the course of analysis, we learn to see things differently; whereas formerly we had loved our fathers for their strength and despised our mothers for their dependence, we learn now to question the adequacy of this picture. Whereas formerly we had been inclined to see certain aspects of our behavior as expressions of love, we now see them as expressions of hatred. And so forth.

All of this happens, not because we learn new facts about ourselves, but because we learn to organize what we already knew in a different way, to see certain aspects of our behavior as instances of repression or denial, to reconstruct the whole in the light of *this* analogy rather than *that* one, according to *this* theme rather than some other.

6.56 In the end, we may say either that it is Freud's achievement to have recognized that we have a strong unconscious tendency to repeat earlier emotional attachments, dramatic situations, and traumas, to construe our present experience according to patterns laid down in the past, to repress certain painful memories, and so forth (all of which are summed up in the notion of a dynamic unconscious), or that the interpretation of contemporary events and meanings on the analogy of events and meanings from the past allows us to make sense of our lives in new—and perhaps necessary—ways, that it makes the burden of our life more bearable: it gives us satisfaction; it allows us to go on.

APPENDIX A:
The Method of Grammar

1. This is a description of the method of grammar as I understand it from Wittgenstein's later (post-1930) writings and published lectures,[1] and especially as it is exemplified in his *Philosophical Investigations*.[2] That this description departs significantly from most of the accepted interpretations of that method, that it bears little similarity to what goes on in contemporary analytical and linguistic philosophy, is a measure of the degree to which I think Wittgenstein has been misunderstood. Still, it is not my purpose here to defend a particular reading of Wittgenstein's philosophy. This is a work about Freud, not Wittgenstein. I believe—as Wittgenstein himself believed[3]—that his main contribution to contemporary thought was in his creation of a new rhetorical and pedagogical method, rather than in the construction of a new philosophical theory (whether about meaning, language, mind, social practices, or whatever). I also believe that this method can—and ultimately must—be extracted from Wittgenstein's own work and interests, that it must be made to stand on its own merits and judged by the fruits that it yields. That is what I have tried to do in this book. I am convinced that the method as I describe and use it here is more or less what Wittgenstein recommends, but whether it actually is so is perhaps less important than whether the exposition is found to be helpful.

2. Generally speaking, "method" is directed toward the question "how to proceed" in the accomplishment of a desired end; it is a way,

---

1. In order to avoid confusion, I use the word "grammar" to designate Wittgenstein's new conception of philosophy, that is, philosophy conceived as the attempt to bring clarity and order to our understanding of language.

2. "We now demonstrate a method," Wittgenstein writes, "by examples; and the series of examples can be broken off" (PI, 1:133).

3. "As regards his own work, he said it did not matter whether his results were true or not," Moore tells us; "what mattered was that 'a method had been found' " (ML, 316).

technique, or process for *doing something*. The questions are, then, What are the ends and aims of the method of grammar? What is it intended to do? What does it actually accomplish?

There are, I would suggest, three general aims, or ends, of the grammatical method:

(1) *Grammar dissolves specific philosophical problems*; it breaks the hold of false analogies. Insofar as philosophical problems arise from a misunderstanding of the forms and uses ("the grammar") of particular linguistic expressions—and especially of misunderstandings based on false analogies (e.g., "all chickens have wings" and "all men seek pleasure," or "I have a sensation of red" and "I have an apple")—they are resolved by obtaining a clear view (*Übersichtlichkeit*) of the sense and conditions of our statements. Grammar breaks the hold of false analogies by *showing* the deep grammatical conditions of sense. "The concept of perspicuous representation [*übersichtlichen Darstellung*] is of fundamental significance for us," Wittgenstein writes. "It earmarks the form of account we give, the way we look at things" (PI, 1:122). Grammar dissolves philosophical problems by allowing us to see how they arise from particular misunderstandings of our linguistic forms. (Generally speaking, our mistake in this case is to see similarity where we ought to see difference. Because our language presents a fairly uniform appearance and our grammatical forms a certain regularity, we tend—quite literally—to *see* conceptual, logical, and figural relations in terms of a very restricted number of grammatical categories and performative rules; in so doing, we fail to recognize the enormous complexity that underlies these apparently simple constructions, or the broad range and diversity of their applications. "What confuses us," as Wittgenstein writes in the *Investigations*, "is the uniform appearance of words when we hear them spoken or meet them in script or print. For their *application* is not presented to us so clearly. Especially when we are doing philosophy!" [PI, 1:11]. Grammar teaches us to see differences.)

(2) *Grammar alleviates the compulsion to view conceptual problems in a particular way*; it dispels linguistic illusions. Philosophical problems arise not only from our failure to understand how our language works—and the conditions of its application—but also from certain qualities intrinsic to the character of language itself, especially from the *pictures* that language imposes on us, pictures that seduce us into false imaginings (the picture of the mind as something inside the head, of time as a river, of logic as something pure and crystalline, of unconscious thoughts as hidden causes, etc.). Almost invariably, in doing philosophy, we view conceptual problems through the medium of distorted linguistic images, images that are deeply embedded in our linguistic forms and that

direct our thinking—often compulsively—in strange, cramped, and inappropriate ways (the obsessive attachment to a single form, one that typically takes the form of the expressions like "must" or "cannot": for example, "logic *must* be the ground of things" or "thoughts *cannot be* unconscious"). Referring to his own early obsession with the essence and general form of propositions, Wittgenstein writes, "A *picture* held us captive. And we could not get outside it, for it lay in our language and language seemed to repeat it to us inexorably" (PI, 1:115). Grammar is an attempt to free ourselves from linguistic pictures, "a battle against the bewitchment of our intelligence by means of language [*ein Kampf gegen die Verhexung unsres Verstandes durch die Mittel unserer Sprache*]" (PI, 1:109). By making us aware of their source and influence, grammar *deliteralizes* these pictures; it allows us to see the picture *as a picture* and thus breaks our fascination with it. (It follows that the real concern in grammar is not with philosophical problems as such but rather, as Henry Staten notes, with "the *compulsion* which those problems exercise over us,"[4] with the subtle but unrelenting pressure they exert on our lives and thinking, the obsessions they breed. Grammar alleviates these obsessions by deliteralizing the pictures that fuel them.)

(3) *Grammar changes our conceptual sensibility.* The compulsion to think philosophically is bound up with our way of seeing things and, ultimately, with our forms of life; hence, we must learn to live and to see differently. To the extent that they are grounded in and reflective of certain basic human sensibilities, the true resolution of philosophical confusions entails more than a change in our conception of language or in our linguistic habits; it demands, finally, *a fundamental transformation of human sensibility and character*, a change in our basic forms of life such that certain kinds of questions—certain kinds of intellectual and conceptual problems—simply do not arise. Grammar, then, is directed against those tendencies in us that give rise to the *need* to philosophize; it aims not at understanding or belief or the achievement of the "right opinion" about things (e.g., about language, meaning, mind, or human nature) but at *transformation*.[5] (One might even speak here of the aim of grammar as the achievement of a certain kind of

4. Staten, *Wittgenstein and Derrida* (Lincoln: University of Nebraska Press, 1984), 67. While I am less than sympathetic to his attempt to link Wittgenstein to Derrida and deconstructionism, Staten's account here of the method of grammar—especially, in chapter 2, "Wittgenstein Deconstructs" (64–108)—is surely one of the most brilliant and insightful in the literature.

5. "The way to solve the problem you see in life is to live in a way that will make what is problematic disappear," Wittgenstein writes in one of his notebooks (CV, 27).

wisdom, or "sound human understanding."[6] For it is finally a matter of learning to live in the absence of the problematic, of being restored to a world unimparied by cramped obsessions and destructive illusions of philosophy. "The real discovery," says Wittgenstein, "is the one that makes me capable of stopping doing philosophy when I want to.—The one that gives philosophy peace, so that it is no longer tormented by questions which bring *itself* in question" (PI, 1:133). The method of grammar is both the source and the process of this discovery.)

3. If these are its general aims, what are the characteristic features of the method of grammar? How does it proceed? What does it do?

Most fundamentally, perhaps, *grammar is a description of language*, but one that "gets its light, that is to say its purpose, from philosophical problems" (PI, 1:109). (Note the implication that until there is some kind of problem, there is no need for grammar and nothing for grammar to do; grammar is a response to philosophical problems, whether implicit or explicit.) Grammar describes language in such a way as to reveal the deep grammatical conditions of sense; grammar *displays* these conditions. Just as a diagram may represent semantic, logical, and grammatical relations pictorially (i.e., spatially), so grammar, we might say, represents semantic, logical, and grammatical relations discursively (i.e., in the unfolding of the text). This is the whole point of the description. (It sounds strange that a text should be able to "re-present" these relations, but no less strange than the fact that we are able to represent them spatially in diagrams, models, and so forth.)

In contrast to traditional philosophy, the question in grammar is not "What is truth?" or "What is knowledge?" but "What do you mean when you say *x*?" And the answer to this question is not a proposition but a description of how *x* is commonly used in the language. Grammar describes the rules for ordinary usage, including the activities, or "forms of life," within which our language is embedded.

To invoke one of Wittgenstein's favorite metaphors, a language is like a great city, "a maze of little streets and squares, of old and new houses, and of houses with additions from various periods; and this surrounded by a multitude of new boroughs with straight regular streets and uniform houses" (PI, 1:18). The purpose of grammar, on this metaphor, is to provide a map of the city; grammar lays out the significant syntactical, semantic, and logical relations among different terms and segments of our language, especially those which are tangled and complex. In

6. See James Edwards, *Ethics Without Philosophy: Wittgenstein and the Moral Life* (Tampa: University Presses of Florida, 1982), esp. 207–16.

grammar, as in cartography, a good representation is one that allows us to survey broad segments of the terrain, one that allows us to see these relations clearly, that provides a perspicuous, or synoptic, view of that terrain. What we lack in philosophy, according to Wittgenstein, is precisely this synoptic view; hence, he says, "we encounter the kind of difficulty we should have with the geography of a country for which we had no map, or else a map of isolated bits. The country we are talking about is language, and the geography is its grammar. We can walk about the country quite well, but when forced to make a map we go wrong" (YB, 43). Grammar is this project of linguistic mapmaking: even though we are competent speakers of the language, we do not understand its geography; grammar lays out the geography of our language in a way that allows us to survey the terrain.

4. *Grammar has no distinctive method, domain, or object*; it is nothing but the resolution—through clarification—of philosophical problems. "There is not *a* philosophical method, though there are indeed methods, like different therapies" (PL, 1:133). Grammar is merely a series of loosely related but open-ended techniques for resolving these problems; whatever allows us to *see* the deeper grammar of our forms of expression, whatever reveals the false analogies and pictures that guide our thinking, belongs to grammar. While this process is not blind, neither is it something that can be circumscribed by rules. There is no set way of proceeding in this kind of presentation, beyond some very general guidelines like "Look at the use in ordinary language," "Describe the term in context," and "Compare this use to that of other, formally analogous terms and expressions." Moreover, description alone is often insufficient; sometimes what is needed is more of the order of a grammatical aside—a joke, for example, or an ironic comment, or an imaginative or satirical presentation ("What if. . . ?"), or even something in the imperative mode ("Don't think! Look!").

Nor is it correct to say that language is the object of grammar (as we might say that language is the object of linguistics, or the literary text the object of criticism). Grammar gives no comprehensive account of language (or meaning or truth or whatever) but only illuminates the grammatical contexts within which philosophical puzzles arise. "Your questions refer to words; so I have to talk about words," Wittgenstein declares in the *Investigations* (PI, 1:120).

Grammar as such presupposes *nothing* about the relation between language and the world (or anything else, for that matter). It does not presume that all theoretical questions are merely questions of language or that questions of reference can be reduced to questions of usage—or, more especially, that everything *is* language. ("Language *as opposed to what?*" Wittgenstein asks in one of his lectures.) Grammar proceeds from the idea that at least *some* of our questions—and particularly our questions in philosophy—arise from confusions about the way language works. (The question whether someone else can "know" my pain, for example, arises from a confusion about our use of terms like "pain" and "to know" and so forth. Since it belongs to the grammar of the expression "my pain" that it cannot—logically—be experienced by someone else, it makes no sense to ask whether someone other than myself might "know" it. This, however, is a statement about *how we use language* and not a statement of fact. [If we cannot imagine things otherwise than as they are, we are dealing with a question of grammar, not facts.]) The method of grammar is simply a way of describing what we do when we use words, of describing how language actually works, according to what conventions, rules, and so forth—just as we might describe the activities of players in a game or the rules by which they play. (Are there *any* conditions under which a rook may jump over another piece in chess? Are there *any* conditions under which it would make sense to say, "You know my pain," or "You are now knowing my pain"? Grammar recommends that you try to imagine situations in which you might want to say this—and then to see that no matter what you imagine, your statements are nonsensical.)

Thus, although it has characteristic features and aims, grammar is not definable in the way that, say, calculus, logic, physics, or even aesthetic criticism is definable. Grammar is a particular kind of presentation of and critical reflection upon what we mean when we try to say something; it is neither more nor less than the attempt to understand the sense and proper application of our language, the attempt to clarify the meaning of our forms of expression, especially—but not only—when we speak philosophically.

5.   Because it is merely descriptive, and descriptive only of ordinary language usage, *grammar is not factually informative.* "In grammar you can discover nothing. There are no surprises. . . . We can do only one thing—clearly articulate the rule we have been applying unawares" (WVC, 77). Grammar proves nothing; it asserts nothing; it tells us nothing that we did not already in some sense know. "It is . . . of the essence of our investigation that we do not seek to learn anything *new* by it," Wittgenstein writes in the *Investigations.* "We want to *understand* something that is already in plain view. For *this* is what we seem in some sense not to understand" (PI, 1:89). Grammar does nothing more than make explicit our latent, intuitive comprehension of grammatical rules

and relations; it brings to awareness things known but unrecognized, things that have escaped our notice precisely because of their familiarity. It is these common, familiar things, things so familiar that we fail to take note of them—and not the abstract, esoteric realities of metaphysics— that, according to Wittgenstein, constitute the true ground of philosophical inquiry; it is these things, he says, that are at once the "most striking and most powerful": "The aspects of things that are most important for us are hidden because of their simplicity and familiarity. (One is unable to notice something—because it is always before one's eyes.) The real foundations of his enquiry do not strike a man at all. Unless *that* fact has at some time struck him.—And this means: we fail to be struck by what, once seen, is most striking and most powerful" (PI, 1:129). Later he links this directly to the task of grammar, understood in this context as the description of our natural practices: "What we are supplying are really remarks on the natural history of human beings; we are not contributing curiosities however, but observations which no one has doubted, but which have escaped remark only because they are always before our eyes" (PI, 1:415).

Grammar, we might say, *tells* us nothing, but it *shows* us something profoundly important, something that allows us to make our way around.

6. *Grammar is not hypothetical or explanatory*. It is concerned not with the truth or falsity of propositions but with their sense.[7] Grammar displays the conditions and possibilities of sense in our language. By exhibiting these conditions, grammar, in effect, sets a limit to what can and cannot legitimately be said; it thus "stops us asking illegitimate questions" (L I, 111). But grammar sets forth no hypotheses about how language works, no explanations of meaning; it does not *state* what these limits are—it *shows* them. Grammar proposes nothing, it explains nothing; it has nothing to do with anything "hidden" or concealed. In grammar, everything is displayed, as it were, *on the surface*. "Philosophy simply puts everything before us, and neither explains nor deduces anything.—Since everything lies open to view there is nothing to explain. For what is hidden, for example, is of no interest to us" (PI, 1:126).

7. Insofar as it is concerned with the apriori *conditions* of our linguistic practices, with showing the *possibilities* of sense in language, prior to

7. "That one empirical proposition is true and another false is no part of grammar," Wittgenstein writes in *Philosophical Grammar*. "What belongs to grammar are the conditions (the method) necessary for comparing the proposition with reality. That is, all the conditions necessary for the understanding (of sense)" (PG, 88).

experience and statements of any kind, *grammar can be described as a form of transcendental inquiry.*[8] Grammar comes, as it were, before facts; it is an investigation of the conditions of making meaningful statements, and hence an investigation into the conditions of facts as such. "All I can give you is a method," Wittgenstein says in one of his lectures; "I cannot teach you any new truths. It is of the essence of philosophy not to depend on experience, and this is what is meant by saying that philosophy is *a priori*" (L II, 97). As he puts it in the *Investigations*, grammar is directed "not towards phenomena, but, as one might say, towards the *'possibilities'* of phenomena. We remind ourselves, that is to say, of the *kind of statement* that we make about phenomena" (PI, 1:90). Grammar describes "what is possible *before* all new discoveries and inventions" (PI, 1:126).

Like Kant, Wittgenstein believes that philosophy is not a matter of experience ("sense perception"), or empirical inquiry, but an investigation of the *formal, a priori structures of possibilities of experience*, though for him these structures are practical and institutional rather than, as for Kant, ideal and mentalistic. They belong to our linguistic practices and to our forms of life—to the rules that govern linguistic and other forms of symbolic behavior—rather than to "the mind."[9]

8. *Grammar provides a synopsis of trivialities.* Grammar consists in "assembling reminders for a particular purpose," in making explicit our natural knowledge of the conditions and relations of sense (PI, 1:127). Grammar merely presents an overview, or "synopsis," of these relations. "What we find out in philosophy is trivial," says Wittgenstein in one of his lectures; "it does not teach us new facts, only science does that" (L I, 26). Nonetheless, he adds, "the proper synopsis of these

8. Stephen Toulmin was among the first to argue that Wittgenstein's concern with a "transcendental" form of inquiry—that is, his concern *to delimit the scope and boundaries of the sayable*—was a persistent feature throughout both his earlier and later philosophy. "Wittgenstein's preoccupation remained throughout what it was in the beginning," Toulmin writes, "a preoccupation less with the foundations of knowledge, than with the nature and limits of language. He was above all a 'transcendental' philosopher, whose central philosophical question . . . could be posed in the Kantian form, How is a meaningful language *possible at all?*" (Allan Janik and Stephen Toulmin, *Wittgenstein's Vienna* [New York: Simon and Schuster, 1973], 221).

9. In a sense, the very concept of "grammar" is misleading, since it seems to imply that what is involved is purely a matter of language and linguistic usage. In fact, if one attempts to define what grammar is, one very quickly finds oneself describing *what people do*, for language is deeply embedded in complicated human activities, customs, and institutions. As Wittgenstein puts it in *Zettel*, "How words are understood is not told by words alone" (Z, 144).

trivialities is enormously difficult, and has immense importance. Philosophy is in fact the synopsis of trivialities"[10] (L I, 26).

9. *Grammar is incontrovertible.* A grammatical description sets forth the obvious but unrecognized facts about language, facts so trivial that they tend to go unnoticed. Ideally, such a description should be immediately transparent and incontrovertible; it is "wrong" only when it contradicts common sense or the conventions of ordinary language. "If one tried to advance *theses* in philosophy, it would never be possible to debate them," Wittgenstein writes, "because everyone would agree with them"[11] (PI, 1:128). In grammar we do not draw conclusions, for grammar "only states what everyone admits" (PI, 1:599). In grammar, we move in a realm where we all share the same ideas, beliefs, and opinions because we all share the same basic forms of life. "On all the questions we discuss I have no opinion; and if I had, and it disagreed with one of your opinions, I would at once give it up for the sake of argument because it would be of no importance for our discussion. We constantly move in a realm where we all have the same opinions" (L II, 97). There are no disputes in grammar, though there may certainly be good and bad grammatical analyses. The test is whether *something gets done.*

10. *Grammar gives an order to our conceptions of things.* "The problems [of philosophy] are solved," according to Wittgenstein, "not by giving new information, but by arranging what we have always known" (PI, 1:109). It is the purpose of grammar to provide such an arrange-

10. Moore gives the following account of the same lecture: "He also said that he was not trying to teach us any new facts: that he would only tell us 'trivial' things—'things which we all know already'; but that the difficult thing was to get a 'synopsis' of these trivialities, and that our intellectual discomfort can only be removed by a synopsis of *many* trivialities—that 'if we leave out any, we still have the feeling that something is wrong' " (ML, 323).

11. Wittgenstein makes roughly the same point, but at greater length, some five years earlier, in his conversations with Waismann and the Vienna Circle: "If there were theses in philosophy, they would have to be such that they do not give rise to disputes. For they would have to be put in such a way that everyone would say, Oh yes, that is of course obvious. As long as there is a possibility of having different opinions and disputing about a question, that indicates that things have not yet been expressed clearly enough. Once a perfectly clear formulation—ultimate clarity—has been reached, there can be no second thoughts or reluctance any more, for these always raise from the feeling that something has now been asserted, and I do not yet know whether I should admit it or not. If, however, you make the grammar clear to yourself, if you proceed by very short steps in such a way that every single step becomes perfectly obvious and natural, no dispute whatsoever can arise. Controversy always arises through leaving out or failing to state clearly certain steps, so that the impression is given that a claim has been made that could be disputed" (WVC: 183–84).

ment. By making previously unrecognized grammatical and logical relations explicit, and by doing so in a perspicuous manner, grammar *gives an order* to our knowledge of language and linguistic practices. As Wittgenstein puts it in one of his lectures, grammar involves "something like putting in order our notions as to what can be said about the world," and it can be compared to "the tidying up of a room where you have to move the same object several times before you can get the room really tidy" (ML, 323). Grammar arranges the items of our knowledge, like furniture in a room; it places things side by side, like books on a shelf. It thus allows certain kinds of comparisons to be made, certain similarities and differences to be noted. In the case of most philosophical problems, according to Wittgenstein, this is all that is really needed:

> Some of the greatest achievements in philosophy could only be compared with taking up some books which seemed to belong together, and putting them on different shelves; nothing more being final about their positions than that they no longer lie side by side. The onlooker who doesn't know the difficulty of the task might well think in such a case that nothing at all has been achieved.—The difficulty in philosophy is to say no more than we know. E.g., to see that when we have put two books together in their right order we have not thereby put them in their final places. (BlB, 44–45)

In a critical passage from the *Investigations*, Wittgenstein summarizes many of these points as follows:

> It was true to say that our considerations could not be scientific ones. It was not of any possible interest to us to find out empirically "that, contrary to our preconceived ideas, it is possible to think such-and-such"—whatever that may mean. (The conception of thought as a gaseous medium.) And we may not advance any kind of a theory. There must not be anything hypothetical in our considerations. We must do away with all *explanation*, and description alone must take its place. And this description gets its light, that is to say its purpose, from the philosophical problems. These are, of course, not empirical problems; they are solved, rather by looking into the workings of our language, and that in such a way as to make us recognize these workings: *in despite of* an urge to misunderstand them. The problems are solved, not by giving new information, but by arranging what we have always known. Philosophy is a

battle against the bewitchment of our intelligence by means of language. (PI, 1:109)

The notion of "arranging" indicates, once again, the open-ended character of grammar in contrast to the insistence, in most of traditional philosophy, on an absolute, final form of truth. Grammar provides an arrangement of our knowledge—not *the* arrangement, but only one of many possible arrangements: "We want to establish an order in our knowledge of the use of language," Wittgenstein says later, "an order with a particular end in view; one out of many possible orders; not *the* order" (PI, 1:132). The real difficulty in grammar is "to say no more than we know," to recognize this process of ordering *as itself the solution* and not something that is merely preliminary to it; the difficulty, in other words, is to know when to *stop*:

> Here we come up against a remarkable and characteristic phenomenon in philosophical investigation: the difficulty—I might say—is not that of finding the solution but rather of recognizing as the solution something that looks as if it were only a preliminary to it. "We have already said everything.—Not anything that follows from this, no, *this* itself is the solution!"
>
> This is connected, I believe, with our wrongly expecting an explanation, whereas the solution of the difficulty is a description, if we give it the right place in our considerations. If we dwell upon it, and do not try to get beyond it.
>
> The difficulty here is: to stop. (Z, 314)

11.   *Grammar has no (immediate or direct) effects on our actual use of language*; it does not change or in any way interfere with our accepted practices (except, of course, to the extent that it has effects on the way we do philosophy). It is no part of grammar to *reform* language or linguistic practices, whether in our everyday life or in the technical languages of the sciences: grammar "leaves everything as it is" (PI, 1:124). This is not to say, however, that a grammatical analysis has no consequences for how we use language; it is only to say that these consequences are indirect and that they are incidental to the analysis as such. "Say what you choose," Wittgenstein writes, "so long as it does not prevent you from seeing the facts. (And when you see them there is a good deal you will not say.)" (PI, 1:79)

12.   *Grammar is contextual*; it takes the "scene of language"—the actual, concrete situations of language use—as the locus of meaning,

rather than the word, sentence, or the text. Grammar is contextual because meaning is; meaning only occurs through the regular, systematic conjunction of words and rule-governed activities. "Our use of language is like playing a game according to the rules" (L II, 32). Grammar is, in part, the attempt to describe these rules, to make them manifest and render them explicit. In order to describe them, however, it is necessary to refer these rules back to the concrete activities that make up the game. Hence, for a grammatical analysis, the basic unit of meaning is the game taken as a whole—that is, the unity comprising *both* the actual words and expressions, together with the specific contexts, activities, or situations in which they are used. This is what Wittgenstein means by the notion of a "language game" (*Sprachspiel*):[12]

> We can also think of the whole process of using words [as described in the builder's game of "block," "slab," etc.] as one of those games by means of which children learn their native

12. It is generally accepted that Wittgenstein uses the term "language game" in at least two different senses: first, as the basic unit of a grammatical description (the language game as something found and described), and second, as an ideal—generally simpler or more primitive—construction that allows different kinds of grammatical comparisons to be made (the language game as something hypothetical and invented; the heuristic role of the ideal). Used in the latter sense, the language game is a tool that allows us to see certain features of our language that might otherwise remain obscure, or, on occasion, to rid ourselves of the idea of necessary forms of language. Wittgenstein writes, for example: "I shall in the future again and again draw your attention to what I shall call language games. These are ways of using signs simpler than those in which we use the signs of our highly complicated everyday language. Language games are the forms of language with which a child begins to make use of words. The study of language games is the study of primitive forms of language or primitive languages. If we want to study the problems of truth and falsehood, of agreement and disagreement of propositions with reality, of the nature of assertion, assumption, and question, we shall with great advantage look at primitive forms of language in which these forms of thinking appear without the confusing background of highly complicated processes of thought. When we look at such simple forms of language the mental mist which seems to enshroud our ordinary use of language disappears. We see activities, reactions, which are clear-cut and transparent. On the other hand we recognize in these simpler processes forms of language not separated by a break from our more complicated ones. We see that we can build up the complicated forms from the primitive ones by gradually adding new forms" (BlB, 17). And, from one of his lectures: "Games or languages which we make up with stated rules one might call ideal languages, but this is a bad description since they are not ideal in the sense of being 'better.' They serve one purpose, to make comparisons. They can be put beside actual languages so as to enable us to see certain features in them and by this means to get rid of certain difficulties" (L II, 99). (See also L II, 101, 105.) I believe, however, that this particular understanding of a language game had become secondary by the time of the writing the *Investigations* (though not entirely abandoned—see, e.g., PI, 1:130) and that in Wittgenstein's later philosophy "language game" comes more and more exclusively to mean the actual activities and instances of language use, the "object" of a grammatical analysis.

language. I will call these games "language-games" and will sometimes speak of a primitive language as a language-game.

And the processes of naming the stones and of repeating words after someone might also be called language-games. Think of much of the use of words in games like ring-a-ring-a-roses.

I shall also call the whole, consisting of language and the actions into which it is woven, the "language-game." (PL, 1:7)

A particular use of language—say, stating a proposition—is like a move in a game, and the proposition is itself like a piece in the game, a knight in a game of chess, for instance; it is meaningful only if it represents a legitimate move within the game, that is, only if it is allowed by the rules of the game, or, to put it differently, if it has an application, a use, within a language game. Hence, like the function or "value" of a piece in a game of chess, the meaning of an expression is always contextually dependent and situational, spatial and temporal rather than mental and instantaneous:

We are talking about the spatial and temporal phenomenon of language, not about some non-spatial, non-temporal phantasm. [Note in margin: Only it is possible to be interested in a phenomenon in a variety of ways]. But we talk about it as we do about pieces in chess when we are stating the rules of the game, not describing their physical properties.

The question "What is a word really?" is analogous to "What is a piece in chess?" (PI, 1:108)

Elsewhere Wittgenstein notes that "just as a move in chess doesn't consist simply in moving a piece in such-and-such a way on the board—nor yet in one's thoughts and feelings as one makes the move: but in the circumstances that we call 'playing a game of chess,' 'solving a chess problem,' and so on," so the meaning of any particular word or expression can only be determined in the context of the language game in which it occurs (PI, 1:33). Hence, the language game is primary and fundamental for Wittgenstein; it is, as it were, the "proto-phenomenon": "Our mistake is to look for an explanation where we ought to look at what happens as a 'proto-phenomenon.' That is, where we ought to have said: *this language-game is played*" (PI, 1:654). Since it is the primary datum of analysis, the language game is not subject to explanation in terms of anything else. The question is not one of explaining a language-game by means of our experiences, but of noting a language-game.

". . . Look on the language-game as the *primary* thing. And look on the feelings, etc. as you look on a way of regarding the language-game, as interpretation" (PI, 1:655–56).

As something fundamental and irreducible, as that beyond or beneath which analysis cannot go, a language game cannot be grounded in anything beyond itself. It is not based on grounds; it is properly neither "reasonable" nor "unreasonable." It is simply there, as Wittgenstein says, "like our life" (OC, 559).

13. *Grammar is rhetorical.* To the extent that it aims at a change in our way of seeing—as opposed to conveying information of some sort or demonstrating the truth of a thesis—grammar is essentially a form of *persuasion*; it is *rhetorical* rather than demonstrative. Grammar says, in effect, Look at things *like this*, not like that. Indeed, the whole point of the grammatical presentation is to persuade us to see things differently. (This is an important part of the reason grammar cannot be confined to a mere description of rules for linguistic usage, why it must also be a form of representation, a mode of presentation that *displays* rather than merely describes the conditions of sense; for the aim of grammar is not merely to change our way of thinking about things—our way of conceptualizing philosophical problems, for example—but also, and more radically, to alter our conceptual sensibility, to change the way we *see* conceptual relations, prior to any interpretation or reflection. Grammar is not a matter of statements *about* language; it is a presentation in and through language. The point is to *exhibit* the relevant logical and grammatical relations--and this exhibition should in itself be significantly persuasive, should change our way of looking at things.)

It should be clear that calling grammar rhetorical does not mean that it is irrational, arbitrary, or, as it were, mere persuasion (any more than aesthetic criticism, for instance, is irrational merely because it is not based on strictly logical principles).[13] Through the perspicuous use of examples and models of comparison, of tropes and figural language, similes and analogies, and through its epigrammatic, serial mode of presentation, grammar shows our language in a new light; it reveals formerly hidden grammatical differences. In the process, it leads us to look at things in a new way. "What I'm doing is . . . persuasion," Wittgenstein says. "If someone says: 'There is not a difference,' and I say: 'There is a difference' I am persuading, I am saying 'I don't want

13. For an exceptionally perceptive discussion of the relation of Wittgenstein's method of grammar to aesthetic criticism, and of the relation of both to psychoanalysis, see John Casey, *The Language of Criticism* (London: Methuen, 1966), esp. 1–34.

you to look at it like that' " (LC, 27). Grammar changes our way of looking at things. Like good aesthetic criticism, it persuades us to see things that we had not seen before, to notice things that we might otherwise deny or ignore.

14. *Grammar is aesthetic.* Grammar proceeds, then, by criticism and elucidation, by perspicuous presentation, rather than—for the most part—by theorizing and argumentation. Grammar is thus best conceived on the model of *aesthetics* rather than science, according to a style of thinking in which conflicts of opinion are resolved, not by deduction or appeals to evidence, but by the pointed presentation (*Darstellung*) of further and more-refined descriptions and examples[14]—for what is at issue in such conflicts is, once more, not the *facts* but our *way of viewing* the facts. "The solution of our problems consists in eliminating the disquieting aspects generated by certain analogies contained in our grammar," Wittgenstein writes in one of his notebooks. "Philosophy changes aspects—by bringing out different analogies—inserting connecting links, etc."[15] Similarly, in *Zettel*, Wittgenstein compares the effect of grammar to placing an alternate picture before our eyes, where the point is not to understand but to *see* ("Look!"):

> I should like you to say: "Yes, it's true, that can be imagined, that may even have happened!" But was I trying to draw your attention to the fact that you are able to imagine this? I wanted to put this picture before your eyes, and your *acceptance* of this picture consists in your being inclined to regard a given case differently; that is, to compare it with *this* series of pictures. I have changed your *way of seeing* [*Anschauungweise*]. (I once read somewhere that a geometrical figure, with the words "Look at this," serves as a proof for certain Indian mathematicians. This looking too effects an alteration in one's way of seeing.) (Z, 461)

14. In one of his notebooks Wittgenstein himself remarks on "the queer resemblance between a philosophical investigation . . . and an aesthetic one. (E.g., what is bad about this garment, how it should be, etc.)" (CV, 25). On the other hand, as James Edwards has observed, there is at least one crucial difference between aesthetics and grammar: in the case of aesthetics, the acceptance of a new perspective involves a change in one's aesthetic judgment; in the case of grammar, it involves, not the substitution of one judgment for another, but the end of philosophical judgment as such. (See Edwards, *Ethics Without Philosophy*, 142.)

15. Quoted in G. P. Baker and P.M.S. Hacker, *Wittgenstein: Understanding and Meaning* (Chicago: University of Chicago Press, 1980), 277.

15. *Grammar is an art*; it is a skill that is mastered only through practice. To the extent that there is no single, clearly definable method for the resolution of individual problems, and to the extent that such a resolution proceeds primarily on intuition and a certain acquired mastery, it may be said that grammar, like therapy, is more an *art* than a technique. "I think I summed up my attitude to philosophy when I said: philosophy ought really to be written only as a poetic composition," Wittgenstein once wrote. "It must, it seems to me, be possible to gather from this how far my thinking belongs to the present, future, or past. For I was thereby revealing myself as someone who cannot quite do what he would like to be able to do" (CV, 24). Grammar, like poetry, is, strictly speaking, impossible: it tries to show more than we can ever say.

Because "style" is properly neither more nor less than the *form* of discursive representations, it follows that there can be no separation, in a grammatical analysis, between the method and the manner of presentation. Grammar *is* what grammar *does*; in grammar, there is no distinction between the form and the content of analysis.

APPENDIX B:
On Sense, Nonsense, Hypothesis, and Grammatical Rule

1. It is sometimes argued that a grammatical approach—being limited to questions of sense and nonsense—actually accomplishes very little. In one sense this is true, but in another and more significant sense, it indicates a serious misunderstanding. Typically, the claim is that grammar is concerned solely with questions of *coherence* to the exclusion of questions of *truth* and that this severely restricts its philosophical value. In respect to psychoanalysis, the argument runs, even the harshest critics have rarely charged that it is incoherent, that its claims make no sense; rather, they have wanted to deny its claims are *true*—and to this issue, grammar has nothing to contribute. After all, what has really been said once one says one *could* play a particular language game? Is coherence really enough for truth?

The answer, of course, is that coherence is *not* a sufficient condition for truth—but also that this is completely beside the point, since grammar is not about the business of demonstrating logical coherence in any case. Grammar clarifies language usage, not logical conditions and relations. Grammar, we might say, is *antecedent* to truth; it tells us what *kind* of truth is at stake in a proposition, prior to questions whether the statement actually meets those conditions. The issue is not one of internal logical consistency or empirical verification but of *actual or possible applications*. (Which is *not* to say that internal logical contradictions, or contradictory facts, are irrelevant!)

In relation to psychoanalysis, the question is not "Can this game be played?"—obviously, it can—but "What does playing this game amount to?" that is, "What *kind* of game is it?" The problem is not to determine whether the propositions of the theory are internally consistent but rather to find out *what kind of propositions they are*, what role they play in the language game.

What we investigate in grammar are the *conditions* of something being called true or false, prior to anything factual. "How do I know that red can't be cut into bits?" is not a question we can sensibly ask; "How do I know that the unconscious exists?" may or may not be a legitimate question, according the sense we ascribe to it. The question of sense precedes the question of truth. "I must *begin* with the distinction between sense and nonsense," writes Wittgenstein. "I can't give it a foundation" (PG, 20).

2.   We distinguish, then, between the *sense* of a proposition and its *validity*. The former concerns the *grammar* of the propositional statement, its conformity to—or deviance from—accepted rules of linguistic usage; the latter pertains to the truth or falsity of the proposition, its relation to *facts*.

   A judgment about the *sense* of a proposition involves an appeal to *conventions*, or standards of usage, in grammar. A judgment about the *validity* of a proposition involves an appeal to *evidence*.[1]

3.   The rules of grammar, we might say, are independent of the facts, or states of affairs, that we describe *in* our language. "We cannot say of a rule that it conforms to or contradicts a fact" (YB, 65). Rules are in this sense "arbitrary," since nothing about the factual world compels us to adopt one rule rather than another. (For example, if we say that the statement "It is both green and red" is nonsense, this is not because it is contradicted by reality but only because this statement has no application, no use, in our language; in other words, what determines it as nonsense is not, in Wittgenstein's phrase, "a standard of usage in nature" but only "a standard of usage in grammar" [YB, 65]. In short, *we just don't talk that way*.)

4.   This should not be taken as an *explanation* of sense: grammatical rules *describe* conventions (forms of linguistic usage); they do not *explain* them. A rule does not "constitute," or "determine," the sense of a proposition, but rather it serves as a standard by which that sense can be judged. (We say that "a yardstick *determines* the length of a rod." In one sense, this is true; in another sense, not.)

5.   What does it mean to say of something that it is "nonsense"? We are inclined to think that there are different kinds of nonsense, that there

---

1. But note that these two aspects of a proposition, its sense and its validity, are not unrelated; the *sense* will determine the *kinds of evidence* relevant to judgments about its validity. As Wittgenstein puts it, "The way a proposition is verified is part of its grammar" (L II, 126).

is a difference, say, between strictly grammatical nonsense (e.g., "The was it dog no," or, less obviously, "This is both green and red at once") and pure gibberish (e.g., "Ab sur ah"). According to Wittgenstein, however, this difference is inconsequential; nonsense is nonsense, he says, "the only difference being in the jingle of the words" (L I, 64). In the end an expression either makes sense or it doesn't; there is no such thing as "degrees" of nonsense.

To say of a particular expression that it is "nonsense" is to make a judgment about its use, to say in effect that it has none or that it is excluded from use. "When a sentence is called senseless, it is not as it were its sense that is senseless. But a combination of words is being excluded from language, withdrawn from circulation" (PI, 1:500).

6. Grammatical rules may exclude particular expressions in one of two ways: first, when what is heard is immediately recognized as nonsensical (e.g., "Ab sur ah"), or second, when certain operations—those of grammatical analysis, for example—allow us to recognize it as nonsense (e.g., "Only my pain is real"). This latter implies a distinction, then, between the surface grammar and the depth grammar of a word or expression: the surface grammar refers to what we immediately understand about a word, its meaning, use, and syntactical possibilities—"the part of its use . . . that can be taken in by the ear"; the depth grammar, on the other hand, pertains to the unsuspected diversity and specific character of these uses (something familiar but generally unrecognized) together with the largely hidden conditions of its sense—that is, the wider context of rules and practices that define correct and incorrect usage in language (PI, 1:664).

7. The question of sense or nonsense thus hinges on the question of use.[2] Certain (syntactically correct) sentences that are excluded as

2. This is one of the main differences between Wittgenstein's earlier and later writings. In his later writings, Wittgenstein is concerned with the investigation of how words and expressions are actually *used*, rather than with the investigation of linguistic forms (and particularly, the form of a proposition). Hence, for the later Wittgenstein, the boundary between sense and nonsense is not something given but something that must be *drawn*, and it can only be drawn on the basis of criteria such as "use," "function" "purpose," and so forth: "To say 'This combination of words makes no sense' excludes it from the sphere of language and thereby bounds the domain of language [*Gebiet der Sprache*]. But when one draws a boundary it may be for various kinds of reason. If I surround an area with a fence or a line or otherwise, the purpose may be to prevent someone from getting in or out; but it may also be part of a game and the players are supposed, say, to jump over the boundary; or it may show where the property of one man ends and that of another begins; and so on. So if I draw a boundary line that is not yet to say what I am drawing it for" (PI, 1:499).

nonsensical can conceivably be given a sense by redefining our grammatical rules in such a way that the sentences find a use (i.e., by changing our *criteria* for judgments of sense.) For example, it is conceivable that the expression "It is both green and yellow" could be given a sense if we were to make it a rule that "green and yellow can be in the same place at the same time" (YB, 64). This statement—though contradictory in our present language—is not contradicted by nature, for nature as such tells us nothing about how one color relates to another. This is a corollary of the fact that the rules of grammar are arbitrary, since it is these rules alone that prescribe what is and is not possible to say in language (i.e., the rules of grammar are independent of the facts that we describe *in* language).

Wittgenstein compares a rule for the use of a word to the length of a rod that serves as a unit of measure. Insofar as one chooses this length for practical reasons, it is clearly *not* arbitrary (since it is presumably better suited for a particular purpose than other alternatives); but neither is it necessary in the sense of being somehow "determined" by the facts, for another length, even perhaps less practical or efficient, could serve the same function.

"We say that though no man sits in this chair someone could. This means roughly, 'The sentence "Somebody sits in this chair" makes sense,' that is, there is a logical possibility of someone sitting in it" (YB, 69). So, too, in a different grammatical system, it might be possible for certain hydrogen atoms to have six times their normal valence, but this system would doubtless be less practical than our current system of chemistry.

Some systems are practical, others impractical; those which are practical are retained, whereas those which are impractical are rejected—very often with the judgment that they are "false." In fact, however, the rejection of a grammatical system is like the rejection of a unit of measure: it makes no sense to call this standard either correct or incorrect, true or false. (This is part of what we mean when we say that rules are antecedent to truth.)

8.   There is a difference, then, between rejecting a hypothesis as "false" and rejecting a symbolism, or grammatical system, as "impractical"—though, as Wittgenstein reminds us, "there are transitions from one to the other" (YB, 70). Suppose, for example, a planet that is predicted in one hypothesis to describe an ellipse fails to do so; in this case, we may say either that the original hypothesis ("All planets move in elliptical orbits") is wrong or that there is some further variable that causes this particular planet to move irregularly (e.g., the gravitational effect of

another planet somewhere nearby). Moreover, our choice between these two alternatives is, in a sense, arbitrary (since either could be made consistent with *some* system of explanation, though one might be considerably less complicated than the other). "Here we have a transition between a hypothesis and a grammatical rule," Wittgenstein comments. "If we say that whatever observations we make there is a planet nearby, we are laying this down as a rule of grammar; it describes no experience" (YB, 70). (Compare Freud's use of the term "unconscious psychical processes" to account for psychological slips and disruptions of one sort or another: if we say there *must* be a cause, this is a matter of grammar, not evidence. [Freud's determinism.])

If we accept a particular statement as a rule—and therefore as unfalsifiable—then we might be forced to make "a queer alteration," for we will "have to model everything else to account for it"; in other words, this statement becomes *paradigmatic* for making other descriptions[3] (YB, 70). It becomes part of the standard by which other propositions are judged true and false, relevant and irrelevant.

9. We describe the difference between a hypothetical proposition and a grammatical rule according to the *role* that each plays in the language or in a particular language game. Statements of rules function as standards of sense, and their role is accordingly paradigmatic and normative: they "set up" a language game. Hypothetical or factual propositions, on the other hand, convey information of some sort; they tell us something about the world. They are statements to be judged true or false on the basis of evidence; they are, as it were, moves *within* a language game.

Since what matters is not the *form* of the proposition but its *function*, its role in the language game, it may be hard—or even, at first glance, impossible—to tell whether one is dealing with a rule or a hypothesis; it is only by actually observing the practice—only by seeing how the game is actually played—the one learns how the various propositions function within it. ("Deciding whether a sentence is used as a hypothesis or as a grammatical rule is like deciding whether a game is chess, or a variety of chess distinguished by a new rule entering at a certain stage of the game," says Wittgenstein. "Until we get to that stage, there is no way of telling which game is being played by looking at the game" [YB, 70].)

The statement "There are six primary colors" sets forth a grammatical

---

3. For an interesting discussion of this example—and its relevance to falsification criteria—see Imre Lakatos, "Falsification and the Methodology of Scientific Research Programmes, in *Criticism and the Growth of Knowledge*, ed. Imre Lakatos and Alan Musgrave (Cambridge: Cambridge University Press, 1970), 100–103.

rule; it says, in effect, that it makes no sense, according to the grammar of colors, to speak of a seventh primary color (i.e., by the rules of *this* language game, statements about a seventh primary color are excluded as "nonsense"). Once again, however, this is not a restriction imposed by nature but merely a matter of convention. "It is not a fact of nature that seven primary colors cannot be arranged on the corners of a regular polyhedron," but we can reasonably ask whether the expression "seventh primary color" has any legitimate *use* (YB, 66). By contrast, the statement "There are six books on this shelf" plays an entirely different role in our language. In this case, it makes perfect sense to ask whether this statement is true and to use specific procedures to find out.

10.   "Suppose," says Wittgenstein, "the standard of a foot length was a rod in my room, and suppose the Greenwich rod agreed exactly with this rod. To say 'The Greenwich rod is as a matter of fact a foot long' is to assert a proposition, whereas at present it does not make sense to say this. It is a definition" (YB, 70). If the Greenwich rod is the standard for measuring feet, then to say, "It is a foot long," is to court nonsense, for all we can really say is, *"This is what we mean by 'a foot.' "* As Wittgenstein puts it in the famous passage from the *Investigations*, "There is *one* thing of which one can say neither that it is one meter long, nor that it is not one meter long, and that is the standard meter in Paris.—But this is, of course, not to ascribe any extraordinary property to it, but only to mark its peculiar role in the language-game of measuring with a meter-rule" (PI, 1:50). In other words, to say it once more, the role of certain statements is paradigmatic and grammatical rather than hypothetical and factual; such statements function as a *means of representation*, as "something with which comparison is made" rather than as something that is itself represented, something that might be judged true or false, correct or incorrect.

11.   Summarizing, we might say that there are two essential characteristics of a grammatical or paradigmatic statement: (1) it makes an assertion about an object, event, or process (i.e., it has the *form* of a proposition: it ascribes predicates to subjects); and (2) its truth value, or validity, depends exclusively on conventions of linguistic usage rather than on appeals to evidence of some sort. (To deny that two plus two equals four is not to disagree with a widely held opinion about a matter of fact; it is to show an ignorance of the meaning of the terms involved.) Grammatical statements are really not propositions at all but, as it were, recommendations for the use of words; they tell us how language, or a

particular form of expression, is supposed to be used, what are and are not correct applications of this language.

Whether a given statement is grammatical depends entirely on its role within the language game. The most direct way of determining this role is by asking, with respect to its truth, "How do we know?" or "How do we find out?" (Compare, on the one hand, "How do we know that 3 + 3 = 6?" or "How do we determine whether this color is *really* red?" with "How do we know there are six books on the shelf?" or "How do we find out what color the books are?")

12.   Compare the following statements:

All rods have length.	All roses have thorns.
I cannot feel your pain.	I cannot feel the music.
My thoughts are private.	My finances are private.
All bachelors are unmarried.	All bachelors are miserable.
My name is C.	His name is D.
Light travels in straight lines.	Light floods the room.
Molecules are composed of atoms.	Books are composed of pages.
There are unconscious mental processes.	There are reflex processes.

Although both sets of statements have the same grammatical form, their *uses* are very different: the statements on the left are true by definition, or according to convention (i.e., they are all, in different ways, *necessarily* true); the statements on the right are factual propositions that may or may not be true (i.e., if true, they are only *contingently* true).

13.   Now, I want to suggest—and it is an important part of this work to show—that virtually all of the core propositions of psychoanalytic theory function, for the most part, paradigmatically rather than hypothetically. Among these paradigmatic statements, I would include the following:

1. the proposition that all mental acts are purposive;
2. those propositions referring to unconscious purposes, ideas, affects, fantasies, and acts of volition;
3. those propositions that describe, or pertain to, the distinction between primary and secondary processes;
4. propositions about the nature of unconscious wishes or impulses (i.e., as erotic or aggressive);
5. propositions descriptive of intrapsychical conflict; and

6. those propositions that refer contemporary mental acts and events to infantile prototypes.

All of these propositions—as they are used in the context of psychoanalytic theory and practice—are essentially paradigmatic rather than hypothetical (hence, we might say that they are not really propositions at all); they function, for the most part, not to convey factual information but to set forth certain standards of sense and meaning ("grammatical rules"). Thus, is we adopt them as "true," we do so on grounds other than those of empirical evidence; by the same token, if we reject them as "false," it is not because they are contradicted by factual evidence but because we fail, for whatever reason, to find them persuasive. Either way, our judgment here concerns, not the truth or falsity of certain propositions, but the acceptance or rejection of a particular form of representation or symbolism, "a grammatical system."

We can compare this to the choice of a unit of measure: if we choose to measure in meters rather than inches, this does not mean that it is *false* to say that this table is thirty-six inches high; if I choose to deny the reality of the unconscious, this does not mean that it is *false* to say that dreams express repressed and unconscious wishes.

It is wrong to treat the rejection of a unit of measure as if it were a rejection of the proposition "The table is three feet high rather than two" (YB, 69). This confusion pervades not only a great deal of the current debate about the nature and status of psychoanalytic claims but indeed much of the philosophy of the human sciences as a whole.

APPENDIX C:
The Concept of "Seeing As" in Wittgenstein

1. The notion of "seeing," as I use it in this work, together with the concepts of "seeing as" and "seeing an aspect," are based on Wittgenstein's influential discussion of these ideas in part 2 of the *Investigations*. What I offer here is less a summary of that discussion than an attempt to formulate what I take to be the main conceptual points, especially as they bear on my reading of Freud.

2. At the very outset, Wittgenstein makes a distinction between two different uses of the word "see": (1) the case of "I see this" (followed by a description, painting, or copy of some sort) and (2) the case of "I see a likeness between two faces" (PI, 2:193). The first he calls "seeing"; the second, "seeing as" or "seeing (noticing) an aspect": "I contemplate a face, and then suddenly notice its likeness to another. I *see* that it has not changed; yet I see it differently. I call this experience 'noticing an aspect' (*das Bemerken eines Aspekts*)" (PI, 2:193). According to Wittgenstein, there is a "categorical difference" (*kategorische Unterschied*) between the objects of sight in these two cases. The next twenty pages of the *Investigations* describe this difference.

   In the course of his discussion, Wittgenstein cites a number of different examples of "seeing as," of which the most famous is undoubtably Jastrow's "duck-rabbit" drawing.[1] The question is, If I see a duck, while another person sees a rabbit, or if I see both at different

---

1. Other examples include the following: (1) reversible perspective figures (e.g., puzzle pictures, the ascending-descending staircase projection, and the double cross); (2) multiaspect figures (e.g., the schematic cube and the triangle); (3) ambiguous figures (e.g., the upside-down face, reversed words, the galloping horse, interpreting hexagons, and the animal transfixed by an arrow); (4) familiar likenesses (e.g., the rabbit running by, the friend in crowd, and hidden faces); and (5) pretend fantasies (e.g., the chest that the children take as a house).

times, is my perception in each case changed, or is it the same? For Wittgenstein, the answer is neither yes nor no. " 'Seeing as. . . ,' " he writes, "is not part of perception. And for that reason it is like seeing and again not like" (PI, 2:197). In particular, through his analysis of the concepts of "seeing" and "seeing as," Wittgenstein shows that in many cases—but not all—seeing is found to involve more than "having a visual impression."[2]

The relevant points of this analysis are the following.

3. *"Seeing as" is not the same as interpreting*, though we *can* see according to an interpretation. What constitutes seeing the Jastrow drawing now as a rabbit, now as a duck? Do I see something different each time, or do I merely interpret what I see differently? Wittgenstein decides in favor of the former, because, as he says, "to interpret is to think, to do something; seeing is a state" (PI, 2:212). Moreover, when we interpret, we form hypotheses that are subject to verification, whereas "seeing as . . ." can no more be verified than "I am seeing red" (PI, 2:212). On the other hand, it is perfectly possible that the same illustration—an isometric cube, for example—might appear several places in a textbook and each time be seen differently: as a glass cube, an inverted open box, a wire frame, and so forth, according to the accompanying text. "So we interpret it, and *see* it as we *interpret* it" (PI, 2:193).

4. *"Seeing as" is not our primary perceptual relation to the world*, or to our everyday experience. "One doesn't *'take'* what one knows as the cutlery at a meal *for* cutlery; any more than one ordinarily tries to move one's mouth as one eats, or aims at moving it" (PI, 2:195). And "I cannot try to see a conventional picture of a lion *as* a lion, any more than an F as that letter. (Though I may well try to see it as a gallows, for example.)"[3] (PI, 2:206)

2. It is worth emphasizing that the point of this discussion, for Wittgenstein, is *not* to elaborate a theory of perception or epistemology or even to examine the concept of "seeing" as such; rather, it is intended as an exploration of a particular kind of inner experience and its relation to our use of symbols. As Wittgenstein later makes clear, the importance of the discussion lies in the close analogies between the concepts of "seeing an aspect" and "experiencing a meaning" (PI, 2:214).

3. This idea that "seeing as" refers to a particular and limited experience and not to our perceptual relation to the external world contradicts any attempt to generalize it into an epistemological doctrine. Norwood Hanson, for example, drawing on Wittgenstein's distinction between "seeing" and "seeing as," attempts to show that virtually *all* seeing involves an element of construction and, hence, in his view, has a component of "seeing as." In *Patterns of Discovery*, Hanson writes, "Not only do scientists see things as being of a certain sort . . . but . . . the situation could not be otherwise. It is a matter of logic, not merely a matter of fact, that *seeing as* and *seeing that* are indispensable to what is called, in science, *seeing or*

5. *"Seeing as" does not properly belong to perception*; it is both like and unlike our ordinary understanding of "seeing." The report of a perception, for instance, commonly takes the form of "I see x" or "It is an x"; the report of an experience of "seeing as" indicates the possibility of a *change* in aspect, for example, *"Now* I am seeing x," *"Now* I am seeing it *as* an x," or just *"Now* it's an x":

> I am shown a picture-rabbit and asked what it is; I say "It's a rabbit." Not "Now it's a rabbit." I am reporting my perception.—I am shown the duck-rabbit and asked what it is; I *may* say "It's a duck-rabbit." But I may also react to the question differently.—The answer that it is a duck-rabbit is again the report of a perception; the answer "Now it's a rabbit" is not. Had I replied "It's a rabbit," the ambiguity would have escaped me, and I should have been reporting my perception. (PI, 2:195)

> "But this isn't *seeing!*"—"But this is seeing!"—It must be possible to give both remarks a conceptual justification. (PI, 2:203)

6. *What changes in an aspect change is the organization of the visual impression,* not the visual impression itself.[4] (Note that "organization" in this context is purely another way of describing *how* the visual impression is perceived; that is, seeing is not only the having of a visual

---

observing" (147). In his later work, *Perception and Discovery*, Hanson makes the same point even more strongly when he argues that "almost everything we usually call *seeing* involves as fundamental to it what I, following Wittgenstein, have called *seeing as*" (105).

Again, it is important to stress against such interpretations that Wittgenstein's real point is *strategic* (i.e., aimed at resolution of specific philosophical puzzles—in this case, the puzzle surrounding our use of the concept of "seeing") and *limited* (i.e., relative to specific instances and contexts of language use—in this case, descriptions of the experience of "seeing" and "seeing as"). Moreover, the idea that "seeing as" involves the perception of an internal relation *between* different objects (relations of resemblance and difference) suggests that it *cannot* be generalized to include *all* forms of perception.

In short, Wittgenstein's point, unlike Hanson's, pertains to a limited instance of perceptual experience, not to perception in general.

4. Hanson proposes a useful distinction between what he calls variable-perspective figures (e.g., an isometric cube, rhomboid, staircase, tunnel) and variable-aspect figures (e.g., Jastrow's duck-rabbit, white-black cross, Koehler's goblet, young woman–hag). According to Hanson, only the latter display a true "change of aspect," whereas the former are best described in terms of shifts in perspective. For the present purposes, however, we may ignore this difference—as indeed Wittgenstein himself does—and consider all of these figures as instances of multiple, or "variable," aspects. (For discussion, see Hanson, *Perception and Discovery*, 85–90.)

experience but also the way in which the visual experience is had.) A change of aspect is expressed as a *new* perception, while the perception in fact remains unchanged:

> The change of aspect. "But surely you would say that the picture is altogether different now!"
>
> But what is different: my impression? my point of view?—Can I say? I *describe* the alteration like a perception; quite as if the object had altered before my eyes.
>
> "Now I am seeing *this*," I might say (pointing to another picture, for example). This has the form of a report of a new perception.
>
> The expression of a change of aspect is the expression of a *new* perception and at the same time of the perception's being unchanged. (PI, 2:195–96)

7. As they are for all inner processes, *the criteria for the experience of "seeing as" are—as linguistic criteria in general must be—outward and public*, though they cannot be the same as those for perceptual experience in general. For although the usual criterion of having a certain visual impression is simply the representation of what is seen (the concept of what is seen and the concept of the representation of what is seen are, as Wittgenstein says, "intimately connected"), the content of the experience of "seeing as" *cannot* be represented, since the organization of the visual impression—*how* something is seen—is not itself subject to representation. Hence, the criterion for "seeing as" can only be either (1) the description, or report, of the perception ("Now it's a rabbit," "A rabbit!" "The sphere seems to float," "It floats!" etc.) or (2) particular kinds of behavior (some indication of "knowing one's way about," certain gestures, "fine shades of behavior," etc.) (PI, 2:202–3).

In the case of *my* experience of "seeing as," the description of the impression is the description of the object, and the description of the object is thus the only criterion for having the impression. When the aspect changes, the description changes: " 'And is it really a different impression?'—In order to answer this I should like to ask myself whether there is really something different there in me. But how can I find out?—I *describe* what I am seeing differently"[5] (PI, 2:202). "Then is the copy of the figure an *incomplete* description of my visual experi-

---

5. But as Wittgenstein later reminds us, "You must remember that the descriptions of the alternating aspects are of a different kind in each case" (PI, 2:207).

ence?" Wittgenstein asks. "No.—But the circumstances decide whether, and what, more detailed specifications are necessary"[6] (PI, 2:199).

8.   Seeing is something that is, for the most part, immediate and given, but *"seeing as" requires imagination.* "It is possible to take the duck-rabbit simply for the picture of a rabbit, the double cross simply for the picture of a black cross, but not to take the bare triangular figure for the picture of an object that has fallen over. To see this aspect of the triangle demands *imagination*" (PI, 2:207). Indeed, the basic difference between "seeing as" and "seeing" turns on the relation of "seeing as" to images and to the imagination. "The concept of 'an aspect' is akin to the concept of 'an image' [*eine Vorstellung*]. In other words: the concept 'I am now seeing it as . . .' is akin to 'I am now having *this* image.' " Both "seeing as" and imagining (*die Vorstellung*) are subject to the will, whereas "seeing" is not. Thus, it makes sense to say, "Imagine *this*," and "Now see the figure like *this*," but not "Now see this leaf green" (PI, 2:213).

At the same time, however, imagination is not something that is simply *added* to perception; rather, it is what makes this perception what it is. "Doesn't it take imagination to hear something as a particular theme? And yet one is perceiving something in so hearing it" (PI, 2:213) (This is related to the difference between a visual impression and the way the impression is organized, or between *having* a visual experience and *how* the visual experience is had; the former, we might say, is purely perceptual, whereas the latter involves something more, something like imagination.) Nor is "having an image" the same as "seeing an aspect": for what is perceived in seeing an aspect cannot be represented; it can only be described. (And this is related to the fact that what is seen in the dawning of an aspect is not a quality of the object but a relation *between* objects.)

9.   There are certain logical conditions for the experience of "seeing as" that are different from those of seeing. In the first place, *"seeing*

---

6. Similarly, in *Zettel*, Wittgenstein suggests that the criterion be found in the *consequences* of the experience—and, of course, if there are no consequences one way or the other, then it makes no difference whether I have actually had the experience or merely think that I have: "Don't I see the figure now like this, now another way, even when I do not react verbally or otherwise?

"But 'now like this' 'now another way' are words, and what right have I to use them here? Can I show my right to you or to myself? (Unless by a further reaction.)

"But I surely know that they are two impressions, even if I don't say so. But how do I know that what I say is what I knew? What consequences follow from my interpreting this as that, or from my seeing this as that?" (Z, 213) *as"—the experience of seeing something as something—requires familiarity with what is represented* (presuming, of course, that the figure is representational). You cannot see a figure as a goblet unless you know what a goblet is. "You only 'see the duck and rabbit aspects' if you are already conversant with the shapes of those two animals. There is no analogous condition for seeing the aspects A [the two aspects of the 'double cross']" (PI, 2:207).

Second, and more important, in most cases *"seeing as" requires certain skills, habits, and dispositions, and therefore a certain kind of training*; it requires, in Wittgenstein's words, *"mastery of a technique"*: "It is only if someone *can do*, has learnt, is master of, such-and-such, that it makes sense to say he has had *this* experience" (PI, 2:209). For instance, in order to see a certain figure as a schematic cube, I must not only be familiar with actual cubes (i.e., what they look like), I must also know the different ways in which cubes can be represented (i.e., how they can be "connected to" figural representations); and in order to know that, I must have mastered certain basic techniques of projection. Put differently, confronted with the figure of a cube, I must be capable of making particular applications of it, of dealing with the figure *as* I see it. " 'Now he's seeing it like *this*,' 'now like that' would only be said of someone *capable* of making certain applications of the figure quite freely" (PI, 2:208). So, too, in the case of the duck-rabbit figure: not only must I be knowledgeable about the shapes of ducks and rabbits, I must also know the basic techniques by which such things are represented.

It follows that what we mean by "experience" in the experience of "seeing as" is significantly different from what we ordinarily understand by the term, for the fact is that we don't ordinarily think of experience as something that is conditioned by our capacity to *do* things. To quote Wittgenstein in full:

> The substratum of this experience [of seeing this as the apex, and that as the base of a triangle] is the mastery of a technique.
>
> But how queer for this to be the logical condition of someone's having such-and-such an *experience*! After all, you don't say that one only "has toothache" if one is capable of doing such-and-such.—From this it follows that we cannot be dealing with the same concept of experience. It is a different though related concept.
>
> It is only if someone *can do*, has learnt, is master of, such-and-such, that it makes sense to say he has had *this* experience.
>
> And if this sounds crazy, you need to reflect that the *concept*

of seeing is modified here. (A similar consideration is often necessary to get rid of a feeling of dizziness in mathematics.)

We talk, we utter words, and only *later* get a picture of their life. (PI, 2:208–9)

Thus, we might say that the concept of "seeing as" has *"more* than purely visual reference," that it also necessarily refers to certain conditions (abilities, training, dispositions, etc.) that do not relate to, or at least cannot be confined to, purely visual experience (PI, 2:209).

10. *What is perceived in seeing an aspect is not a property, or quality, of the object but "an internal relation between objects."* Wittgenstein writes, "The color of the visual impression corresponds to the color of the object (this blotting paper looks pink to me, and is pink)—the shape of the visual impression to the shape of the object (it looks rectangular to me, and is rectangular)—but what I perceive in the dawning of an aspect is not a property of the object, but an internal relation between it and other objects" (PI, 2:212). In other words, the process of seeing something *as* something almost invariably involves two components:[7] namely, the original object and that which the original object is *seen as.*[8] As it occurs in variable-aspect figures (e.g., the duck-rabbit), "seeing as" is the function of a relation between a gestalt, or sense configuration, and the two congruent figures ("picture duck" and "picture rabbit") which it can be seen as. (This relational definition of "seeing as" is crucial to our own understanding of what occurs in psychoanalytic interpretation, of its persuasive power and its "objective" validity, as well as of the more general relation between psychoanalysis and aesthetics.)

11. *The capacity to see something as something is a contingent fact about ourselves,* something that need not have been so. We see the schematic cube as the object itself. We regard the photograph as the

---

7. The only exception that comes to mind are reversible-aspect figures that are also nonrepresentational, such as the double cross.

8. Once again, a comparison to Hanson is illuminating. For Hanson, "seeing as" is a necessary component of our perception of objects. To use Hanson's favorite example: Kepler, in contrast to Brahe, sees the sun *as* stationary, the earth *as* moving. For Wittgenstein, on the other hand, "seeing as" characterizes a kind of seeing that involves a perception of likeness; hence, the example of Kepler fails to fit. In Wittgenstein's conception, Kepler sees the sun (moving), but he does not see the sun *as* anything; that is, he does perceive the kind of "internal relation" that Wittgenstein regards as an essential characteristic of "seeing as." For Wittgenstein, what is at issue in the Kepler case is an instance not of "seeing as" but of grammatical innovation; it concerns how we use such terms as "movement." "earth," "sun," and so forth, not how our visual field is organized. (See, e.g., L II, 98, and Z, 215.)

actual man, the landscape, or whatever, yet "we could easily imagine people who did not have this relation to such pictures. Who, for example, would be repelled by photographs, because a face without color and even perhaps a face reduced in scale struck them as inhuman" (PI, 2:205). The question then arises, "Could there be human beings lacking in the capacity to see something *as something*—and what would that be like?" (PI, 2:213). This leads to an exploration of what Wittgenstein calls aspect blindness, that is, the inability "to see something *as something*," a condition we can imagine as being similar to lacking a "musical ear" (PI, 2:214).

12.   For Wittgenstein, the importance of the notion of "aspect blindness" lies in the close analogies between the concepts of "seeing an aspect" and "experiencing a meaning." The particular experience that sometimes accompanies our use of language—what might be called an experience of meaning—can be described in terms similar to those of "seeing an aspect." In poetry, for example, I do not merely *read* the words, but I *feel* them, as if their meaning were an intrinsic part of their character. If I say "March" to myself and mean it first as an imperative, then as the month, I experience the word in a slightly different way each time. The question is, What would I be missing without this experience? "We want to ask 'What would you be missing if you did not *experience* the meaning of a word?'

"What would you be missing, for instance, if you did not understand the request to pronounce the word 'till' and to mean it as a verb,—or if you did not feel that a word lost its meaning and became a mere sound if it was repeated ten times over?" (PI, 2:214)

The answer is, You would be missing a great deal, but not the ability to use language as such. For however important our experience of words, of their familiar physiognomy—our feeling at times that a word has "taken up its meaning into itself," it is not this experience that determines its meaning. "The meaning of a word is not the experience one has in hearing or saying it, and the sense of a sentence is not a complex of such experiences" (PI, 2:181). I may have certain personal associations to particular words, I may experience Wednesday as "fat" and Tuesday as "lean," but this does not affect the meaning of the words themselves.[9] For to say that there is something that can be described as "an experience of meaning" is not to say that meaning *is* an experience.

9. Wittgenstein writes, "Here one might speak of a 'primary' and 'secondary' sense [*Bedeutung*] of a word. It is only if the word has the primary sense for you that you use it in the secondary sense" (PI, 2:216).

"Meaning is not a process which accompanies a word," Wittgenstein writes. "For no *process* could have the consequences of meaning" (PI, 2:218). And this is, of course, the conclusion toward which Wittgenstein has been driving all along, throughout the entire discussion of "seeing" and "seeing as," of aspect blindness and experiencing a meaning.

BIBLIOGRAPHY

Abraham, Nicolas (1969). "The Shell and the Kernel." Trans. Nicolas Rand. *Diacritics* (March 1979): 16–29.

Archard, David (1984). *Consciousness and the Unconscious*. La Salle, Ill.: Open Court Publishing.

Aristotle (1954). *"The Rhetoric" and "The Poetics" of Aristotle*. Trans. Ingram Bywater. New York: Random House.

Baker, G. P., and P.M.S. Hacker (1980). *Wittgenstein: Understanding and Meaning*. Chicago: University of Chicago Press.

——— (1985). *Wittgenstein: Rules, Grammar, and Necessity*. New York: Basil Blackwell.

Benveniste, Émile (1966). "Remarks on the Function of Language in Freudian Theory." In *Problems in General Linguistics*, trans. Mary Elizabeth Meek. Coral Gables, Fla.: University of Miami Press, 1971.

Bettelheim, Bruno (1983). *Freud and Man's Soul*. New York: Alfred A. Knopf.

Black, Max (1964). *A Companion to Wittgenstein's Tractatus*. Ithaca, N.Y.: Cornell University Press.

Bouveresse, Jacques (1973). *Wittgenstein: La rime et la raison*. Paris: Les éditions de Minuit.

Bouwsma, O. K. (1982). *Toward a New Sensibility: Essays of O. K. Bouwsma*. Ed. J. L. Craft and Ronald Hustwit. Lincoln: University of Nebraska Press.

——— (1986). *Wittgenstein: Conversations, 1949–51*. Ed. J. L. Craft and Ronald Hustwit. Indianapolis, Ind.: Hackett Publishing Co.

Brown, Norman O. (1959). *Life Against Death: The Psychoanalytic Meaning of History*. Middletown, Conn.: Wesleyan University Press.

Burke, Kenneth (1941). *The Philosophy of Literary Form: Studies in Symbolic Action*. Baton Rouge: Louisiana State University Press. Rev. ed., New York: Vintage Books, 1957.

——— (1966). *Language as Symbolic Action: Essays on Life, Literature, and Method*. Berkeley and Los Angeles: University of California Press.

——— (1969). *A Grammer of Motives*. Berkeley and Los Angeles: University of California Press.

Casey, John (1966). *The Language of Criticism*. London: Menthuen.

Cavell, Stanley (1969). *Must We Mean What We Say?* Cambridge: Cambridge University Press, 1976.

Chalmers, A. F. (1976). *What Is This Thing Called Science? An Assessment of the*

Nature and Status of Science and Its Methods. St. Lucia: University of Queensland Press.

Cioffi, Frank (1969). "Wittgenstein's Freud." In *Studies in the Philosophy of Wittgenstein,* ed. Peter Winch. New York: Humanities Press.

———— (1970). "Freud and the Idea of a Pseudo-Science." In *Explanation and the Behavioural Sciences,* ed. Robert Borger and Frank Cioffi. Cambridge: Cambridge University Press.

Drury, M. O'C. (1973). *The Danger of Words.* London: Routledge and Kegan Paul.

Edelson, Marshall (1984). *Hypothesis and Evidence in Psychoanalysis.* Chicago: University of Chicago Press.

———— (1988). *Psychoanalysis: A Theory in Crisis.* Chicago: University of Chicago Press.

Edwards, James (1982). *Ethics Without Philosophy: Wittgenstein and the Moral Life.* Tampa: University Presses of Florida.

Feyerabend, Paul (1975). *Against Method: Outline of an Anarchistic Theory of Knowledge.* London: New Left Books.

Freud, Sigmund (1895). "Project for a Scientific Psychology." In *Standard Edition* 1:295–397. London: Hogarth Press, 1966.

———— (1900). *The Interpretation of Dreams.* In *Standard Edition,* vols. 4 and 5. London: Hogarth Press, 1953. German edition, *Die Traumdeutung.* Frankfurt am Main: Fischer Taschenbuch Verlag, 1982.

———— (1901). "On Dreams." In *Standard Edition* 5:631–86. London: Hogarth Press, 1953.

———— (1901). *The Psychopathology of Everyday Life.* In *Standard Edition,* vol. 6. London: Hogarth Press, 1960.

———— (1905). *Three Essays on the Theory of Sexuality.* In *Standard Edition* 7:135–243. London: Hogarth Press, 1953.

———— (1911). "The Handling of Dream-Interpretation in Psycho-Analysis." In *Standard Edition* 12:91–96. London: Hogarth Press, 1958.

———— (1912). "A Note on the Unconscious in Psycho-Analysis." In *Standard Edition* 12:260–66. London: Hogarth Press, 1958.

———— (1913). "The Claims of Psycho-Analysis to Scientific Interest." In *Standard Edition* 13:165–90. London: Hogarth Press, 1953.

———— (1914). "On the History of the Psycho-Analytic Movement." In *Standard Edition* 14:7–66. London: Hogarth Press, 1957.

———— (1915). "Instincts and Their Vicissitudes." In *Standard Edition* 14:117–40. London: Hogarth Press, 1957.

———— (1915). "Repression." In *Standard Edition* 14:146–58. London: Hogarth Press, 1957.

———— (1915). "The Unconscious." In *Standard Edition* 14:166–216. London: Hogarth Press, 1957.

———— (1916–17 [1915–17]). *Introductory Lectures on Psycho-Analysis.* In *Standard Edition,* vols. 15 and 16. London: Hogarth Press, 1961.

———— (1917). "A Difficulty in the Path of Psychoanalysis." In *Standard Edition* 17:135–44. London: Hogarth Press, 1955.

———— (1923). *The Ego and the Id.* In *Standard Edition* 19:13–59. London: Hogarth Press, 1961.

———— (1923 [1922]). "Remarks on the Theory and Practice of Dream-Interpretation." In *Standard Edition* 19:109–21. London: Hogarth Press, 1961.

———— (1923 [1922]). "Two Encyclopedia Articles." In *Standard Edition* 18:233–59. London: Hogarth Press, 1955.

————— (1924 [1925]). "An Autobiographical Study." In *Standard Edition* 20:7–75. London: Hogarth Press, 1959.

————— (1925). "Some Additional Notes on Dream-Interpretation as a Whole." In *Standard Edition* 19:127–38. London: Hogarth Press, 1961.

————— (1926). "The Question of Lay Analysis." In *Standard Edition* 20:177–258. London: Hogarth Press, 1959.

————— (1933 [1932]). *New Introductory Lectures on Psychoanalysis*. In *Standard Edition* 22:5–182. London: Hogarth Press, 1964.

————— (1937). "Analysis Terminable and Interminable." In *Standard Edition* 23:216–53. London: Hogarth Press, 1964.

————— (1937). "Constructions in Analysis." In *Standard Edition* 23:257–69. London: Hogarth Press, 1964.

————— (1940 [1938]). "An Outline of Psycho-Analysis." In *Standard Edition* 23:144–207. London: Hogarth Press, 1964.

————— (1940 [1938]). "Some Elementary Lessons in Psycho-Analysis." In *Standard Edition* 23:279–86. London: Hogarth Press, 1964.

————— (1985). *The Complete Letters of Sigmund Freud to Wilhelm Fliess, 1887–1904*. Trans. and ed. Jeffrey M. Masson. Cambridge: Harvard University Press.

Gillispie, Charles Coulston (1960). *The Edge of Objectivity: An Essay in the History of Scientific Ideas*. Princeton: Princeton University Press.

Grünbaum, Adolph (1983). "The Foundations of Psychoanalysis." In *Mind and Medicine: Problems of Explanation and Evaluation in Psychiatry and the Biomedical Sciences*, ed. Larry Laudan. Berkeley and Los Angeles: University of California Press.

————— (1984). *The Foundations of Psychoanalysis: A Philosophical Critique*. Berkeley and Los Angeles: University of California Press.

————— (1988). "Précis of *The Foundations of Psychoanalysis: A Philosophical Critique*." In *Mind, Psychoanalysis, and Science*, ed. Peter Clark and Crispin Wright. Oxford: Basil Blackwell.

Habermas, Jürgen (1968). *Knowledge and Human Interests*. Trans. Jeremy J. Shapiro. Boston: Beacon Press, 1971.

Hanley, Charles (1972). "Wittgenstein on Psychoanalysis." In *Ludwig Wittgenstein: Philosophy and Language*, ed. Alice Ambrose and Morris Lazerowitz. New York: Humanities Press.

Hanson, Norwood (1959). *Patterns of Discovery: An Inquiry into the Conceptual Foundations of Science*. Cambridge: Cambridge University Press.

————— (1969). *Perception and Discovery: An Introduction to Scientific Inquiry*. Ed. Willard C. Humphreys. San Francisco: Freeman, Cooper.

Hartmann, Eduard von (1869). *Philosophy of the Unconscious: Speculative Results According to the Inductive Method of Physical Science*. Trans. William Chaterton Coupland. London: Routledge and Kegan Paul, 1931.

Hester, Markus B. (1967). *The Meaning of Poetic Metaphor: An Analysis in the Light of Wittgenstein's Claim That Meaning Is Use*. The Hague: Mouton.

Hilmy, S. Stephen (1987). *The Later Wittgenstein: The Emergence of a New Philosophical Method*. Oxford: Basil Blackwell.

Homans, Peter (1979). *Jung in Context: Modernity and the Making of a Psychology*. Chicago: University of Chicago Press.

————— (1989). *The Ability to Mourn: Disillusionment and the Social Origins of Psychoanalysis*. Chicago: University of Chicago Press.

Hook, Sidney, ed. (1959). *Psychoanalysis, Scientific Method, and Philosophy.* New York: New York University Press.

Ijsseling (1976). *Rhetoric and Philosophy in Conflict: An Historical Survey.* The Hague: Martinus Nijhoff.

Janik, Allan, and Stephen Toulmin (1973). *Wittgenstein's Vienna.* New York: Simon and Schuster.

Jones, Ernest (1953–57). *The Life and Work of Sigmund Freud.* Vols. 1–3. New York: Basic Books.

Kuhn, Thomas (1962). *The Structure of Scientific Revolutions.* Chicago: University of Chicago Press.

—— (1970). "Reflections on My Critics." In *Criticism and the Growth of Knowledge,* ed. Imre Lakatos and Alan Musgrave. Cambridge: Cambridge University Press.

Lacan, Jacques (1964). *The Four Fundamental Concepts of Psychoanalysis.* Ed. Jacques Alain Miller, trans. Alan Sheridan. New York: W. W. Norton, 1978.

—— (1966). *Écrits.* Paris: Éditions du Seuil. Partial English translation, *Écrits.* Trans. Alan Sheridan. New York: W. W. Norton, 1977.

Lakatos, Imre, and Alan Musgrave (1970). *Criticism and the Growth of Knowledge.* Cambridge: Cambridge University Press.

Lemaire, Anika (1970). *Jacques Lacan.* Trans. David Mackey. London: Routledge and Kegan Paul, 1977.

Louch, A. R. (1969). *Explanation and Human Action.* Berkeley and Los Angeles: University of California Press.

Lovibond, Sabina (1983). *Realism and Imagination in Ethics.* Minneapolis: University of Minnesota Press.

MacIntyre, Alasdair (1958). *The Unconscious: A Conceptual Analysis.* New York: Humanities Press.

Malcolm, Norman (1984). *Ludwig Wittgenstein: A Memoir.* 2d ed. Oxford: Oxford University Press.

Miller, Richard (1987). *Fact and Method: Explanation, Confirmation, and Reality in the Natural and the Social Sciences.* Princeton: Princeton University Press.

Nagel, Ernest (1954). "Review of Stephen Toulmin, *The Philosophy of Science: An Introduction.*" *Mind* 63:403–12.

Perelman, Chaim (1982). *The Realm of Rhetoric.* Trans. William Kluback. Notre Dame, Ind.: University of Notre Dame Press.

Perelman, Chaim, and L. Olbrechts-Tyteca (1958). *The New Rhetoric: A Treatise on Argumentation.* Trans. John Wilkerson and Purcell Weaver. Notre Dame, Ind.: University of Notre Dame Press, 1969.

Popper, Karl (1959). *The Logic of Scientific Discovery.* New York: Basic Books.

—— (1962). *Conjectures and Refutations: The Growth of Scientific Knowledge.* New York: Basic Books.

Ricoeur, Paul (1950). *Freedom and Nature: The Voluntary and the Involuntary.* Trans. Erazim V. Kohak. Evanston, Ill.: Northwestern University Press, 1966.

—— (1965). *Freud and Philosophy: An Essay in Interpretation.* Trans. Denis Savage. New Haven: Yale University Press, 1970.

—— (1969). *The Conflict of Interpretations: Essays in Hermeneutics.* Various translators. Evanston, Ill.: Northwestern University Press, 1974.

—— (1975). *The Rule of Metaphor: Multi-Disciplinary Studies in the Creation of Meaning.* Trans. Robert Czerny. Toronto: University of Toronto Press, 1977.

—— (1981). "The Question of Proof in Freud's Writings." In *Hermeneutics and the Human Sciences*, ed. and trans. John Thompson. Cambridge: Cambridge University Press. Originally published in *Journal of American Psychoanalytic Association* 25 (1977): 835–71.

Rieff, Philip (1959). *Freud: The Mind of the Moralist*. Chicago: University of Chicago Press.

Rorty, Richard, ed. (1967). *The Linguistic Turn: Recent Essays in Philosophical Method*. Chicago: University of Chicago Press.

Schopenhauer, Arthur (1883). *The World as Will and Idea*. Vols. 1–3. Trans. R. B. Haldane and J. Kemp. London: Routledge and Kegan Paul.

Sherwood, Michael (1969). *The Logic of Explanation in Psychoanalysis*. New York: Academic Press.

Shope, Robert (1973). "Freud's Concept of Meaning." *Psychoanalysis and Contemporary Science* 2:276–303.

Spence, Donald (1982). *Narrative Truth and Historical Truth: Meaning and Interpretation in Psychoanalysis*. New York: W. W. Norton.

—— (1983). "Narrative Persuasion." *Psychoanalysis and Contemporary Thought* 6, no. 3:457–81.

——. (1987). *The Freudian Metaphor: Toward Paradigm Change in Psychoanalysis*. New York: W. W. Norton.

Staten, Henry (1984). *Wittgenstein and Derrida*. Lincoln: University of Nebraska Press.

Timpanaro, Sebastino (1974). *The Freudian Slip: Psychoanalysis and Textual Criticism*. Trans. Kate Soper. London: New Left Books, 1976.

Toulmin, Stephen (1953). *The Philosophy of Science: An Introduction*. New York: Harper and Row.

Waismann, Friedrich (1979). *Ludwig Wittgenstein and the Vienna Circle: Conversations Recorded by Friedrich Waismann*. Ed. Brian McGuinness, trans. Joachim Schulte and Brian McGuinness. N.p.

Weiss, Fredric (1974). "Meaning and Dream Intrepretation." In *Freud: A Collection of Critical Essays*, ed. Richard Wollheim. New York: Anchor Books.

Winch, Peter, ed. (1969). *Studies in the Philosophy of Wittgenstein*. New York. Humanities Press.

Wisdom, John (1964). *Philosophy and Psychoanalysis*. Oxford: Basil Blackwell.

—— (1965). *Paradox and Discovery*. New York: Philosophical Library.

Wittgenstein, Ludwig (1914–51). *Culture and Value*. Notes comp. and ed. G. H. von Wright, trans. Peter Winch. Chicago: University of Chicago Press, 1980.

—— (1918 [1921]). *Tractatus Logico-Philosophicus*. Trans. D. F. Pears and B. F. McGuinness. London: Routledge and Kegan Paul, 1961.

—— (1929–30). *Philosophical Remarks*. Ed. Rush Rhees, trans. Raymond Hargreaves and Roger White. Oxford: Basil Blackwell, 1975.

—— (1930–32). *Wittgenstein's Lectures, Cambridge, 1930–1932*. From notes of John King and Desmond Lee, ed. Desmond Lee. Chicago: University of Chicago Press, 1980.

—— (1930–33). "Wittgenstein's Lectures in 1930–33." In G. E. Moore, *Philosophical Papers*. New York: Macmillan, 1959.

—— (1931, 1948?). *Remarks on Frazer's "Golden Bough."* Rush Rhees, trans. A. C. Miles. Atlantic Highlands, N.J.: Humanities Press, 1979. Originally published in *Synthese* 17 (1967): 233–53. Second translation, with expanded text, by John Beversluis, in *Wittgenstein: Sources and Perspectives*, ed. C. G. Luckhardt. Hassocks, Sussex: Harvester Press, 1979.

—— (1932–34). *Philosophical Grammar*. Ed. Rush Rhees, trans. Anthony Kenny. Berkeley and Los Angeles: University of California Press, 1974.

—— (1932–35). *Wittgenstein's Lectures, Cambridge, 1932–1935*. From notes of Alice Ambrose and Margaret Macdonald, ed. Alice Ambrose. Chicago: University of Chicago Press, 1979.

—— (1933–34). "The Yellow Book (Selected Parts)." From the notes of Alice Ambrose, in *Wittgenstein's Lectures, Cambridge, 1932–1935*. Chicago: University of Chicago Press, 1979.

—— (1933–35). *The Blue and Brown Books*. From notes of Francis Skinner, Alice Ambrose, and others. New York: Harper and Row, 1958.

—— (1936–45, 1947–49). *Philosophical Investigations*. Ed. G.E.M. Anscombe and Rush Rhees, trans. G.E.M. Anscombe. New York: Macmillan, 1958.

—— (1937–44). *Remarks on the Foundations of Mathematics*. Ed. G. H. von Wright, Rush Rhees, and G.E.M. Anscombe, trans. G.E.M. Anscombe. Rev. ed. Cambridge: MIT Press, 1978.

—— (1938–46). *Lectures and Conversations on Aesthetics, Psychology, and Religion*. From notes of Yorick Smythies, Rush Rhees, and James Taylor, ed. Cyril Barrett. Berkeley and Los Angeles: University of California Press, 1966.

—— (1945–48). *Zettel*. Ed. G.E.M. Anscombe and G. H. von Wright, trans. G.E.M. Anscombe. Berkeley and Los Angeles: University of California Press, 1967.

—— (1946–48). *Remarks on the Philosophy of Psychology*. Vols. 1 and 2. Ed. G. H. von Wright and Heikki Nyman, trans. C. G. Luckhardt and Maximillian A. E. Aue. Chicago: University of Chicago Press, 1980.

—— (1948–49). *Last Writings on the Philosophy of Psychology*. Vol. 1. Ed. G. H. von Wright and Heikki Nyman, trans. C. G. Luckhardt and Maximillian A. E. Aue. Chicago: University of Chicago Press, 1982.

—— (1949–51). *On Certainty*. Ed. G.E.M. Anscombe and G. H. von Wright, trans. G.E.M. Anscombe. New York: Harper and Row, 1969.

—— (1950–51). *Remarks on Color*. Ed. G.E.M. Anscombe, trans. Linda L. McAlister and Margarete Schättle. Berkeley and Los Angeles: University of California Press, 1978.

Wollheim, Richard (1971). *Sigmund Freud*. Cambridge: Cambridge University Press.

——, ed. (1974). *Freud: A Collection of Critical Essays*. New York: Anchor Books.

Wollheim, Richard, and James Hopkins, eds. (1982). *Philosophical Essays on Freud*. Cambridge: Cambridge University Press.

INDEX

www.ingramcontent.com/pod-product-compliance
Lightning Source LLC
Chambersburg PA
CBHW021856020426
42334CB00013B/363